Teaching Skills in Further & Adult Education

D0280040

life

April 1992

City and Guilds Co-publishing Series

City and Guilds of London Institute has a long history of providing assessments and certification to those who have undertaken education and training in a wide variety of technical subjects or occupational areas. Its business is essentially to provide an assurance that pre-determined standards have been met. That activity has grown in importance over the past few years as government and national bodies strive to create the right conditions for the steady growth of a skilled and flexible workforce.

Both teachers and learners need materials to support them as they work towards the attainment of qualifications, and City and Guilds is pleased to be working with several distinguished publishers towards meeting that need. It has been closely involved in planning, author selection and text appraisal, although the opinions expressed in the publications are those of the individual authors and are not necessarily those of the Institute.

City and Guilds is fully committed to the projects listed below and is pleased to commend them to teaching staff, students and their advisers.

Carolyn Andrew and others. *Business Administration Level I* and *Business Administration Level II* (John Murray)

David Minton. *Teaching Skills in Adult and Further Education* (Macmillan)

Graham Morris and Lesley Reveler. *Retail Certificate Workbook* (Levels I and II) (Macmillan)

Peter Riley (consultant editor). *Computer-aided Engineering* (Macmillan)

Tim Roberts. *Wine Appreciation* (Stanley Thornes)

Barbara Wilson. *Information Technology: the Basics* (Macmillan)

Caroline Wilkinson. *Information Technology in the Office* (Macmillan)

Teaching Skills in Further & Adult Education

David Minton

MACMILLAN

City and Guilds

First edition 1991

Published by
MACMILLAN EDUCATION LTD
Houndmills, Basingstoke, Hampshire RG21 2XS
and London
Companies and representatives
throughout the world

Printed in Great Britain by Billing & Sons Ltd, Worcester

Typeset by TecSet Ltd,
Wallington, Surrey

British Library Cataloguing in Publication Data
Minton, David
Teaching skills in adult and further education
1. Adult education. Teaching
I. Title
374.13
ISBN 0–333–54843–4

Contents

Acknowledgements

I should like to take the opportunity of acknowledging how much of what is in this book has been taught to me by the colleagues and students with whom I have worked over the last thirty years in the UK and overseas. Some of these people appear fleetingly in the case studies in the book. Their willingness to share their experiences with new teachers through this book is invaluable.

I am very grateful to Geoff Jones and John Temple who formed a tutoring team with me for their creativity and critical judgements. I was privileged to work with a remarkable group of moderators for the City and Guilds Further and Adult Education Teacher's Certificate courses for many years, and I am also grateful for the support given to me by the officers of City and Guilds.

The author and publishers wish to thank the following for permission to use copyright material:

Geoff Croxon, for the cartoon on page 3.

Fran Chard, for her description of the 'Sculpting' activity.

The table on page 16 is derived from a paper presented in 1989 to the Industrial Society by ECA of London.

Tony Buzan for material from *Use Your Head*, BBC Books, 2nd edn, 1989.

Federal Publications (S) Pte Ltd for two cartoons from *Fun With Chinese Characters* by T. H. Peng, 1980.

Every effort has been made to trace all the copyright holders, but if any have been inadvertently overlooked the publishers will be pleased to make the necessary arrangement at the first opportunity.

Preface

Many people who come into teaching in adult and further education can find themselves 'thrown in at the deep end'. Others, more fortunate, are able to join a suitable programme of teacher education, in particular the City and Guilds Further and Adult Education Teacher's Certificate, with support and guidance from tutors, mentors and peer group colleagues. It is for both categories that this book is designed.

All teachers should accept responsibility for the development and learning of their students. In defining competence in the design and implementation of learning programmes, I have set out what I believe to be good practice, whatever the context. To implement good practice need not be difficult, but it does require commitment.

This book is intended to provide effective guidance and support both for those working on their own and for those who have the benefit of shared learning and group activities. Whatever the content, wherever the context, I hope that the book will provide an exciting and reliable companion and guide to the learning experience.

DAVID MINTON

Part 1

Effective Class Teaching

Introduction: The Teacher's Role

EJ and Spot

We can almost feel EJ's frustration.

Few come to teaching without any experience, although they may not consciously be aware of having had a go at it. People do enjoy teaching others: children, friends, parents, adults, subordinates, dogs, cats, lions. They 'get a kick out of it'.

They feel they have knowledge or skills, something to share. Often they have an enthusiasm for something, or experience to communicate. Usually it is in an ordinary social context, such as wishing to make others feel jealous, perhaps about the great place they've been to on holiday: 'if you go, you must see . . .'. Or in role-modelling: father taking his son fishing, or mother dressmaking with her daughter.

EJ's attitude is typical. 'I can whistle, you can too. You simply do this!'

How many teachers are satisfied with just having got through what they set out to teach without finding out if the students learned anything at all? What's wrong here?

Spot didn't learn to whistle; why? Was it the way EJ set about teaching him? Would EJ have been more successful if he had used a different technique? Does the dog have a problem EJ does not understand, or does not want to understand?

Who says Spot should whistle anyway? Is it for EJ or for Spot? Is EJ concerned with Spot's achievement or only with his own? Is Spot motivated to learn? How could EJ motivate him? Would it help if he whipped the dog, or fed him chocolate? Is EJ expecting Spot to do something he is incapable of doing, or sees no point in doing?

3

We could ask so many similar questions. Teaching can be the most fulfilling and the most frustrating of human activities. But we should always ask: who is it for?

REMEMBER!
. . . A teacher's prime task is to engage the student in the learning process. What the student does to learn is more important than what the teacher does to teach.

Observing

Have you watched parents with a small child? Perhaps you have brought up children of your own. Parents watch and guide their child constantly. They shape its growth. They inhibit antisocial and dangerous behaviour. They encourage the child to achieve skills and understanding, and to develop certain attitudes. They surround the child with actions, words and objects that stimulate responses from the child. And they learn themselves by experience how to get the 'right' response. In fact, they are creating, usually quite unknowingly, a learning environment for themselves and their child. They are learning the job, and growing with it both as people and as parents.

Watch a very young child explore its environment. Then observe older children and adults, and make some comparisons.

REMEMBER!
. . . The first important skill a teacher needs to develop is the ability to observe behaviour in a learning environment.

Exploring

What do you do when you go into a new place? meet new people? arrive in a new town or country? shop in a new store? **You explore**.

Watch the people who come into your class for the first time. What do they do? **They explore the environment**.

They will probably look for clues as to how to behave there, who the other people are, where to sit, what to wear, and so on. The classroom environment is full of such information: the way the furniture is arranged, what it is like, the equipment in the room, the dress of the teacher and the other students, information on the walls and in books – or lack of it.

Why do they look for such clues? Perhaps so that they can modify their own behaviour to fit, avoid being 'out of place'. They want to feel comfortable there.

You can watch them explore their learning environment and gradually adjust to it. And you can take control of what happens if you want to.

REMEMBER!
. . . The basic learning activity is exploring: finding out.

Teaching and learning

As the teacher, what is your part in the learning activity?

This book is primarily concerned with exploring the role of teacher. Teaching is a learning experience for the teacher as much as for the students. You need to use every teaching session as an opportunity to learn: to watch student behaviour and assess the learning that occurred so that you can improve the learning experiences for them. We call this process **evaluating**.

The book is intended to act as your guide: to provide signposts and suggested itineraries, things to do and things to look out for, to help you establish good practice.

In undertaking the teaching of adults you are embarking on a most exciting journey of discovery, of yourself and others, that will last as long as you continue teaching. There will be no point at which you can say confidently, 'That's it! I've got it! I'm now a fully competent teacher.' But if you learn from the experience of teaching you will achieve confidence and skill. You will understand more about how people learn.

The more you understand people, dealing with them, involving them in the excitement of their own self-discovery and learning, the more they will surprise and fascinate you. There is no limit to the fascination of people. That is the great joy of teaching.

Questions

The book is about questions.

Questions alert the brain: look out! new information is coming. A child is full of questions. In order to learn our brains must be alert, searching, looking for answers to questions.

Many textbooks are only about answers – and frequently the reader is not told the questions to which these are the supposed answers. They set out to provide short cuts, to eliminate the necessity of thinking.

Teaching is a journey of discovery – discovery about yourself and other people. You have come for the journey, for the challenge of thinking things through and of problem-solving, for the satisfaction of being effective as a teacher, and doing a good job.

If the book closes down your curiosity and your eagerness to learn more, it will have failed in its purpose.

Cycles

The establishment of good practice means a repeated cycle of preparation, teaching and review. The questions become more searching and more interesting as you come back to them.

When you have observed what people do, you will want to know why they do it. If you set about asking them, you will receive quite complicated answers. You will want to get behind these answers to underlying motivation, to 'real' reasons, and so to value systems, fears, anxieties and social pressures.

CASE STUDY 1

Carol had an evening class who wanted to learn word-processing. The students were all women, most of them in their late thirties or forties, some older and a few in their twenties. They were all experienced typists, employed in local companies.

Why were they there? At the time there was a strong move in the local firms to switch from typewriters to word-processors and the women felt they had to be able to cope.

They showed a great deal of anxiety.

Think about these questions:

1 What do you think they were anxious about?
2 How would that affect what they did and their learning?
3 What would you do to help them if you found yourself in the same position as Carol?

COMMENT

It is important to know what it feels like to be in the situation of the students in the class. If you understand how they feel, and the barriers and anxieties they bring with them, you will be able to help them overcome the barriers and learn successfully.

We each have a perception of ourselves, our status, our potential or lack of it: our self-image. American education values a good self-image highly; a great deal of effort goes into improving it.

If you cut down a mature tree, you can count the growth rings year by year. You can distinguish the good years for growing from the bad years. Although the tree is largely what was determined by its genes at conception, it was shaped by accident and weather, by where its roots have sought nourishment, by the nutrients or poisons that it found, by disease or by competition with other trees.

People are far more complex than trees, but each is the result of how far environment and experience have promoted or inhibited growth, realised or stunted potential, and shaped his or her self-image.

For many, formal education has failed to stimulate their creativity and damaged their self-confidence. It has convinced them that, compared with others, they are stupid or at least not clever, and so engendered mental blockages. Many adults have a fear of formal education, teachers and exams. They have developed complexes and barriers to learning. One of the great delights of adult education is to see students make quite startling discoveries about themselves.

You will probably learn as much about yourself as about anything else as you reflect on the experiences of teaching that you will undertake, and work through the activities and tasks in this book.

Models

Learning is unstoppable.

You learn all the time – otherwise you could not cope with new situations as they arise. If you did not learn, you could not deal with the world. You would constantly stub your toe on the same step or burn your fingers, miss the chair when you go to sit down, turn the wrong knob on the television set. Learning is also cumulative. Once you have dealt successfully with an experience you find it easier the next time you encounter a similar situation.

When we walk into a room or encounter, say, a new machine for the first time, we look for clues to help us to categorise it. We have 'models in the head' about most things. They enable us to learn quickly how to deal effectively with the new place or machine or people.

Where do our models come from, including our models of ourselves? We are constantly creating them and modifying those that we already have from our experiences.

We hardly have to think about it usually. We instantly recognise a room as, for instance, a sitting room or a kitchen. Equipment and layout tell us how we are to behave there. We do this by transferring learning from one experience and context to another.

It is not true, however, that when we consciously set out to learn something, we can always do it easily. Why the difference? Why is it often apparently hard to learn things? There must be special factors at work preventing learning from happening.

One reason is the way, already mentioned, that the past experience of many people has unfortunately convinced them that they will not be able to deal with it very easily, if at all. They have formed a poor self image and created barriers that stop them from learning.

As teachers we can improve learning by bringing the process to the surface so that we can look at it. We can try to understand what is going on for the students and for us. We must try to see it, and feel it, from the students' point of view.

Reflecting on our own learning experiences will help us to do that – for example, how we felt on our first day at work: what happened for us, and how we changed as we learned.

Growth through experience

We talk about growing with the job. Learning is growth through experience. We need to grow as teachers and stimulate growth in our students. There is no short cut. Of course, some grow and flourish more quickly than others do. This is not simply a matter of luck. It is more a readiness to learn – to reflect on experience and to explore alternative methods and approaches. It may depend on creative problem-solving, ability to adapt and willingness to take risks.

It depends crucially on our belief in ourselves.

REMEMBER!
. . . Maturation is an important part of learning processes that cannot be hurried.

1 How to Use the Book: Learning Through Activity

REMEMBER!

. . . Learning is most effective at a point of need.

Learning requires activity on the part of the learner. You have to do something in order to learn. Reading is one such activity. But when we read, our concentration span is often quite short and so we soon stop taking things in. We need to pause frequently and review what we have read – to try to process it for ourselves in some way. There has to be time for it to become part of our own perception.

You will find learning activity in every section of the book. Some learning activities require simply a change of approach, variety in what you are doing; some ask you to do something – to get up and do it – such as rearranging furniture to improve the environment where you or students are attempting to learn.

It is important to do these things. It is the way to learn, and the way to develop competence.

There is a pattern in the learning programme in the book. The learning activities are integrated into that programme. Undertake them as soon as you can after you have read the appropriate section. They relate to two aspects of learning.

1 The first, described as **Activities**, concern your own needs and self-discovery. They will enable you to explore your strengths and to build up confidence, skill and understanding, and will help you get yourself properly organised and working in methodical and efficient ways. Activity 1, below is an example.

2 The **Tasks** focus on your preparation for teaching: these will help you develop the good practice to be effective.

3 In addition, **Case studies** are set out with questions to draw out the lessons that may be learned. Merely reading the case studies will not extract the benefit that may be had from using the experience of others. You must think about what happened and why, and compare that experience with your own. It is even better if you can share your thinking in a peer group discussion.

ACTIVITY 1 | Your model of teaching

You come to teaching with your own 'model in the head' of what teachers do and why, and of how learning happens for the students.

You will also have feelings about what you want to learn from any book on teaching or from training sessions you may attend.

Learning is change of many things including knowledge and ideas, beliefs and attitudes, insights, skills, habits, approaches that we make to our work and to other people, our self-image. We need to monitor these changes in ourselves and our students.

To observe change we have to know what the initial state is that is to grow and change. We also need to bring to the surface what we think and how we behave in order to have a view of it.

So it is important to work through the following questions now before you read on.

1 What do you consider to be the role of the teacher of adults?
2 Analyse and explain your 'model in the head' of teaching and learning and how they relate to each other. (It may help if you describe students in a context that is familiar to you: how the class works, and what are the expectations of both students and teacher.)
3 Write down what you feel you need to learn in order to be an effective teacher of adults. Decide what your priorities will be, with your reasons.

TASK 1: Building up teaching materials

You will need to keep materials in order and develop a system to file your work. This can be done using ring binders or boxes.

It is a good idea to have a file for your own learning materials, such as completed tasks in this book and other materials you will want to gather. These should be filed in date order so that you can later reflect on your own learning by reviewing your work.

You will need another file for lesson plans and teaching/learning materials.

You should also have a box-file for the audio-visual aids (AVA) and other resource materials you use or gather together for your classes.

Learning paths and maps

You must tackle learning a bit at a time, in digestible amounts. But these will only make sense if they link in successfully to what you have already learned and to your perception of things – your world as a whole. Your perceptions will change with time.

You will find in any case that you and your students select, quite unconsciously, from whatever learning experiences you provide. You (and they) select those bits you can make sense of and can link with present knowledge and understanding. The rest will probably be ignored, at least for the present.

For example, you can easily overwhelm your brain with information about the assessment of student learning. You will find that when you actually need to assess what your students have learned in a particular context, you will search for an appropriate method. By using that method, even if you do it quite badly, you will come to some understanding of how it works; you are then ready to try to explore assessment processes in more detail.

This book has been designed to plot a learning path and to guide you through it. But all individuals have specific needs, and each will modify the design and use it in a way that suits them. That is inevitable.

Consider again exploring an unfamiliar town or building or store. You may start by looking at a map. The map is an abstraction. It made perfect sense to the person who drew it. But it may only really make sense to you *after* the experience of visiting the place. We can use a map to help us explore physically and so come to understand both the town and the map.

A design-plan is understood thoroughly only if you make something following the instructions in the plan, whether it is a dress pattern, a recipe for a pudding or a drawing of a machine part.

The same is true of a book of this kind. To undertake any task in teaching – or in anything else – you must define the task. This involves asking appropriate questions and seeking information. If we ask the wrong questions, or the wrong kind of questions, our perceptions of what we are about are likely to be distorted.

The book should enable you to identify questions in relation to the tasks that teaching requires. These become more searching as experience increases and you encounter new contexts and different groups of students.

Growth cycles

Learning and growth are cyclical. We constantly revisit areas of experience, redo the same tasks, practise the same skills. We grow to be a whole person through this experience.

The learning programme in the book reflects cyclical reality. Learning will be more successful if you undertake the Activities and Tasks in the order set out in the book. There is an order of precedence in which we need to accomplish things. But nothing is once for all. Every group and every class you teach should be approached through repetition of the Tasks: it is by repetition that we embed good practice.

To learn, we need to know what it is we are setting out to learn. Afterwards we need to revisit the learning to fix clearly in our minds what has been learned, and so link it to other learning.

REMEMBER!

... A teacher's prime task is to engage the student in the learning process. The student must take an active role in order for learning to occur.

The structure of the book

The book is in three parts, related to increasing responsibility.

Part 1 assumes that you will be responsible for ensuring effective learning for a learning group, whether it be a class, a workshop or a ward. It is concerned to establish the way of setting about the job, the good practice. To do that you have to understand certain principles and you must develop confidence and other positive attitudes. You need to take control of your own learning and of the conditions under which your students will learn.

To help you, there is advice on 'micro-lessons'[1] with a peer group, as part of a course programme perhaps, to gain insight and confidence. You are then guided through the various aspects of what is involved in dealing with your own students: preparation, running the class, controlling what happens and the environment, communication and the use of feedback and assessment. Good practice is defined through performance criteria – to provide a model in the head of what you are trying to achieve. There is considerable emphasis on evaluating your teaching and on what happens for you and your students.

Part 2 builds on the learning in Part 1, but requires greater depth and breadth. It develops as a case study of your own learning as you design and plan a learning programme for your students. The programme will develop over a defined time span, with a series of teaching sessions. By reflecting on what happens you build up your insight into your role. The purpose is constantly to refine and improve what happens.

The expected performance will be to more demanding standards than in Part 1, since there is growth and increasing maturity. There is much more advice in Part 2 on methods and approaches to help you.

Part 3 provides a survey of educational psychology and theories of learning as they have developed this century. The model of practice set out in the book is based on an understanding of these. I have chosen to present the theory after you have had enough experience to enable you to read it critically, and to compare it with what happens for you and your students. For this reason emphasis is placed also on developing your study skills. But

---

[1] A lesson is a structured and organised learning experience designed to achieve agreed learning goals: usually it is one of a sequence. In this book, the term micro-lesson is used to mean a simulated lesson with a peer group of student teachers, lasting between fifteen and thirty minutes. Its purpose is to promote development of the necessary behaviours of teachers set out here and in Chapter 4. Emphasis is placed on transferability of the learning to some 'real' context.

the book is yours. You may wish to explore various parts in an order that meets your perception of what your needs are.

ASSUMPTIONS

The following assumptions are made about you as student and teacher.

1 You will be functioning in a teaching context where you can undertake tasks in relation to a real teaching situation.

2 You will have some responsibility for a learning group and for designing a learning programme/sessions for them.

3 You will have the opportunity to undertake teaching assignments, in order to develop your competences in the various aspects of the teaching process, and to match your ability against performance criteria.

4 You will have some opportunity to share with others in team and/or group work, so that you will get critical but supportive feedback on what you are doing.

5 You will be able to find a mentor who will support you.

6 You will be able to reflect on the learning and gradually build up a picture of good practice.

2 Learning to Learn: Developing Study Skills

REMEMBER!
. . . Study skills are essential.

To study successfully, you need to decide what you need to know or what it would help you to find out, where you can best and most easily find the information, and how to make the best use of it.

Teachers need to establish rules and a work-orientated environment for students in order to create positive working behaviour. What is true of students is true of our own behaviour.

No two people are the same, nor are the contexts of their work. And every learner must take responsibility for creating the conditions under which he or she will work and study. Major factors are:

- space-management
- time-management
- self-management.

Space-management

You need personal territory for study, just as you need a kitchen for cooking. Make it easy. Like a carpenter, work with the grain of the wood. Get to know yourself and how you work best. Set out a territory, adopt a system that suits you and establish rules and a pattern to follow.

Not everyone is tidy. Some work better with clutter around them, and still seem to know where everything is. That is what matters. Don't waste energy and time looking for things when a need arises. A good idea or good thinking may disappear while you look. Many do find it easier to have a 'proper system' of shelves and files.

ACTIVITY 2 | Preparation for study

Write down the things you will need to do where you study. How easy will it be to do them? You could be systematic about it, and make a table:

Things to happen here	How easy? (ring your score)	What I need to do
Reading	a b c d	Have a reading lamp
Making notes	a b c d	
Writing	a b c d	
Typing	a b c d	

And so on.

Is there enough light to read by? What kind of light do you need? Poor light leads to eyestrain and tiredness. Will the chair be an upright hard chair? and if so, will it give back support if you type or use a word-processor? Or will it be an easy chair? Is there space to establish your territory, to spread out what you need? Will you need extra space on shelves, or room for a machine? Are things to hand when you need them? No carpenter would work without a bench and a tool rack.

Distraction

You need to pay attention to what you are doing. Some people find 'wallpaper' music helps. Some work better in silence. Some prefer to look out on to a busy road, others choose a blank wall. Some find that looking at a wall makes them feel shut in; they will work better sitting on the other side of the desk with space in front of them. Colour has a strong effect on some people, pictures on others. Try things out; experiment to find what improves your sense of well-being. Things distract us, maybe irritating little things. Set aside specific time for yourself, so you can say 'this is my study time'.

Goals or people: time-management

Brain behaviour appears to show pattern-making and rule-making. How goal-orientated are you? Can you shut out distraction and get things done? Or are you easily diverted?

Are you more person-centred or more goal-centred in the way in which you think and behave? If so, you may place greater value on human transactions than on tasks you need to do, and will find it hard to concentrate on what needs doing. How will you handle that?

Some people appear to be sequential in their behaviour, dealing with one thing at a time. Others are happier to have many things on the go at once. The table below compares the two kinds.

Sequential people	Multi-task people
Try/do one thing at a time: time is tangible and divisible	Try/do many things at once: time is intangible and elastic
Concentrate on the job	Easily distracted; like interruptions
Take time commitment seriously, emphasise keeping to schedule	Think time commitment good, but put much more emphasis on human transactions
Emphasise promptness/timing: but only make casual, short-term relationships	Timing is flexible related to assessment of who it is: prefer long-term relationships
Strong preference for keeping to plans and getting the job done	Change plans/details easily and often: commitment is to people not to jobs

Sequential people tend to plan by hours, set priorities and list actions: things to do and when. They do not find it hard to set targets and goals, and to concentrate on the job. In social affairs they tend to be punctual; they regard keeping to time as important, and they establish a schedule and stick to it. They have a strong preference for order and promptness, and are strongly goal-orientated. They find long-term relationships hard and suffer fools badly.

Multi-task people have an elastic view of time. Their goals are imprecise and confused by all the different tasks they have in hand. They tend to be distracted easily and invite interruptions – they may even create them themselves. They acknowledge system, schedules, agendas and deadlines as desirable but not pressingly important. In social affairs, they make judgements about individuals in regard to time-keeping, promptness and punctuality. They constantly change their decisions, plans and arrangements. They are interested in people, not the job, and in maintaining relationships: that is, they are strongly people-orientated.

You will no doubt recognise people you know of both these types. They tend to be intolerant each of the other. People, however, are tall or short – or any size in between. Honestly assess your own characteristics to help you get yourself organised.

Teachers need to be strongly people-orientated. They need to be able to establish relationships and commitment – to inspire trust and liking in their students. But to be a good manager you must get things done. Find a rhythm that will suit your personality.

Time-management and stress-management are related. Imposing schedules on yourself that are impossible for you, maybe because they do not fit with your personality or your style of working, can lead to stress. Equally, disorganisation is very stressful for the person who likes order. In the end it is much better to set targets and keep to schedules if you can, since stress increases with failing to do things that need doing. You must somehow develop goal-seeking behaviour.

Time is precious. Set yourself short-term goals. Plan ahead, but not more than three weeks ahead. Plan regularly, and revise your plan every day. Check where you are and what you need to do *now*.

Reflective diary

ACTIVITY 3

You cannot reflect on learning experiences you cannot remember.

Teachers need to be keenly aware of how learning happens for them if they are to help their students learn. As you explore the role of teacher, you need to monitor change as it occurs for you.

I once read in an examination script: 'The village school consisted of one teacher and seven other children.' There is real truth here! As a teacher you will be learning all the time:

- from decisions you make: what goes well and what goes badly
- what takes you by surprise
- what you find you can do easily or what proves hard
- what students do: what they find difficult or master easily
- what you observe and what you learn about yourself
- how people behave as individuals and groups
- sudden insights when your perception of something changed.

1 At the time these things happen, you need to make a note for yourself with the salient facts. Note too what you feel.
2 Keep a diary in which you record later reflections on your notes, while they are still fresh in your memory.
3 Later still, look back and see if your view has changed. See if it now forms part of a pattern that begins to make sense.
4 Later again, try to organise your learning experiences into some structures or patterns: such as

student behaviour
learning activities and teaching techniques
important insights.

The purpose of the diary

The principal purpose is to encourage you to reflect on learning experiences: what it felt like, what you observed, how it may have looked to others, and what you intend to do after you have thought about it.

What the diary is for is much more important than what it looks like. It must make sense to you when you come back to any entry. It can be in any form as long as it makes sense to you. You can write it or record it – on a pocket cassette recorder perhaps. It may be in a book or card index file or on a word-processor.

Date each entry so that you can monitor changes in the way you perceive things, so that you can see how your ideas develop with experience.

To see what this means try to recall a few occasions when you were acutely aware of having learned something – when your learning was accelerated. You might have said: 'Oh! I see it now', as something that was puzzling you fell suddenly into place, giving you a new way of perceiving it. This often happens. It is like the moment when we see the picture as we assemble a jigsaw puzzle. Perhaps you realised why someone you knew was behaving oddly, or you found out the purpose of the unlabelled button on the television set. Or you might have discovered something about yourself, an ability you did not know you had. You might have surprised yourself by tackling a problem: 'I didn't know I had it in me'.

CASE STUDY 2

Once I was looking for a residential adult centre in an unfamiliar town. I had a map, which I had misinterpreted. I was sure the place was a large house approached up a drive behind a gate on to the road. That was my 'model in the head' of what I was looking for – what I expected to see. Two people I asked gave me directions, and I still walked straight past the place. Why? In fact it was part of a terrace of houses along the road. I did not see what I expected to see: I walked past it.

Consider occasions when you failed to see something. Why was that? What were you expecting to see?

3 Observing Other Teachers

ACTIVITY 4

Class visit

1 Find a colleague or a teacher in a context you are familiar with: the more experienced the teacher, the better.

2 Negotiate with the teacher an opportunity to visit one class he or she is teaching. Students and teacher will need to know why you want to come and what you will be doing. Even experienced teachers may be a little reluctant to have an observer in the class. This is because any intruder into a class may be disruptive, even someone who just sits at the back and does nothing. Once groups form and gel, any visitor remains an outsider and affects group behaviour.

3 Find out as much as you can from the teacher, so that you have a view of the class before you visit it. Make a record along the following lines:

Date of visit:

Class and teacher:

The students:	male/female, numbers, ages, employment status, married/unmarried, and so on
	any specific groupings (for example, nurses, apprentices)
	any other factors the teacher thinks important
The purpose:	relationship to any course, intended outcomes, qualifications aimed at, job prospects, who pays
The place:	what environment, special features/equipment
The time:	time of day, frequency of meeting, and so on

Learning goals for this class:

The visit: building a picture

Armed with the above information, you can prepare for the visit.

When you visit someone's class, you need to make it clear to the teacher and students that you are going to avoid making value judgements as far as possible.

Your purpose is to share an experience with teacher and students: **to observe as accurately as you can what actually happens – what is going on in the class**.

Inevitably you, the teacher and the students will all have your own feelings about the experience. Quite often these strongly influence what happens.

You are extending your experience by sharing that of others. In order to do that, you have to be receptive and alert. You must arrive at the experience with a questioning attitude. You cannot simply be passive and 'let things happen'.

The information you have will help you to make sense of what you observe. It will help you to recognise what is happening in the class if you have a preliminary picture of it to take with you. Without it, you may miss important aspects of what is happening or be puzzled by what you observe.

Go armed with questions.

Set out below is a structure to enable you to get the most out of the experience. Discuss this beforehand with the teacher, who may point out things in relation to a particular context that may have been omitted from this set of questions, designed as they are for general application.

BUILDING UP A PICTURE

Make notes for yourself along these lines, but invent the questions you think are important.

Environment:	room: size, condition, age, lighting, heating etc.
	furniture/equipment: what is present, layout, desks or tables
	purpose: what is it designed for? what style of teaching/ learning?
	constraints: problems for learning activity
Students:	dress, groupings, age
	any things that surprise you
	relationships with the teacher/within and between the groups
Activity:	teacher activity
	student activity
	how they relate
	note timings and change of activity: movement, breaks and so on

Other:

[Leave some space for post-experience comment.]

Sharing perceptions

What you should take away from the experience is a picture that you can reflect on in private. This will arise partly from what the teacher tells you beforehand and partly from what you see. It is important, of course, to keep an open mind.

You need factual statements, rather than judgements. Avoid making notes such as: 'the students were bored' or 'were excited', or 'the teacher explained the topic very well'. You cannot know how the students felt or how they saw what the teacher did.

How far the environment, equipment, learning/teaching material and behaviour help or inhibit intended learning are judgements. Don't try to guess *why* the students or the teacher behaved as they did. Just note carefully *what* they did.

Factual statements concern such things as the environment, the dress of students and teacher, the equipment and resources used, and the behaviour of students and teacher – what they did, their level of activity, the sequence of events and so on: how learning was achieved, and what the students did in order to learn.

You want to observe what actually happens, rather than what you may go expecting to see. Just as I missed the adult centre because I was expecting to see a different kind of building, you may fail to see important things because you are looking for and expecting to see something else. This problem is worse if the context is very familiar.

But no two people will perceive the same experience in the same way. Each comes to it with an individual mind-set and questions. Clearly, we all select from what we hear, smell, touch and so on. It is just impossible to take it all in.

In discussion with the teacher after the experience, you can share and compare your perceptions of what took place. You can ask the questions that have occurred to you as you watched – about why certain things happened, maybe, and especially about student learning activity.

Reflecting on the experience: consolidation

Avoid sharing your feelings with the teacher. You can explore your own feelings in your reflective diary, and later with a group of your peers if you have an opportunity.

To discover what you have learned you will have to wait a while, thinking about what happened, and getting it into perspective. *Then* try to set down what you have discovered. This will help to consolidate the learning. What does this mean?

We have to revisit an experience, we have to rehearse it again, in order to consolidate it in our memories. But we cannot do that unless we shape it some way – in pictures and in words. We may have visual memories and sounds, but usually we frame things and thoughts about them in words.

Consolidation is this revisiting. One of the most effective ways of revisiting an experience is to share it with someone else, tell them about it, and probably then respond to questions. Tell them what happened and how you felt about it. This is normal human behaviour.

Using the peer group

It is very helpful to share the experience of observing a class with a group of your peers, and especially if they had similar experiences to tell you about. The effort you make to explain what you saw, heard and felt will concentrate and focus the experience for you.

REMEMBER!
. . . You will probably discover that you do not know what you think until you hear what you say.

Later reflection

Your views of what happened when observing that class will change with time and you should try to be aware of any changes in your perception. Telling the peer group and listening to their comments will help to bring these into focus.

Look at your previous comments in your diary. What has changed?

4 Micro-lessons or Peer Group Teaching

What are micro-lessons? What are they for? How should they work?

Once, in a restaurant in Villefrache in the Beaujolais, I had a dish of the most delicious garlic mushrooms. Madame ran the restaurant, Monsieur did the cooking. Foolishly, I asked Madame for the recipe.

'Monsieur, it is not what, it is who,' she said.

The difference between one dish of garlic mushrooms and another depends on who has cooked it. I had asked the wrong question. Asking wrong questions is what people do most of the time. They get unhelpful answers. **First find the questions**.

There are no foolproof recipes for a good lesson. There are only teachers. So we must concentrate on 'who'.

Teaching behaviour depends critically on teaching experience. Teacher educators have little control over real classes that teachers teach, so they choose to use simulations: here they can control what happens, what teachers are asked to do, and the conditions and pressures that they face.

It has become standard practice to set up simulations in training for anything. You probably know that airline pilots are trained on a simulator: a highly sophisticated, expensive piece of technological wizardry that puts the trainee through an experience that feels like the real thing. All the senses – sight, hearing, balance, movement – are used to create a grand illusion. The pilot is then put under stress. From normal take-off and landing, the pilot is made to deal with emergencies, engine failure and so on, to ensure that he or she will be able to cope whatever happens. Whenever a pilot changes from a familiar aircraft to another, from flying fighter aircraft maybe to civilian passenger planes, a simulator is used. A minimum number of flying hours must be clocked up before a certificate to fly is awarded, and it is much cheaper and more effective to do it on a simulator. (Of course, the trainees must also fly.)

With the realisation that present training and testing for car drivers do not prepare people at all adequately for real driving – indeed avoid putting them into situations that require rapid response and ability to cope under stress – there is a move to using technological simulators in this field too. If you have ever been on rides in theme parks such as Disney World, you will be aware of what it feels like to be in one of these things. I use the words 'feels like' because these methods are experiential; the trainee/participant goes through a learning experience. The simulation experiences are intended to change people's behaviour.

It is recognised that changing behaviour means changing not only what people do, but the way they think about it – their attitudes to themselves and the things they are asked to do. To take an extreme example: if I propose to walk across a plank suspended far above the ground between two high buildings, I must know that I can do it – I must have a belief in my ability. How do I get the knowledge or the belief unless I actually do it?

People learning to walk the tight rope start close to the ground and go on to using a safety net until they are confident enough to do without it. Someone who is frightened of water can't be taught to swim by being thrown into the deep end of a swimming pool; even if the victim survives, the fear is likely to remain.

The astonishing thing is that most people do cope with such an experience. People do survive their first terrifying drive on the motorway, where they have to react much faster, deal with so much more baffling information and suffer from so much more aggression than their training set out to prepare them for.

One effect can be that they learn bad behaviour, become equally aggressive say, or discover techniques to defend themselves from the dangers they perceive. These then inhibit good practice. We should think about that in relation to learning to teach.

As a way of learning, immersion has certain advantages. We do not usually make tiny steps in learning – we make leaps from one state of being to another. If we try to use a gradual approach, the learner usually gets way ahead of us and is likely to become bored. So long as my motivation to succeed is high enough, I can go through hell and high water. From the point of view of my self-image, succeeding against the odds, overcoming fear and solving problems is very effective. In the end I have to risk drowning in order to swim.

But there are bound to be casualties, since there is a level of risk. Who calculates the risk? What is an acceptable casualty rate? We reduce the risks as far as possible with airline pilots since the costs of failure are very high. But we accept a scandalous rate of failure and casualties on our roads. And what about our classrooms?

Air crashes are still put down to pilot error. However experienced pilots or brain surgeons are, they still have to take risks, and they make mistakes in their professional judgements.

We rely on professional judgements in pilots, doctors and teachers. The judgements they make are based on their knowledge and experience. They depend critically on the depth of that experience and the learning that has occurred as a result.

Simulation in teaching

The simulations that teacher educators use vary widely. Their choice may well depend on their 'model in the head' of what teachers do – on assumptions they make about how learning happens or how it is transferred from one context to another.

There was a fashion in teacher education to analyse teaching into an array of teacher skills, which could be developed and perfected in isolation and then somehow brought back together into a 'global performance'. Micro-training is a better description of this training. Sophisticated set-ups were built at great expense to allow this to happen. A commonly used method was to use modelling: that is, allowing students to watch a teacher in a micro-session using the skills and then video-recording them practising the skill so that they could evaluate their performance against that of the model and so improve it.

But the problem of transfer to a real situation remained. Since the use of skills is only one part of what makes it possible for me to be effective in a given situation, I must integrate my skills with all the other things I need. In teaching, it is what the students do in order to learn that matters. A skilful performance by the teacher, impressive as it may be, will be of no value unless it also engages the students actively in learning.

Early arguments for 'competency training programmes' were based on the assumptions that underlie this approach to training. Since it is impossible, they say, to practise all the skills a teacher needs at once, let us develop them individually. There is, I believe, a misconception here of how changes in behaviour occur. If I practised for ever the individual skills needed to walk my plank between my two buildings (whatever I analysed them to be), when it came to setting off across the plank my fear of falling would drive my skills away. After all, I could walk across the plank easily without training if it were on the floor.

There is no doubt, however, that there are important skills that teachers need to acquire and practise. I believe they are best practised at a point of need – that is, with your own students. What then should we do in micro-lessons?

Planning micro-lessons

The micro-lessons described here occur within a teacher peer group who are attempting to achieve agreed learning goals in a training programme.

PURPOSE

What are micro-lessons for? There are many answers:

- to provide enrichment of the learning through sharing ideas
- to provide the opportunity to experiment and take risks
- to provide feedback by evaluating the effectiveness of what occurs
- to learn experientially as both student and teacher
- to challenge assumptions about how learning can be promoted
- to develop confidence and insight
- to encourage a creative, student-centred approach.

Each micro-lesson should be approached as a simulation of a real class but with constraints of time. It would not be sensible to ask your peers to role-play your students as they are in reality. Your peers have to be themselves. The 'teacher' must deal with the learning needs that they have, not those that some others might be supposed to have.

The constraints of time and place are real. They provide the same challenges as in any other teaching situation: the production of teaching/learning material, the need to think through what is to happen, and the response and ability to adapt to feedback. But there is also a chance for formal feedback and evaluation from the 'students', to let you know how it felt for them, what worked and what didn't, what they learned and what they failed to learn.

You must learn from the experience as a whole. The intention is to create a class experience not dissimilar from the real thing. This is most important, since in a simulation what matters is to be able to transfer learning from the simulated experience to the real one. One should illuminate the other.

One thing you might well learn is that learning can be fun.

All this is easier to understand from examples. I am grateful to those students who have allowed me to use their ideas and to report on their micro-lessons.

CASE STUDY 3

Sandra, a teacher of students with learning difficulties, thought about what she wanted her peer group to learn. This group was made up mostly of part-time teachers from a wide variety of backgrounds: nursing, hairdressing, motor vehicle work, catering, plumbing, engineering, computing and special needs. Indeed, the advantages of groupwork of this kind derive from the richness of experience and challenge in the group.

It was clear to her that very few of them had experience with handicapped students, particularly the sort of students she worked with. Sandra decided that if they were to find themselves working with such students they needed to know what it felt like to be unable to learn – and that she would put them through the experience.

She produced work-cards for each 'student' which gave simple instructions as to what each had to do – written in letters of the Greek alphabet. She also provided paper, patterns, scissors and so on, since they had to try to make something.

The class had fifteen minutes to complete the task on the work-cards: this was the time allowed for the micro-lesson. Sandra had thought carefully about the time constraint. She said nothing to them except that they should read what was on the cards and get on. Of course, they could not read the cards. Here is an example:

τηκ θε σκισσορs ιν θε λεφτ ανδ.

The class asked her to explain it to them.

'Why? can't you read it? It's in English.' Sandra then read it.

'Oh! is that what it says?'

The instructions deliberately made them clumsy by setting them to do things backwards or upside down, using the left hand if they were right-handed and so on. They made a mess of it. They laughed at their own clumsiness and what others were doing. It was fun.

But it was serious learning too. At the end, Sandra asked them what they had learned. They said they knew now what it was like to have a learning difficulty, what it felt like to be clumsy and unable to cope.

One engineer said, 'But you haven't taught us anything.' You may imagine what a good discussion arose from that remark.

What can we learn from a case study like this? Here are some questions to think about.

1 What would you have said to the engineer at the end?
2 What model of teaching did he have that made him say that?
3 What model of teaching was Sandra using?
4 Do you sympathise with the engineer's point of view? if so, why?
5 Why did this class of adults laugh so much when they could not do what they were trying to do? What can we learn from this about adult learners?
6 Can you think of ways of exploiting an idea like Sandra's in your own classes?
7 Could you plan a micro-lesson along these lines?
8 Make a note of ideas you could use: come back later to them.

COMMENT

Sandra was new to teaching, but she had had years of experience in helping Scouts and other people. She started with a simple question and a simple idea.

REMEMBER!

... Try to be straightforward: avoid being complicated and 'clever'.

Sandra thought through what she wanted the group to learn, how they should learn it and what they had to do in order to learn. She set up a learning experience for them to go through. It involved them in attempting to do something and so discover things about themselves that they did not know.

There were clear learning goals. Sandra knew what they were. She could have made it clear to the group what they were to learn, but she felt it would affect the process of discovery. They were able to say afterwards, and confirm, what they had learned. Usually, it is better to share the learning goals at the beginning. Sandra was right, of course.

The method she chose involved her in considerable preparation of the cards and materials. But during the session she had little to do, and could concentrate on watching the learners and giving a hand when asked. The students were very busy; it was entirely learning activity, mostly discovery learning, on their part. There was a lot of variety too in what happened in the class in fifteen minutes. The students could say what they had learned at the end to consolidate.

REMEMBER!

. . . Preparation pays off. Thinking through and preparing properly matter even more than enthusiasm and giving a good performance.

Sandra came into her own mainly during the final session when she made them consolidate what they had learned by getting them to tell her about it.

Finally, she was able to exploit the comment made by one of the group to tie up the principles on which she was working and to make them clear.

The students went away from the experience changed in important ways. It had made them think. They had found out things about themselves and others that were important. It almost certainly affected the way they thought about student learning difficulties.

All this stemmed from just fifteen minutes of learning experience. This was learning by leaps: a great deal of important learning is of this kind.

CASE STUDY 4

Tony, who was in the same group, taught plumbing. He decided not to follow the easy option of giving a mini-introduction to pipework but to share an enthusiasm of his, a working hobby that he pursued with his wife on market days. He went round the markets dealing in antique pottery. He was very knowledgeable about pottery, and had a good collection.

The room was set out with comfortable chairs and some tables. Tony set up on the tables a representative sample of plates. He had made photocopies from a catalogue of the makers' marks that are usually stamped or printed on to the bottoms of plates and show the manufacturer and the year of manufacture.

Armed with these, groups of two or three students were asked to identify and date sets of plates. They moved around the tables to do this, picking up the plates and examining them closely, looking for and comparing the makers' marks.

At the end, Tony marked the groups' scores and helped them to understand where they had gone wrong. He revisited the learning with them and consolidated it. He communicated his own enthusiasm, and talked about the feel and look of the glazes, the patterns and so on.

In the evaluation afterwards, there were expressions of genuine enthusiasm and excitement about what they had found out. It had opened their eyes to a whole new area of interest they had not known existed. Some brought their own plates the next week to be identified and dated. And so did I. I was particularly fascinated by a Toby jug I had which turned out to be French, not English as I supposed. I have continued to learn. So have they.

Consider the following questions.

1 What preparation did Tony have to do?
2 Tony's input of information came after the students had had the opportunity to discover about the marks for themselves. What do you think was the

advantage of that? Would they have learned better or worse if he had given a lecture first?

3 What was the advantage of doing it in small groups?
4 What was the point of marking the scores?
5 What lessons can you learn that you can apply in your class?
6 Make a note to yourself about these things. Review it later.

COMMENT

Most teachers rely heavily on only one of their students' senses: hearing. Usually they do so without any idea how to develop the listening skills such reliance requires.

It is a great pity, since for most people hearing is a poorly developed and inaccurate faculty. We are even worse at listening: our concentration span is about fifteen minutes. We are much better at seeing than we are at hearing things, particularly since television has replaced radio as our main leisure activity. Seventy per cent of what we learn we learn through seeing. It was probably because our ancestors relied so much on their eyes that they took to walking on their hind legs, to give themselves a better view of the world. And most teachers ignore the importance of touch, of handling things.

If you really want to know about something, you try to explore it with all your faculties. You look at it closely, you pick it up, feel it, weigh it in your hand, smell it, even taste it maybe. A baby does all these things as it explores its world. This is what the students did with these plates.

Tony loved pottery, the feel of it, the look, the different glaze mixes that were used, and how the different makers produced the tell-tale characteristics. He communicated its sensuousness to us. His plates were the products of loving craftsmanship.

Most real-life learning is of this kind. People explore, walk through their environment, handle objects, smell, touch, feel. Most adult classes are about hands-on activities, 'doing it' learning. Teachers and textbooks tend to make it academic. Why do we so often take the fun, the exploring, the doing, out of it?

There was a great deal of cognitive learning in the class. I now know something about china marks. I can recognise the differences in plates and glazes which I certainly did not know before. I wanted to know more. My interest had been aroused. I had been shown how to set about learning more also.

Tony's class ran over its allotted time. When something so good was happening, it would have been stupid of me as the tutor to stop it too soon – and that is another lesson. The ability to adapt is most important. Often teachers are trapped by their own rigidity and determination to get through what they had planned, and stop student learning just as it was about to take off, to everybody's annoyance.

CASE STUDY 5

A small group of students wanted to try an experiment in learning with their peer group. They had learned about the difference made to learning by using structure.

They used two low tables set in different parts of a large room. On each of the tables a collection of the same things was displayed. On one table, the many objects were set out in random order, deliberately jumbled up with no possible logic to connect them. But on the other, they were grouped so that a learner could easily recognise the category to which each object belonged. For example, ink, pen, paper, a book and paper-clips were placed together; so were a screwdriver, screws, a tape-measure and a hammer.

The students were selected randomly into groups. Each group was then allocated one area of the room and not allowed to see the other. Members of the two teams were to compete in trying to memorise the contents of the table in front of them. The contents were covered with a cloth. The cloth was removed and they were asked to look at the table and its contents for two minutes. The cloth was put back and they were then individually to write down as many of the objects as they could remember.

The scores were then added up and people were invited to talk about the difficulty they had in memorising the objects. The team who tried to memorise objects that were randomly distributed on the table had had great difficulty, but the other group, with objects set out in categories, found it not too hard. Neither team, of course, knew that the thing had been rigged. They were amazed that one team had done so much better than the other.

Of course, the real learning came when each team was shown what the other had to learn. 'Oh well! if I'd had that . . .'.

Again, in this case the learning goals were known to the persons who devised the game, but were only divulged to the students at the end when they had perceived them for themselves.

1 What do you think was the advantage of having a small group plan a micro-lesson together?
2 This was a game set up as a competition between teams. What do you think might be the advantage of that approach?
3 How do you think the losing team felt when they saw the arrangement on the table for the other team?
4 How effective do you think this approach might be in getting students to learn some important principle?

COMMENT

Games are very powerful learning tools. The competitive element, if used well and properly controlled, can create a strong motivation towards achieving group or individual goals and can improve the level of achievement overall. Used badly, however, games can be disruptive of co-operative, friendly relationships.

The peer group here had come together well by the time this game was devised, so that everyone in the group was able to relate well to the others. Even so, the losing team felt they had been cheated. This probably had something to do with self-image.

What is important is that the learning was highly experiential. In fact, it was much more powerful for the losing team than for the students who found it quite easy. We often learn a great deal more from working hard to do something than from a task that is easily accomplished, and if we have to come back from failure.

CASE STUDY 6

Fran taught personal relationships and coping skills with various groups, including mentally retarded students. She wanted to show her peer group how she set about getting people to understand how relationships develop – for instance, what might go wrong within a marriage and why. Here is her description of the activity, given to the students at the end of the experience as a handout.

SCULPTING

Begin with two willing volunteers. Choose any situation you like. You could choose the family, because it is a common experience. If you want to explore conflicts and relationships at work, you could choose that instead. In the description that follow I assume you are looking at family relationships.

1 Place your two volunteers in positions which you feel convey the relationship that would exist between a couple in a newly formed relationship. Ask the group to tell you what the postures suggest – affection, closeness, protective, absorption and so on.
2 Now move the time scale on – two years perhaps – and introduce the first child (another member of the group).

You can do the rest of the exercise in one of two ways: *either* continue to position additions to the group and explore feelings, *or* allow additions to stand where they feel most natural. If you are working in a real situation with a group it is best to use the second method because you can explore why they have stood in that position – for example, closer to one person than another.

3 Continue to add 'family members'. They need not all be children; some can be elderly relatives, for instance. Either use volunteers, or choose people if you know them well. You can also remove members – perhaps a sister who has married, a brother who has moved away to take a job, a partner who leaves home and then comes back, one member who has died.
4 At each new addition/subtraction, explore with the group their feelings about the changed situation and how they would prefer the relationship to develop. Let them adjust their postures and then talk with the other group members to see how they now feel.

5 At intervals, encourage the group members who are observers rather than participators to say what the groupings suggest to them. See if 'family members' agree with their viewpoints/impressions.

6 Finally, ask the first couple to stand exactly where they are while the others return to their seats. Explore with the whole group how the original body postures of the 'parents' have changed and what this might indicate about the changed nature of the relationship. Why has it changed? How could this be avoided.

Fran conducted the exercise above for about fifteen minutes. The peer group found it entertaining. At the end, comment was hardly necessary, but it led to a fascinating discussion.

1 What advantage do you think there might be in getting people to 'be' someone else and to try to express their feelings about it? (This was *not* role play, which would require the students to play out a scene of some kind, but a worldless 'sculpting' of postures to express feelings/relationships.)

2 Fran was using examples of 'body language' here. What do you think is meant by that phrase? Why is it so important?

3 Was the teacher able to predict what would happen? How far should she have tried to control and shape what people chose to do? What effect would that have had on the learning?

4 How well would you need to know your students in order to use this kind of technique successfully?

5 What effect do you think the experience had on the learners?

6 Can you think of other ways to use an idea of this kind?

7 Make a note of any ideas/thoughts you could use.

COMMENT

Such complex ideas as the relationships between people and how they change with time and different pressures are very difficult to deal with. Usually they become abstractions, or get bogged down in anecdotes and discussions of people's personal problems.

This method was marvellously powerful in creating an abstraction and at the same time allowing individuals to explore relationships in their own way. It produced striking visual images and made people walk through the experience. It was as fascinating for the observers as for the participants.

People were encouraged to draw their own conclusions: there was no ready-made moral, no advice from Fran. My own conclusion was that you have to work hard to hold a relationship together if so much is going on to force people apart.

What we discover for ourselves may be much more creative learning than what other people tell us.

This was another example of a simple but powerful idea well used.

CASE STUDY 7

John needed to explain a particular concept to his class of apprentice plumbers. He wanted his students not only to be able to apply a formula but to understand how to calculate heat loss from a building, and hence how much heat you needed to put into it. They had to visualise the problem: the rooms were in three dimensions and heat loss in six directions – through the four walls, the ceiling and the floor – and they needed also to take into account the number of rooms inside a house.

He felt it would be a good idea to try to explain the principle to people who knew very little about plumbing in a micro-lesson: to experiment with them first before doing it with his students. He and I agreed that it could be done by using a doll's house. So he managed to get hold of a large doll's house and brought it to the class.

The students were asked to examine the house in small groups and then to work out in their groups what factors had to be taken into consideration in designing heating input into the house, and in particular to discover the problems of heat loss. Each group was asked to come up with a solution to the problem.

It took them very little time to analyse the heat loss problem, and their solutions were quite fascinating. They saw that insulation was as important as heat input and the reasons why.

So the students told the teacher what the problem was, and jumped way ahead in understanding other principles as well.

1 What was the advantage of using a physical object?
2 Why do we find it so hard to deal with abstract ideas?
3 Would it have helped if the students had known formulae for calculating heat loss/heat input?
4 What was the advantage of setting them the task in teams?
5 What do you understand by a 'principle'? Why are they so important to grasp? Why are they sometimes so hard to grasp?
6 Can you think of ways of using this idea?
7 What principles do you need to get across? Write them down and think of ways of achieving that.

COMMENT

It is usual to present principles to students as abstractions, but a principle is much better understood in a concrete situation. When you explore something physically in the round, you are using all your faculties rather than just that part of the brain that deals with language and concepts. Equally, you will create your own abstraction in language that makes sense to you. There are marked differences in the ability of groups of students to deal with abstractions. We need to observe carefully how hard it is for any particular group: their difficulties will depend critically on their experience, and also on their ability to visualise something as a mental model. Many people find this extremely hard.

Creative use of micro-lessons

Micro-lessons allow us to rehearse teaching techniques on a small scale and get the feel of how they work, without the fear of the consequences of failure.

It is important to take risks – to try, and maybe to fail. We can learn a great deal from such experience. For instance, if the students had become really angry when they found they had been tricked in the game with the objects on the tables (unlikely, but possible), the teacher could have explored with them why they felt like that, and think of ways of dealing with it.

The only way you will find out what tremendously good things can happen in micro-lessons is by taking part in them. However many examples I might give, they will lack the excitement and challenge of being there as either student or teacher, sharing the learning of others and matching your experiences with theirs.

Micro-lessons do not have to be confined entirely in time or space. It is perfectly acceptable to set the group things to do before your micro-lesson, perhaps as a game.

For instance, if you want to interest them in local history, it is good to get them to some simple research first. You could ask them during the week, whenever they are about the district, to look out for things of interest, anything that catches their eye and that might have a history to it. At the lesson, get the class to tell you what they spotted and then show them how and where they could find out about their observations. You will no doubt be able to explain many of them, but if there are gaps in your knowledge, you can use them to advantage too.

All this focuses their attention – they arrive with questions to alert the brain. A catalogue history lecture on the town might evoke nothing but yawns. They also develop the ability to observe and to research for information. The questions are theirs, not yours or those of a history book. It's all much more fun.

Another approach is to give them a list of places to discover, or questions that can only be answered by searching through the town. 'What is on the weather-vane on the Town Hall?' 'What colour is the lion on the White Lion?' It is possible to make it competitive too: you could even award prizes!

Take risks. Be inventive. And, whatever you do, prepare thoroughly.

Effectiveness

There are numerous examples of successful and inventive lessons. Peer group work can bring about a startling release of creative energy once people stop worrying about their own performance and concentrate instead on student learning.

Many micro-lessons involve demonstrating techniques. A lesson is about learning; it is not a challenge to the teacher to prove something. Most of the many demonstrations I have seen were adequately done, but a fair number were so 'clever' that all they did was convince the students that this was a kind of magic they could never learn. Others encouraged the students to believe just the opposite.

It is hard for teachers to remember what it was like when something they now do easily was difficult for them to do at all. Their present skill has come naturally without their having to think about it. All skill learning is like this. With sufficient practice it is a matter of habit, 'memory of the muscles', so that the concentration of the skilled person can be given to other things such as the design of the object that is being created, while the skill takes care of itself. Skills, after all, are not an end in themselves; their purpose is to enable us to create something, maybe a meal or a table or a document.

It is also hard to slow down: to demonstrate a skill at a pace that the students can 'see'. At the same time you have to ensure that all the students can see what you are doing and this can be hard if you have to demonstrate on a flat surface to twenty people, or if you have to have your back to them – working at a lathe, say, or with a 'patient' on the floor or on a bed.

To be effective, demonstrations must provide opportunity for the students to have a go. So the students must be able to learn the skill/techniques quickly. For example, catering students can learn to make quite reasonable 'roses' by peeling tomatoes thickly with a sharp knife, well within the fifteen minutes allowed. Students can learn to do a fireman's lift or simple resuscitation, or how to find someone's pulse and measure the heart rate, or how to bandage an arm – or almost anything that is simple, easy to follow, and achievable by the students within time constraints. There are many things you cannot learn in fifteen minutes: how to use a typewriter or a computer or how to write a poem. But I did once learn a Cantonese children's song that taught me Chinese numbers.

Obviously, you have to decide where your lesson is to happen, and what equipment or resources you will need. You cannot plaster a wall or lay bricks in classrooms designed for ordinary teaching, any more than you can reasonably ask students to dice a macedoine of vegetables on a desk. I have seen wet clay presented on large trays with desks protected by polythene so that people could experiment with it. But if you want to throw a pot on a wheel you have to go to the wheel; you cannot bring it to the class.

You do not have to be trapped in the normal classroom. But if you are going to ask students to meet in a specialist environment, they need to know where it is, and it may be important that they wear the 'right' clothes: they must know in advance and come prepared. All this requires thinking through, planning and organising.

Evaluating micro-lessons

Ask before:

- What are the students setting out to learn?
- What are you going to get them to do in order to learn that? What preparation do you need to do, and by what time?
- How will they know what they have to learn and whether they have succeeded or not?
- How will you know whether they have learned what you intend? How will you consolidate the learning?

Ask after:

- Did it go as intended?
- What actually happened?
- Why?

Evaluation must be seen as entirely concerned with consolidating the learning. We are trying to learn about learning, and what the teacher's behaviour and thinking has to do with it.

A micro-lesson is always about learning, not the performance of the teacher. Evaluation must be concerned with how effective the learning was, not with scoring the various teacher skills. So let us be clear what micro-lessons are for. They are not part of the assessment of competence as a teacher. If they are used for this purpose most of the excitement and fun will disappear, and so will much of the potential for learning.

Evaluation is an opportunity to revisit a learning experience, so that the group can take a reasoned view of what actually happened and why, and draw some conclusions from it.

First, you must establish the facts – this is where sharing the perceptions of the group is valuable. Consider again the advice on observing a class on page 19. You can compare the teacher's idea of what happened, what she or he noticed and felt, with those of the students. If they are different, so much the better.

How did the students feel when trying to learn using the method chosen? Did they feel threatened? confused? stimulated? Was it easy or hard? challenging? infuriating? Were they amazed at their ability or depressed by their failure? If some succeeded and others did not, what was the difference? Why so?

Perhaps there was some sex stereotyping. In some exercises women generally seem to do better than men, and in others not so well. If that does happen, it could lead to asking why that might be so: does it relate to self-image? to experience? to conditioning?

I am not going to suggest all the possible questions. But that in the end is what it is for: to discover the questions. It is no help to learn theories about how people learn if you have no practical experience against which to test them, and to judge their validity.

You need to look consciously at how you learn, how you feel about what is happening to you, if you are to understand how it is for your own students. The more experience of teacher–student interactions you have, the more fascinating the questions become.

Task 2 sets out some structured ideas for planning a micro-lesson. In Task 3 you will evaluate one by reflecting on the experience.

TASK 2: Preparing a micro-lesson (checklist)

LEARNING GOALS
1 Clarify for yourself what you want the students to learn.
2 Set these out as statements of learning goals. For example:

The students will

- locate a fracture in a limb
- make a sling
- make the patient comfortable.

Make the statements simple.

3 Try to ensure that what you describe can be done in the time, and can be easily observed happening.

METHOD
1 Think about how the students are going to learn.
2 Try to ensure they will learn, as far as possible, by being required to do something actively.
3 Think about what they might enjoy attempting to do.
4 Are they going to work individually or in groups?
5 Will there be any element of competition?
6 How practicable is it? Where can it be done?
7 What are the things they and you will need?
8 How much organisation time will you need for room/equipment?
9 Will you need a specialist room? How do you organise that?
10 What information will the students need beforehand? Map? What clothes to wear? Ingredients? Anything else?

INPUT
1 What do you have to provide as input to get it going?
2 Will this be you talking, or will there be instructions?
3 Will you need to demonstrate something?
4 What time will you need to do your bit?
5 How much time do they need? What is to be the balance?
6 How much can be prepared beforehand – handouts? overhead projector transparencies?
7 Will they need anything a week before, or to do anything in advance?
8 How will you grab their attention? How will you make them want to learn?

PREPARATION

1 Make clear for yourself what you need to make or prepare.
2 Give yourself deadlines – 'do this by' such and such a day. Have a checklist.
3 Have it all together and ready. Make sure everything works!
4 Have a cue-sheet, showing teacher activity, student activity and timings.

CONSOLIDATION

Ensure there is time to focus on what they have learned.

TASK 3: Evaluating micro-lessons (checklist)

FACTS

1 What did you expect to happen? Did it happen that way?
2 What actually happened? Can you describe it?
3 Did the students understand what they had to do? and do it?
4 How well did they do it? Did anything surprise you?
5 What would you do differently next time?

LEARNING GOALS

1 Restate for yourself what you wanted them to learn.
2 Do you think your view of that has changed? Why?
3 Did they achieve the goals? Did they know? How did you?
4 What else did they and you learn?
5 Did anything about the learning surprise you?

METHOD

1 Was the method you chose appropriate for the learning?
2 How active or passive were the students?
3 Did you get the balance right, do you think?
4 Did they enjoy what they did? Why, or why not?
5 Were there any problems? Could you have foreseen them?
6 How well did you cope with making it all happen?
7 Did they co-operate, or was there any tension?
8 Did you get the practicalities right?
9 Did they have the right things to learn with? Was the place right?
10 How could you have improved what happened?

INPUT

1 What about your preparation and what you actually did?
2 Did it take too long? Was it clear?
3 Was there too much information to absorb? Was it confusing?
4 Was everything ready? Did it work? What else did you need?
5 Did the environment support the learning or cause problems?
6 If you did it again, how would you change it?

CONSOLIDATION
1 What did they learn?
2 What did you learn?

5 Teams

Why is it so important to practise working as part of a team?

We live in a technological society. Our students need to function well within that society and to do so they need to have certain skills, knowledge and attitudes that relate to problem-solving. This is a cumulative learning experience for us individually: we build up our confidence to tackle problems in a creative way.

We all need to try to predict what will happen. We cannot deal with things or people unless we have some hypotheses, guesses, to guide us. Suppose you are driving a car at night down a dark road. You see lights coming towards you. From experience you can make a reasonable guess as to what those lights are. You predict how the oncoming car, not the lights, will behave – that it will keep to the side of the road away from you. On the basis of this prediction, you are able to decide what you should do. Of course, you could be wrong!

When you are faced with new and challenging circumstances, with problems you are unfamiliar with or where your theories are not in fact working very well, you are forced to try out new ideas or new tactics. If the lights coming towards you present a totally unfamiliar pattern that makes no sense to you, you cannot make any predictions or take action. You might be best advised just to stop and wait to see what happens.

If there are other people in the car, you can consult with them. Perhaps, if you put your heads together, you will come up with a workable hypothesis and an action plan.

This is normal human behaviour. We are social animals. We work best in groups rather than on our own. The only way in which we can explain how an animal as physically weak as *Homo sapiens* came to dominate much stronger animals is in terms of this combining of strength and talent. The most terrifying animal in the jungle is a column of ants on the march. Here, truly the whole is much greater than the sum of the parts.

Individuals alone are less likely to solve problems than are groups. We have seen that management is essentially the harnessing of the energies of groups of people that have agreed goals that they are committed to achieving together. Those countries that value the group more than individuals have achieved technological dominance in the last few decades.

If we want our students to be able to become adept at problem-solving and developing the insight, skills and confidence needed, we have to encourage them to work in teams, to share and to support each other. One thing an employer will always value highly is a good team member. What is true of students is true of teachers.

Apart from any other consideration, it is much more fun. It is also very satisfying to achieve particular goals together with a group of colleagues. We learn so much from each other. This also provides a point of challenge, testing our ability fully.

Setting up a team exercise

First, there must be a context in which the team exercise will occur. It is much easier to practise the skills as an extension of the micro-teaching. It needs a whole day to do it properly.

Identify teams of three or four teachers and invite them to plan a learning activity to last about 30–45 minutes. Of course, planning and preparation must take place well ahead of the day.

All the same considerations apply as for micro-lessons (or, indeed, for planning learning of any kind). What is special is the greater potential for creative thinking and design of the learning. Again, the model is:

- explore ideas
- choose one and shape it
- design a session
- implement the learning
- evaluate it with the group.

CASE STUDY 8

Karen, Christine and Frances planned the following exercise. They thought of a simple task like answering the telephone and how difficult people find it to do it well.

They set up a large room with telephone sets, putting them into six different contexts in different parts of the room. They wrote instruction cards, each defining a different situation and a problem using telephones. The situations included:

asking a difficult bank manager for a loan
answering the phone in a busy shop with one insistent customer on the phone and another in the shop
dealing with an answering machine
having a one-sided conversation
taking down instructions by telephone

The teachers started proceedings with a role play of a secretary who committed every possible error in dealing with the phone. It alerted the students to problems they might encounter and was fun to watch. It created a good atmosphere.

Students then went round in pairs to experience all the situations. The team positioned an observer at each station to note what students did as they followed the instructions.

At the end the students reported what they had discovered and the observers what they had observed. The learning was then agreed in relation to certain principles.

COMMENT

The team exercise was fun. Students explored a range of different but perfectly realistic situations, and discovered quite a lot of important principles about communicating by telephone.

Having observers meant that there was an opportunity to take different views of the same experience. The observers were able to compare different people doing the same tasks. The participants could explore their own feelings. And sharing the experience with a partner allowed the students to extract maximum benefit from the whole exercise.

The teachers learned a great deal also about generating ideas and about making students work together as a team.

TASK 4: Planning a team exercise

Plan a team exercise as a micro-lesson, or a class with some of your colleagues working as far as possible as a team – to gain the experience.

Implement and evaluate the plan.

What have you learned?

6 Getting Started

What are the students going to do in order to learn?

Teaching

There is a great deal more to running effective learning sessions than the ability to maintain control of the class or to deliver your material clearly, or even to manage the learning activity you have devised. All these skills are required and no class is likely to be successful without them. But these are all about what *you* are going to do.

In developing your skills and competence as a teacher, you must constantly keep in mind that **you are there principally to engage the students in a learning process**. Whatever you do, however well you do it, their learning depends critically upon what *they* do in order to learn.

This must be your starting-point for planning learning sessions. If you are anxious about your own ability to manage, how well you are performing, what the students think of you – or how critical your head of department or tutor is going to be of your performance – it may prove very difficult to avoid concentrating largely on what you do and ignoring what the students are doing.

In observing other classes, therefore, concentrate your attention on the students: how they are responding to what the teacher is doing, on the balance of activity – that is, who is doing all the work in the class.

Think about the role of a doctor with a patient. The doctor has to deal with needs of individuals, listening carefully to what the patient says, asking questions in order to elicit helpful information, and then making a professional judgement about the patient's needs in order to prescribe a course of therapy.

The responsibility for getting well lies with the patient as much as with the doctor, however. The doctor may prescribe a regime, advise a change of life-style, perhaps, or of eating habits or work patterns, but it is what the patient chooses to do that affects progress. If he or she goes on over-eating, refuses to take the pills and muddles and/or abuses their use, it is the patient who is to blame (though, of course, the doctor must ensure that the patient understands what the instructions mean).

I remember a surgeon saying to me: 'A surgeon can only do damage. It is the body that must do the healing.' The body's capacity to heal itself amazed him. He set me thinking about teaching.

It requires effort on the part of students to learn, and a commitment to doing it. A teacher must create the right conditions for learning to happen and find ways to motivate the students. A teacher should be able to generate lively excitement about the subject and communicate enthusiasm.

Often enough, you will feel the need to do much more. You will want to be certain the students get it right. But in doing so you may well take away the excitement that comes from intellectual or physical challenge. You may do all the thinking and all the work, only requiring the students to sit quietly and listen.

Learning

REMEMBER!
. . . Unless the student makes the effort to learn, learning is unlikely to happen.

What makes someone want to learn, to move on from where they are now, when it obviously requires a lot of effort? Who will want to change unless they are somehow discontented with the way things are now? Perhaps the teacher should be like the grit that gets into the shell of an oyster. How does it feel for the oyster? an itch? an irritation? a pain? The result, whatever it is, is a pearl which may be very beautiful.

A learner has to worry at the thing. Many teachers will provide the pearls ready-made. Students are asked to value them highly for what they are, and to store them in their bags. But they are only borrowed, put into the bank. It is the pearls the students make themselves that they really value, that matter for them, and that will have a significant effect on their thinking, behaviour and self-esteem.

7 Lesson Preparation

In the next few chapters we are going to consider separately each part of the process involved in preparing for and teaching a class, beginning here with the preparation of a lesson.

Any new experience is difficult to grasp as a whole because there is such an enormous amount of information, so many different and confusing things to try to take in all at once. Initially we explore and deal with the bits as they arise. Only later can we try to make sense of it all, when we have an opportunity to look back over our experiences and try to get them into perspective.

You will have had this happen to you many times. With anything new, whether it is trying to read a book, to make some new thing that you have never tried to make before, or to visit an unfamiliar town or a supermarket, there has to be a learning period.

We can, however, try to adopt a strategy that will enable us to deal with the new experience more effectively. With a book, for instance, we could decide first of all what information we want and then search the book for it, rather than just plough through what the author thought we should be told. We can approach a film or television programme with the same questioning attitude; all too often, we are completely passive in the cinema or in front of the television set.

Think about starting a new job. What happens when you arrive? You can wait to be told by your new employers whatever it is they feel is necessary or important for you to know. Of course, this will be important information. But the trouble is they cannot start from what you already know and what you don't know, nor can they address their remarks to what *you* feel it is important for you to find out (or in a sequence that will suit you), unless you tell them. They cannot know what difficulties you find as you try to come to terms with the job. You must say what is worrying you.

From past experience, we can identify for ourselves what we feel it is important for us to find out. And we can then set out to discover these things, and so make sense much more quickly of the experience.

Think about that from the point of view of your students as they join a new class. If you look at things not only from the point of view of the teacher taking on the new class, but also as the students coming to the class may see it, you will recognise what needs to happen early in the proceedings.

You need to share with the students your perception and theirs of what the class is about, find out where they are starting and what they perceive as their learning needs. I asked you to do this for yourself early in this book.

So we need to ask ourselves certain kinds of question when we start thinking about teaching a class – and to go on questioning as we gain experience by teaching the class. What questions? They are of the kind: who? what? where? why? how? when?

TASK 5:   Finding the questions

Preparation pays off: thinking it through, having things ready.

In preparing to teach we need to ask questions such as these:

WHO?
Who am I going to teach?
What age are they? What is their background?
Why are they in this class?
What do they want, or what do they need to learn?
Why do they need to learn it?
What are they going to learn?
What do they know, or what can they do already?
What are they expecting from me?

WHAT?
What are they going to learn?
What do they have to do in order to learn that?
What do they need in order to do that?
What are they going to learn with?
What do I have to do in order to provide that?
What do I have to do to help them learn?

WHERE?
Where are they going to learn, or where am I going to teach?
What kind of support and help will they find there?
What kind of difficulties are they likely to find there?
What equipment can they and I use?
How do I get hold of it, set it up, find out how to use it?
What reorganisation and preparation must I do?

WHEN?
How much time have I or they got for each class? and for the programme?
What time of day will it happen?
How often will they meet?
What might be the effects of time of day or frequency?

HOW?
Where are they starting from? Where should I start?
How are they going to learn?
How am I going to teach? What pace of learning?

How will we agree our learning goals?
How will I get them working and committed?
Can I assume they will want to learn what I teach?
How do I engage them in the learning?
How far can I trust them to be responsible for learning?
What kind of problems are they likely to have in learning?
What can I do to make what they have to do easier to do?
How can I anticipate these problems and make it easier?
How shall I know whether they are learning – and what?
How shall I get feedback, and how shall I use it?
How should I adapt what I do to what they need?
How flexible should my learning/teaching programme be?

How will you answer the questions? Initially, by asking your employer. When you meet your class, in discussion with them.

In discussion of micro-lessons I focused on 'how' and 'where' questions in relation to planning learning for the student group. In planning for your own class, you have to consider so many other factors, such as motivation and purpose, needs and expectations, effects of the teaching environment, time of day and group dynamics. **The context of the teaching has to be clearly understood.**

Questions must still be simple and direct. They must lead to useful, clear answers, and so to action you can take. There is no real point in trying to discover information you cannot use when planning your teaching programme.

Who?

In very many contexts, students are not used to teachers showing interest in discovering their views, or being concerned to draw them into discussion about the learning process. Many may resist if you ask questions about them personally. They may take the view that you are the expert and they expect you to make the course interesting for them: how can they contribute if they don't know about the subject?

But they do know about themselves, which you do not. Most people will in fact welcome the chance to talk about themselves and what they feel they need. Teachers often report that their students were grateful and welcomed the opportunity to talk to a teacher who 'wanted to know about me'. This is the critical starting-point of a process of **building up a spirit of trust between students and teacher**.

If it goes wrong or is handled badly, it may make things harder. It is perfectly possible to find out most of what you need to know without asking the students at all. If your class is part of a larger programme, the other teachers, or the head of department, will know what you want to ask. Of course, they may not have asked the students their views either. And it is valuable to compare what the teachers think with the students' own views.

|| Consider ways in which you might find out about your students.
|| Write down the options and think about what you have to do.

What?

Learning goals should be set out clearly. 'What are the students going to learn?' is the important question. 'What am I going to teach?' can only be answered after that.

Your students will expect you as the person with knowledge and experience to have a clear idea of what they are supposed to be about, what they have to learn. That is the starting-point.

It does mean that they should know what they are trying to learn. They should also know what you are trying to teach. And these must be the same. Frequently and unfortunately, they do not appear to be the same. So many classes fail simply because the students did not know what it was the teacher was trying to teach them. It is not unusual for students to come to class with a fixed expectation of what they will learn and how – and for the teacher and students to have a mismatch of expectation. This is why it is so important that all agree what they are about.

This is a process of sharing. Telling them is not enough. You do have to ensure that they understand what is intended, and that they agree that it is what they are ready to set about learning.

In preparing a teaching programme, you have to make assumptions. Make clear to yourself what the assumptions are that you use. Look carefully at them again once you have met the students and worked with them to check where the assumptions might be wrong. It is easy to continue with a lesson style and structure based on the wrong assumptions. Be ready to admit when it is necessary to change; that depends on readiness to observe what actually happens in your classes.

Clarify for yourself what you want the students to learn. It will be best to have a general statement of overall learning first for a programme, with more detailed statements for lesson plans within the programme. They and you need to know where they are going and how they are going to get there: and what they need to learn along the way. This will help you to sequence learning and activity in a helpful way; and to provide the essential links to make the learning easier to perceive and assess.

Once the learning goals are agreed, type them up and ensure that each student has a copy.

Learning goals for a lesson should be given to the students at the start of the lesson so that they know what they are to learn, and you and they can assess the effectiveness of the learning at the end of the lesson. They can also link learning in one lesson to learning in the next lesson, and so build up a structure. With no idea of the structure, students find it hard to learn.

Learning goals are always a compromise between what the students feel they want to learn, and the teacher's perception of needs – of what they have to do to pass the assessment, for instance. Of course, the assessment should arise from the learning and not be imposed on it.

There must be a working match between the two pressures. **You and your students must share and agree the learning goals.** This is not the same as arriving at the first session or lessons with a blank page and asking them what they want to learn. Even a negotiated programme must start by declaring the options.

TASK 6:   Learning goals

Set out the learning goals for your class. Make the statements simple. You might say:

The students will

understand the various methods and techniques for making x
develop skills necessary for using the techniques
use the techniques successfully to produce examples of x
use the equipment and materials efficiently/effectively
be able to evaluate the quality of the product.

How will you make sure the learning goals are reasonable and make sense?

Who needs to look at them or agree them? your tutor? your head of department? your students? When should that happen?

Ensure that you and the students are committed to achieving the learning goals.

How?

Think about how the students are going to achieve the learning. With the learning goals set out, it is clear the students must use techniques in order to understand them, and use equipment to develop skills in its use. They must produce examples of whatever the thing is they are to make in order to evaluate them.

Consider carefully which learning methods are likely to be the most successful. Why is that likely to be so? What should you do as the teacher? What is your part in the learning process?

There is little value in their seeing a demonstration, however excellent it may be, if they do not have the chance to 'do it themselves'. It is useful to watch someone turn metal on a lathe, for instance, or carve a piece of wood or ice a cake; but to learn how to do these things we have to do them. Our eye–hand co-ordination, our clumsiness, the weight of an object we handle, the speed at which things can happen, can only be known when they happen to us and by our reactions.

Are the students going to learn individually or in groups? Students themselves bring tremendous resources to a class, in the richness of their experience.

What is to be learned in your class must link into and arise out of their experience. How are you going to exploit that experience? How are they going to make sense of it, starting from where they are?

Consider how to promote group sharing through group activities. They can learn so much more together and from each other than on their own. To do this, you have first to establish a group identity that is supportive of each member of the group. You will need to think about how to get people sharing. And whatever you decide, it must be practicable and possible within time available.

Make a list of all the possible ways in which you might teach the class and the ways in which they might learn what you have set as learning goals above. Choose one way. Try to say why that one.

Sketch an outline of what is to happen in your class. Think about who is going to do what, and when. What will they, and you, need?

What preparation is needed to have things ready?

Your role

There has to be energy in a system for anything to happen. Where does it come from? How much of the energy in the class has to come from you? How can you get the students to work in order to learn? If you do all the work, will they actually learn anything? What will be the balance between what you do and what they do?

In the preparation for the class, it is important to decide how much you will need to talk and for how long, how you will get them working and how quickly. What will you need to prepare for them to do that? Time spent preparing teaching and learning materials will be well rewarded by the energy and excitement that it will facilitate in the learning.

Once you have decided what they are going to do, you can think about how much time they will need to do it. Then you can work out how much time you will need to make the input that will get them going.

How much do you need to do? Remember that students can only deal with a limited amount of information at any one time. Trying to cram a whole mass of facts or words or symbols or ideas into them all at once is very ineffective. We need to absorb a few things at a time and do something with them. It is better to have variety of activity in the class.

Even if you want to get through a large amount of information, you will need to present it in sections of no more than fifteen minutes at a time, and then make them do something to learn and assimilate what you have presented. Often a teacher will assume that the students have understood what has been presented and hurry on. Even if they have, by the time they have attempted to grasp the next package the first one is gone.

Try to see it from their point of view. Ask: what is hard here? what is it that a student will find it difficult to understand or do? You can then approach it by tackling that difficulty.

Getting ready

How much can you prepare beforehand, and in what form? What would best help the students to learn, get them active? Would it be better on paper as a handout, or on an overhead projector (OHP) transparency? Do they need to have something in their hands that they can use?

What teaching aids do you need? What do you have to get ready? Where are they? Do you have to make anything or carry it to the room? Are there ready-made materials somewhere? if so, where?

Can you get the room set up before the students arrive? This matters! How much time do you need beforehand to set things up and make sure that they work? There is nothing more frustrating than to have to wrestle in a class with something that won't work: an OHP with a dud lamp, say, or a video machine that doesn't function. It is a good idea always to carry a small screwdriver to repair the plug that has a loose wire. And your own supply of chalk, and pens for use on the OHP. The number of classrooms in which students seem to have eaten the chalk always comes as a surprise. Be prepared.

Lesson plans

Your lesson plan is essentially a cue-sheet. The plan of the lesson should be clearly in your mind, related to the use of teaching and learning materials that you have produced. It is helpful to have a paper that you can refer to from time to time to check where a lesson is going: whether it has got lost or is basically still on the right programme. It is not unusual for teachers to lose their way in a class – nor for them to adhere too strictly to a plan and not respond to student needs.

A lesson plan should state the learning goals for the lesson and give some indication of how you will check if the students have achieved those goals.

It should identify both teacher activity and student activity, with a clear relationship between the two and some indication of the use of time, and also of what both teacher and students will need to use.

Remember that student learning activity is itself an assessment of their ability to cope with the tasks and so of the learning. A reasonable test of someone's ability to produce something, or of skill in using a technique or piece of equipment, is doing it. The students can assess their own performance also.

EXAMPLES OF LESSON PLANS

This section includes examples of lesson plans. Their style suits me, but you should try to develop your own.

There are different approaches. What matters is not the plan itself, but what it is about. The plan is a tool that will enable something to happen. It must be flexible and usable: it should alert you to what needs to be done, and when, and by whom.

The learning process you set up depends on what you may think the whole thing is about – what it is for.

Many lesson plans tell only what the teacher is going to do: what aids the teacher is going to use, the content the teacher is going to cover. They are rather like the micro-lessons in which a video camera points only at the teacher and records what the teacher does. In my view, any video camera should point at the students. What are they doing while the teacher is teaching? After all, what matters is that the teacher observes carefully what the students do – or don't do. Many video recordings made on that basis would be very dull to watch.

LESSON PLAN 1

Class: Evening class in local history, one evening a week for ten weeks
Duration: two and a half hours, Thursday 6.30–9 pm
Location: Adult Centre; classroom with tables and chairs
Equipment: chalkboard, OHP. Photocopying available
Facilities: central 'coffee-break' area with easy chairs
Students: age range 35–55, four men, twelve women
Main purpose: personal interest, no examination.

Session 1:   First evening session: 'Getting Started'.

Purposes: To get to know each other
To share interest and motivation: what do we bring?
To agree learning goals and programme to achieve them
To establish working procedure – set targets.

Learning goals for Session 1

The students will

- share their reasons/expectations in joining class
- agree what we are all setting out to learn
- establish good working relationships as a group
- identify a learning programme and responsibilities.

Evening programme

A: Teacher Activity A (10 minutes at most!)

Welcome students and introduce myself: who, why I'm here
Set up and explain 'ice-breaking' activity
Divide students into pairs (mix up men and women if they have separated themselves out); they may have to move
Provide an 'interview brief' (very short, some cues).   *Paper A*

B: Student Activity B (10 minutes)

Each one of pair to interview the other and change over (5 minutes)
Make brief notes – use my cues as starting-point.

C: Student Activity C (30 minutes)

Each student introduces his/her partner to the class.
(Note: must ensure it's light-hearted and fun. Spot a 'jolly' character to start it off – set the tone.)

D: Teacher Activity D (5 minutes at most)

Tell them what we are going to do after the break.

Coffee break   (Ask them to be back in 10 minutes)

E: Teacher Activity E (20 minutes)

Set out my own interest and background in local history
Outline: how to find information
           what to look for: clues, evidence, gathering information and ideas.
(Note: make it interesting! photos, old newspapers, artefacts on a table to handle: hand around.)

F: Student Activity F (15 minutes)

Students, in pairs again, examine the articles and try to see what can be learned from the ones they look at. They make notes.

G: Student Activity G (30 minutes)

Each pair comes to the front to explain what they discovered.

H: Teacher Activity H (5 minutes)

Consolidation of the learning: what we have learned.
Use students' ideas as far as possible.
Learned about:
how to go about local history
what interest can be found in ordinary things
each other, the group.

I: Teacher Activity I (5 minutes)

Setting up the programme for the 10 weeks
Tell them my learning goals *Paper B*
Learning approach to be used:
individuals or groups to agree the topics to tackle
they share the tasks – agree who will research what
they will prepare and present a paper to the class.
Present my own outline: what I think important and why *Paper C*
Get them to take papers B and C away and think about them
Make their own programme around mine: what to add
                        special interests
                        research each to do.

J: Teacher Activity J (5 minutes)

Agree with them what we will do next week
                what they will do before then.
Complete the register.
Thank them for coming – what a pleasure and so on.

Note to myself: Preparation

1 Set out learning goals   Paper B
2 Design my own outline programme   Paper C
3 Design my cues paper   Paper A

Before the class
Arrive early.
Find the caretaker and make friends.
Make sure the room is comfortable: check heating, windows.
Set up tables and chairs as I want them – committee style.
Set the 'articles' table.
Make sure there are copies of the lesson plan, Papers A, B, C.
Ensure OHP etc is in place and working, in case I need it.
Ensure there is chalk and other things I need.
Find out the drill for coffee, paying etc: when, how, who.
Get the register and make sure I know how to complete it!

LESSON PLAN 2

Class: Full-time course in catering
Subject: communication skills
Duration: one hour, twice a week
Location: drama studio with some tables and chairs
Equipment: lighting, chalkboard, OHP
Facilities: central refectory and student areas
Students: 20 men and women, ages around 17+
Main purpose: to improve interpersonal skills

Purposes: To improve communication skills and confidence in dealing
with clients
To integrate work in accounts with writing skills
To improve team-working
To stimulate good working practice

Methodology: An extended simulation for a term
Class divided into teams: a management game
Each team to 'set up' a catering company for weddings.

Learning goals for course

The students will

- improve their interpersonal and communication skills
- have increased confidence in dealing with clients
- establish good working relationships in teams
- use accounts to improve understanding of need
- understand, have insight into managing a small business.

Programme for sessions

Session 1   Setting up teams and agreeing learning goals
Setting competitive goals and targets
Establishing working practice – team behaviour
Roles and responsibilities

Sessions 2–8   While teams are working, practise skills team by team
Use feedback opportunities: tackle problems.

Sessions 9–10   Presentation by each team of what they have done.

Lesson plan for Session 3

Face to face with the customer – how to handle it

Learning goals (enabling overall learning goals 1–2)
The students will

- be able to establish a welcoming, helpful manner
- explore with the 'customer' what he/she wants
- guide the customer carefully: advise, be helpful
- clarify what is required and agree to cost it.

(Note: in a subsequent session the students will prepare a firm proposal/ estimate to meet the customer's requirements and cost it. The customer will receive different estimates and choose one, taking into account the whole package. The 'bottom line' is whether they can make a profit on a sufficient scale to keep going.)

Programme

Teacher activity:	Make sure teams know what they have to do	
	Check on progress so far and understanding of activity and goals	
	Set up the role play, explaining it	
	Provide a cue-sheet for the role play	*Paper 1*
	Evaluate what happened with the teams.	
Student activity:	Take roles and work them out	
	Observe carefully and note what happens	
	Reflect on what happens, evaluate performance	
Teacher activity:	Explain what each team has to do now.	*Paper 2*

Time allowed for each team: 30 minutes.

Note to myself: Preparation

Design role play guidelines, cue-sheet and guidance Papers 1 and 2.
Set out room to facilitate role play.

To understand the nature of the questions let us consider a few examples of actual classes. The examples are drawn from different countries: contexts change but learning and teaching present similar questions everywhere.

CASE STUDY 9

Karen was to teach typewriting in the Business Studies Department of a college in the United Kingdom. She was new to teaching. Her class was a full-time secretarial group of sixteen-year-olds. They had no experience of producing real documents in a working environment, although they had a level of typing skill. She tried to discover from the other teachers about the students but felt safe in assuming they were like she had been at that age. So she felt reasonably happy about understanding their needs.

As a new teacher, Karen played safe using the model of teaching/learning that she knew best. She had been taught typewriting using a textbook. The textbook had worked for her; why not for these students? What she had not thought about was how many students the method had *not* worked for. She had been highly motivated and able to learn her skills whatever method was used by the teacher. Many students learn from what appears to be very poor teaching.

The textbook provided a 'lock-step' approach. It assumed every student needed to learn exactly the same thing at the same time, in the same way and at the same pace. Clearly, this cannot possibly be true. Individuals have personal learning patterns and learn at a pace that suits them.

Rote-learning has a place. And skills like touch-typing certainly do need repetitive practice. Learning to be a secretary or a typist in the real world requires a very different approach, however. The skills are a means to an end; what matters is the ability to create letters and other documents of a quality an employer needs. And that requires all sorts of other skills.

Karen quickly discovered that some of the students who chose to sit at the front of the class did the exercises in the book at a pace she felt happy with, and at the same pace. Most of the class got left behind, and some who chose to sit at the back did very little work. The room was clearly set up to encourage the approach Karen had adopted. The typists' tables stood in rows facing down a long room to the teacher's desk and a chalkboard at the front. Karen could not supervise the students misbehaving at the back.

The teaching/learning strategy was clearly unsuccessful for most of the students. Karen decided to redefine her learning goals.

What the students needed was not just to learn the orthodox methods of paragraphing and so on from the book as some kind of abstraction, but to have tasks that simulated real world demands and which gave a point to what they tried to do. She decided on a new strategy.

She prepared packages for all the students to enable them to adopt the role of a typist in an estate agent's office. They had to complete all the tasks a typist might undertake in the selling of a house: the advertisements, the house details, design of a brochure with a photograph, a window display, the letters to buyer, seller, solicitor and other agents, and so on. Each had a worksheet identifying what they had to do, as well as other resources.

The pressure and excitement of the simulation radically changed the behaviour of the students. Karen spent a great deal of time in the preparation of the sets of materials, and found herself in the class with little to do except to encourage the students and respond to requests for help from individuals. This happened only occasionally. She was anxious, but as tutor I encouraged her to do nothing and just watch. The 'naughty' students at the back got on as quickly as the ones at the front. One girl made a mistake in typing a letter, dragged it out of the typewriter, looked at her neighbour and said, 'I'll still beat you.'

1 What were the assumptions Karen made about the class?
2 Why did she choose to use the model of teaching/learning she had experienced as a student? Why was it unsuccessful?
3 Try to explain the differences between her first strategy and her second.

4 Why was it more successful in involving all the students?
5 What do you think she had to do to use this method well?

CASE STUDY 10

John was appointed as an education officer to Northern Nigeria. He found himself in an isolated town south of the Sahara desert. The people were Moslem with a strong tradition. English was the language of education and government, but the main language there was Kanuri and many people also spoke Hausa. He was teaching in a government secondary school preparing students to take English overseas examinations.

The young men had passed local examinations in English and felt they were privileged to be at the school. They were keen to do well, since getting the examination passes would open up good jobs for them in the future. But there were strong cultural barriers that affected their learning and John's understanding of them.

He was to teach English, history and health science. History was concerned with the expansion of Europe and the Industrial Revolution. Europe was no more than a word for the students, and at that time an industrial revolution had not happened in that part of Africa. How do you create a feeling for industrial towns or factory life for people who have only known an agricultural society?

Health science was a more promising subject. This required some basic knowledge of the human body: where various organs were, how they worked, what their function was, and especially what part they played in the health of the person – what could go wrong.

Africans tended at that time to be afflicted by most of the diseases that affected people in Europe, plus a profusion of illnesses that were specific to Africa, or which had largely been controlled elsewhere. Many were insect-borne and most were preventable; this was the point of his students learning health science, although they also needed to pass the examination.

John thought about them. What were their needs? Why was it thought they needed to know about the industrial revolution? It was hard for him to convince himself of the necessity, let alone the students.

But they certainly needed to understand health science. John felt he had a high level of motivation on his side. People are fascinated by themselves and their own bodies more than by almost anything else, and these young men had a strong desire to be fit and well. They all had the experience of being ill; most had relatives who had suffered from a whole range of ailments. All had had malaria and knew what many of the diseases felt like when you contracted them. This was not an abstraction, but very real. They also had their own bodies to relate experience to. John decided to use this experience.

The main obstacle to learning health science was the large amount of special vocabulary they had to learn, a 'naming of parts' and medical terms and conditions. And John had no access to organs in bottles or laboratory equipment.

What they needed, he felt, was some way of visualising what the body was like inside. They needed to be able to see how the body worked, how the various parts fitted together as a whole, how the organs and their functions related to the whole 'machine', what a malfunction could do and its likely effect.

His solution lay in a plastic construction kit of the human body that he discovered advertised in a magazine. He sent for the kit. As a group, they had all the bits and a diagram to help them assemble them.

This allowed them not only to see things in the round, but to handle them and try to fit them together in the places they belonged. 'You have the diagram: you have to build it.' They had a great time and they learned the parts very quickly. They were also able then to understand the diagrams in the textbook and draw diagrams themselves to show how the parts worked. They learned technical terms quickly, and passed the examination.

Most importantly, however, they learned health science as 'real' and relevant to them, as practical knowledge related to their own life and well-being. It was not simply something to swot up to pass an exam and then forget.

1 What was the essential difference between what John was asked to teach as history and as health science?
2 Why should this make so big a difference in learning?
3 What factors did John feel he could exploit with them? Why were these so helpful in relation to the learning goals?
4 What was it in the method he chose that made it successful? Would it work with any students in any context?

Using prior learning

One clear advantage of using the energies and resources within the student group is that they will start from where they are and not attempt to start from where the teacher believes them to be – or, as usually happens, from where the teacher is. A teacher can only make assumptions about a group: it is even harder to be clear as to individual learning needs.

To use and integrate prior learning – that is, what they bring with them to the class from experience – the students must use their new information and skills to create new perceptions and behaviour. It is actually not possible to ignore prior learning, because it determines what students select from what is presented to them.

New ideas and new thinking have to link to those that are already there. Skills can only build on previous skill levels. What teachers provide is information and opportunity: to acquire knowledge and skills and to gain insights. Information is usually presented neatly packed as a parcel to take away. Unfortunately, that is all it remains unless the students process it in some way to make it part of their own knowledge structure. Packages remain as useless lumber in the memory if they are simply stored to be repeated as answers to tests, and dumped afterwards. This information only becomes knowledge when they do something with it. Knowledge is a process, a constant change in perception, not just an accumulation of packages. The same is true of skills.

Pace

Students usually do not know what they know, where they have got to in their learning or where they are going. They have to learn to use experience, to reflect on it and integrate the parts. We have to find some way for them to explore their own resources and experience while matching it against new challenges. Equally, we have to help them remove the barriers to learning that previous learning has probably created for them. How fast can the process go?

Pace in learning is a major concern. How quickly can we expect an individual to learn something? Some methods promote learning more quickly than others. Many students in Karen's class in Case Study 9 would hardly have learned anything if she hadn't changed her teaching strategy. Nor will simply learning names for a test change perception of ourselves or our world, as John discovered (Case Study 10).

The methods both chose accelerated the learning dramatically. No doubt Karen's students would eventually have learned how to work properly, perhaps when they were employed in an office somewhere. Karen by using a simulation hastened the process. She also ensured that each one progressed at his or her level of readiness and commitment to learning. It gave them something to do that they found interesting. They all progressed faster and gained insight into the 'why' as well as the 'what' they had to do.

Learning/teaching materials

Most new teachers, and many established teachers, rely heavily on textbooks. The trouble is that this allows the author to decide what students are going to learn and how they are going to learn it. A book is a resource to be used wisely. It is not intended to dictate what happens in class. A crutch can eventually prove a handicap and should then be thrown away.

New teachers frequently lack the courage to take charge, and to take risks. They look for what appears safe. Some adopt a pattern of defensive behaviour. One of the results of relying on a book, of course, is that it takes away the need to think things through.

Similarly, new teachers can find it difficult to challenge what seem to be established patterns in the classroom or workshop. Often a caretaker seems to dictate how a class will run. Some teachers lack the nous or the courage to move the furniture to promote the activity they want to happen, however hard that actually makes it to do.

It is not necessary to try to produce 'professional' teaching or learning materials and aids. Some searching in resource areas in colleges and schools may produce useful stuff. It may be that what you need is available, but in the wrong place. Whatever you make or get, make sure it really is helpful to students. I have seen astonishing effort made by new teachers in producing teaching aids that are far too elaborate for their purpose.

The test is: will it help them learn? Anything can be an aid in the right context. Tony's plates were effective learning aids; so were Sandra's instructions written out in letters of the Greek alphabet. If there is something available which is real, it is better than any simulation of it. The main criterion is: how useful is it?

Usually, you can follow the principle of 'the simpler, the better'. Instructions on a worksheet need to be clear and simple to understand. The less an OHP transparency has on it, the easier it will be to grasp, and the more effective it will be. Look at the cartoon at the beginning of the book. It could hardly be simpler or more effective.

8 Tasks and Performance Criteria

The language used in education, as in all other disciplines, changes with time. Indeed, education more than most other human activities is subject to cycles of fashion. There is at present an increasing emphasis on 'competence'.

You will certainly wish to become a competent teacher. It is one of the purposes of this book to help you define the competence you should have in particular aspects of teaching. I hope in fact you will want to raise your level of understanding and skills well beyond simple competence. Teaching is about decision-making, about creative interaction with students to promote learning.

A teacher is to be judged at least as much by what the students do and what they achieve as by any demonstration of competence in particular aspects of the role. Indeed, there is a danger that too great an emphasis on the teacher's performance will tend to divert attention from the effort to improve student learning. But a teacher who lacks competence in particular important areas cannot do even an adequate job for the students.

REMEMBER!
... What is important is that you are effective in the role.

A teacher cannot exist in a vacuum. Every teacher must teach in a context of a specific learning programme with specific students. This is where we must develop skills and understanding to an acceptable level. But we must also ensure that the skills and insight that are achieved in one context are transferable to any new context.

In attempting to define competence in terms of performance criteria, we must bear in mind that their achievement is part of the process of becoming effective in a particular context. Many factors will determine how effective a person is in any role. Some are definable as performance criteria, while others relate to environmental and contextual pressures, or to interpersonal skills and relationships, to working in teams, to confidence and adaptability. This is where growth in the job is most marked as a teacher gains experience.

Overall, a person's learning and perception of learning is to be achieved by reflection on the experiences which enable him or her to learn. Teaching is such a learning experience. Since its context will be whatever it turns out to be, the performance criteria we define need to relate to *any* context; their achievement will then be transferable. This means that we cannot be over-precise in stating performance criteria by which competence is to be judged.

The term 'performance' is used here to mean 'behaviour as a teacher that can be observed and assessed', preferably in a real teaching situation – that is, a classroom, workshop, laboratory, ward or anywhere else that the teacher has responsibility for the learning of an identified group of students. The 'criteria' are the judgements to be made. We have to rely on judgement in making our assessment. Clearly, the quality of the judgements made will depend on the level of experience of whoever is making them.

There has to be a sharing of perceptions, just as there is in the observing of a class and in micro-lessons. The teacher has principal responsibility for assessing his or her own performance against agreed and stated criteria. But it will be much more valid and constructive if an experienced mentor can be involved, not only in assessing with performance criteria, but in the whole learning process.

What is needed is that you, as teacher, should perceive clearly what is required to be effective in the role you fulfil at the level of responsibility you carry. That is partly defined by a statement of performance criteria, and partly by feedback from a mentor who can share the context in which the teaching occurs.

As you read on, you will encounter statements of performance criteria for each of the aspects of the role of teacher. They are intended to help you understand the principles that are involved in what you do as a teacher; they define 'good practice'.

Study these criteria, and match what you do against them. Where you meet with a clear lack of success in achieving any of them, ask yourself why that is so. Look carefully at what you are doing to evaluate what happens and what needs to happen. And don't ignore the effect of what you as teacher do on the learning of your students, and how it promotes their competence.

TASK 7: Lesson preparation

1 Discover as much as you can about the students in your class and use that information in planning learning sessions. How will you agree learning goals and a programme with them?

2 Design at least one lesson for the group. In developing the ideas and lesson plan(s), think about what you have learned from micro-lessons or from your own experience as a student. You will know your own context and your own students, so you should develop a style of lesson planning that suits you.

Remember, a lesson plan is a cue-sheet. What matters is the thinking that leads to the design. It should, however, define clearly the activity of the teacher and the activity of the students and indicate how they relate together.

You need to state the learning goals clearly, showing how you have agreed them (or will agree them) with your students.

Try to ensure that you have defined the learning process and the activities that will promote it. Show how you hope to get feedback and have some idea of what is being achieved.

Indicate what learning/teaching materials you will use.

TASK 8: Evaluating your preparation

Look critically at your lesson plan(s). Then read through the criteria below.

1 How well do you match up to the criteria?
2 What can you improve?

PERFORMANCE CRITERIA

1.1   Students within the group are identified and information is obtained about their educational background, motivation and personal learning goals. This information is used in planning learning sessions.
1.2   There is a shared perception of learning goals between the teacher and the students, both for each lesson and overall.
1.3   Lessons are planned to achieve specified learning goals.
1.4   Where appropriate, the learning is consistent with requirements of external examining bodies.
1.5   Teaching methods and learning activities are well designed.
1.6   Prior learning is taken into account.
1.7   The lesson(s) will engage the students actively in learning.
1.8   There is flexibility to allow for the different pace of learning of individual students.
1.9   Learning materials and teaching aids are well chosen and are related clearly to promoting the learning.
1.10 Methods of obtaining feedback and assessment are identified.

Good practice

What we are about is the establishment of a pattern of good practice in your preparation for your classes. This implies repetition of the pattern in preparing for *all* your classes.

Don't be too anxious to achieve all the criteria that relate to performance in the first class you take. There is a process of maturation that cannot be hurried. It is by reflecting on your experiences that you will learn. Each time you undertake preparation of a class, you will understand more.

The criteria are not goalposts between which you can shoot the ball once and then feel 'I don't need to do that again.' They are signposts: they point a direction of travel. Every time you attempt to meet them they will show you more of the road. You will find you can always do better.

TASK 9: Evaluating the experience/reflection

Use your lesson plan (or series of lesson plans) in a teaching context and evaluate its effectiveness – what actually happened.

If you have the chance, share the evaluation with your mentor and agree together an evaluation statement. Match perceptions of what happens in your classes to the performance criteria below, and use them to shape what you do.

PERFORMANCE CRITERIA

2.1 The lesson has specified (and/or negotiated) learning goals that are clearly stated and shared with the students.

2.2 The structure and content of the lesson is known by students and takes account of the identified needs of individuals and of the group(s).

2.3 Teaching methods are appropriate to the specified goals.

2.4 Learning problems are identified during the lesson and the work programme (or lesson plan) adapted to take account of them.

2.5 Learning materials and teaching aids are used thoughtfully to promote the intended learning.

2.6 Individuals and groups are managed well. Control of the session is maintained. There is good linking and structure.

2.7 Learning is assessed by the students and the teacher and is consolidated at the end, with clear linking between lessons.

Evaluating a teaching session

You will need to think about the following aspects, in relation to your initial lesson plan.

FACTS

Class: students, course, time, duration, place.

1 What did you expect to happen? Did it?
2 What actually happened? Do you and your mentor agree?
3 If there are differences, make a note of these.
4 How well did students carry out the activity? Any surprises?
5 What was really important in what happened there?

LEARNING GOALS

1 Did your view of those change?
2 Did they achieve the goals? How well? How do you know?
3 What else did they learn? Did anything surprise you?
4 Did they/you consolidate the learning? take it away?
5 How do you expect them to use it? How will they link to next session?
6 Was the method you chose able to provide assessment?

METHOD

1 Was the teaching method you chose appropriate?
2 Did the students *do* much to learn, or were they mainly passive?
3 Did they enjoy what they did? Why, or why not?
4 Did they understand what to do and why they were doing it?

5 Did they have the right things to learn with?
6 Could you have improved the organisation? room? equipment?

INPUT

1 Was it right? Did it take too long? Was it effective?
2 Were the teaching aids/learning materials effective?
3 Were instructions clear? Were there enough? Was there too much information?
4 Was everything ready? Did it work?

COMMUNICATION

1 Did the students work as a group? Was that partly down to you?
2 Were there any problems for individuals or groups? What did you do about them?
3 Did you feel sufficiently skilful? Comment on that.
4 What about the students' attention, their enthusiasm, their concentration?

CONSOLIDATION

1 What did you learn? What would you change, or rethink?
2 What do you need to work on now?

9 Using your Plan in Teaching

Activity 1 asked you to set down what you felt you needed to learn to be a teacher of adults. Many new teachers, when asked this question, replied; 'I need to know how to control the class.' What did they mean and why did they feel it to be a need?

Managing the learning is certainly what it is about. Any manager wants to feel in control, but what is it that you, as a teacher, can control? We shall explore the answer to that question in this chapter. Certainly, you need to control the environment and the learning materials. What about the people?

You cannot manage others if you cannot manage yourself. Self-organisation was mentioned in the discussion of study skills in Chapter 2. We have also discussed other factors in the mechanics of management, such as stating clearly what you and the students are about and preparing competently, so as to have things ready and properly structured.

But you cannot manage people in the same way that you manage a machine or an environment. I believe that the new teachers were afraid of the loss of control, that the fear of students and what they might do pressed on them – that they had little confidence in their own ability to manage them in the class.

Rules

Teachers will adopt defensive behaviour if they feel insecure.

Your students will look to you to lead. That means, at least, that you should know where you are intending to go and how you want to get there. But it also means establishing roles and responsibilities. No groups can work successfully without rules that govern their interactions and behaviour. In establishing the group, you will need to create the framework of understandings within which it works. Usually these are well known to all from previous experience of learning groups. Most of the important rules governing behaviour of groups are unspoken but clearly understood.

Nevertheless, you need to make it clear from the beginning what is acceptable in your class and what is not. This is a matter of observing behaviour and interfering to shape it. If, for example, your class uses computers (or any other equipment) the students must know how to treat it properly, not to abuse or damage it. There are also safety considerations – wearing protective clothing and so on; we shall discuss these later.

Do you allow smoking? Who decides? Do you set deadlines? What about absence? or being late for class? or failing to produce work?

Making clear rules and responsibilities like these will help to create a good working environment, without disruptive actions on the part of individuals upsetting the working of the group.

The essential quality is leadership. Perhaps the teachers above had an image of the teacher as 'boss' and were not sure they had the personality or the presence for such a role. They might remember a teacher they were afraid of: 'you didn't muck about in her class.' Why not a teacher they found stimulating to be with?

Managing

Good management, in industry and business as well as in teaching, consists largely in creating good teams of people working well together to achieve things. This is done in various ways. It helps if people know where they are going, have set targets, schedules and goals to achieve. The managers can then motivate them to accept 'ownership' of the targets, and to harness their energies to work together for a shared purpose. They need to identify strongly with the group, to see their achievement as part of the achievement of others. Will it happen if all the decisions are taken at the top? When managers want robots, they can buy them. People need motivating, guiding and supporting; it must appear to them that they, their ideas and their talents are valued and worth while. The leader can help to give them shape.

Sensitivity: identifying needs and problems

Clearly, we have to work with the consent of students, especially adults. But we need more than passive acceptance: we want active participation and commitment.

If we concentrate in designing our classes on what the students have to do in order to learn, the methods we choose will be student-centred and activity-based. The teacher in the class is thus relieved of a great deal of pressure, and can concentrate on the quite different role of supporter and guide – a reference point to assist the learning. Consider Karen's class again (Case Study 9).

The teacher can also watch the students. This ability to observe and to be sensitive to what is going on is most important. Case Study 11 describes an example.

CASE STUDY 11

Richard taught a GCSE history syllabus to full-time British students of mainly 16/17 years. He was faced with trying to get them to understand the reasons for the partition of India after 1947. They had as much experience of the conditions in India as John's Nigerian students (Case Study 10) had of an industrial revolution – none.

Richard's principal learning goals were descriptive, but he found he needed to get over to these youngsters what it was like to be there: what religious fanaticism means, how people could feel so strongly that they would go out in mobs to massacre hundreds of people of other tribes and beliefs. History is apt to take all the emotion out of events, giving dispassionate accounts and analyses from an Olympian stance. No wonder some students find it boring. People are not like that – in 1947, Indians were driven by the wildest of emotions.

As it happened, there was a level of experience in the class that he could exploit. For some reason (which he did not know), the girls in the class appeared to 'hate' the boys. The messages were clear in their behaviour. The girls came to the class in a bunch separately from the boys and deliberately late. They challenged Richard and the boys when they came in and sat in a group as far away from the boys as they could. Richard did his best to make them take part in the discussions and to get the class working together. But what an atmosphere, and what a conflict!

The problem had to be faced, and Richard adopted a strategy to tackle it and maybe turn it to advantage. He needed to get the girls talking to him and explaining why they felt as they did. Their powerful feelings could also be used to help them understand partition, and why it was thought a necessary solution in India.

They could be helped to see that reasoning with people whose behaviour is driven by hatred and fear and strongly held beliefs just will not work. He hoped that they would find that their own emotions were trivial by comparison and that the problems could be talked out.

1 What was Richard's original approach? What were his learning goals? Why were they unsuccessful?
2 Even if the conflict had not arisen in the class, would they have been appropriate? What other major difficulties were there?
3 Had Richard really thought about what the students needed to learn and how they might learn it?
4 How would you have tackled conflict in the class?
5 What can you learn about observing carefully what is going on in your classes and using it to advantage?

COMMENT

Richard revised his learning goals and his approach to achieving them, while the students by exploring their own emotions could understand those others and what drove them to behave as they did. The girls' anger could have destroyed any possibility of achieving the course learning goals. He prevented that.

However well you prepare, you cannot predict how things will go in any particular class. All experienced teachers will confirm that you can prepare exactly the same material and work for two apparently similar classes; in one class the lesson goes tremendously well, with commitment and excellent learning activity, but in the other it dies. Why? It's very difficult to say. It could be something in the chemistry of the class – the mixture of personalities, perhaps – or the time of day or week, or the way you or they are feeling; it could be something that has happened in another class or in the corridor, or the weather or some other outside factor. You need to be sensitive to what is happening and adapt, change, adopt some new tactic.

Teaching is about complex human relationships: the way groups (and groups within groups) form and feel about each other and about strangers, including perhaps the teacher. Without a relationship of mutual trust linking teaching and students, difficulties are bound to arise.

No doubt, for many people the prospect of teaching is daunting. There are memories of being in a class of difficult students who are making the teacher's life hell. For many there is almost a stereotype image of the teacher doing battle with the class. But it is easier to remember the sensational rather than the routine: of the vast number of classes that happen every day, only a very few become battlegrounds, and not necessarily with the teacher involved.

That does not mean that teachers do not frequently lose control or fail to manage the learning effectively. Some do fail to get organised, to identify clearly for themselves and the students what they are trying to teach, and to motivate or stimulate their classes. Some students do rebel – out of boredom or protest at what they see as a waste of their time. There is much pressure on the teacher to 'deliver'. It can feel like a one-man show.

REMEMBER!
. . . Preparation is all-important.

You will find that your students respond well if you appear ready and well prepared, showing interest in them and involving them in 'ownership' of the learning goals, and if they know clearly what they are to learn and what they have to do to learn. It must be a combined effort: them and you together. They will want to co-operate with you.

Structure and links

REMEMBER!
. . . It is much easier to understand the parts of a thing if you have a view of the whole of it first.

The most obvious evidence to your students of your competence in dealing with their class is your structure. Share it with them.

It is helpful for the class to have copies of your lesson plan, so that they know what is going to happen and what they will be asked to do. They can see what you are going to do, and what that has to do with their learning.

They also need a baseline from which to start. Learning goals for the lesson should be clear to all. At the end of the session they should be invited to assess their achievement of the goals and provide you with feedback on how it was for them. They will then perhaps be able to focus on their own learning needs – what has to happen now, whether they can consolidate the learning or come to terms with it by reflection at home or by more effort.

Whatever we set out to learn has to build up into a structure. The same is true of a programme of classes. They need to build week by week, the learning from one week helping to make sense of the learning from other classes. The student has to be able to see the links. Your structure should make the links plain.

In order to make the links, the beginning and the end of each session are particularly important. At the end, students need to focus on what they have learned, partly to assess their own learning, but also to be able to do something with it: unless something is done with the learning it will quickly disappear. At the beginning of the next class, they need to revisit previous learning to ensure that it links into what they are going to learn now. The first activity of any subsequent class should be to establish this linkage.

And what of the time in between? What happens to the learning in the time between classes? The left-hand graph in Figure 1 (overleaf) shows the rate at which what we have learned evaporates away. Within twenty-four hours we have forgotten 75 per cent of what we learned today. And after a month there will be very little left. This explains why revision is so difficult: you are not really revising at all, but learning everything again from scratch. How then should we tackle the problem of recall?

The more often something is recalled, the easier it is to recall it. What is required is some way of regularly revisiting what you have learned, reviewing it and refreshing your memory. Of course, it will also be processed each time by the brain and become part of understanding a greater whole, linking it to other learning. This process allows students to take control of their learning.

Reviewing is simple. The more frequently we revisit learning, the more easily we will recall it; it becomes familiar. So students should be encouraged to review the learning between classes. The effects of reviewing are shown diagrammatically in the right-hand graph in Figure 1 (overleaf).

Teaching methods and learning materials

Students must be able to deal with the learning activities and materials that you provide. Similarly with your teaching: your style, your language, your visual aids. You should assume nothing.

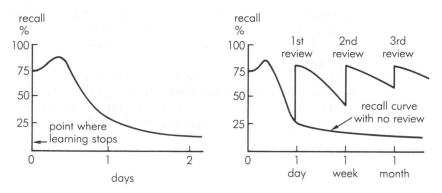

Fig. 1 Learning recall curves (derived from *Use Your Head* by Tony Buzan, BBC Books, 2nd edn, 1989)

Whenever you write anything, come back to it and look at it again and again to try to see it as others see it. You know what you mean, it is clear to you. Will it be clear to your students?

How complicated we can make things when we try! sometimes, particularly, when we present an OHP or a handout in class. The main criterion is that any material you use should be as brief as possible. Get rid of anything that is not absolutely essential for the students to have. Give them the bones, not the flesh – you can build up the flesh in class.

When you put up an OHP transparency or write on the chalkboard, walk to the back of the class and look at it from there. Can they read it? Does it make sense? Is it easy to grasp?

Make your instructions simple, direct, easy to follow. And what of your voice? Just as visual aids are of little use if people cannot see them, so a teacher must at least be audible. Some rooms are very difficult acoustically, and some are full of distractions.

What matters is that the learning is successful, not that you as the teacher feel pleased with how it was for you. Any teaching method may be successful with a particular group under the right circumstances. You need to choose a method you feel comfortable with and can handle effectively. But watch to see how it works.

There is no point in trying to be 'clever'. But think critically about what you are doing – and particularly what they are doing. There may well be alternative ways of approaching the learning that are no more difficult than the one you have chosen, and which could be more interesting and stimulating for you as well as for them. All teachers fall easily into repetitive methods.

There has to be variety of activity in each class and between classes. No activity should go on too long, whether it is the teacher explaining something or the students reading for information or watching a video sequence. There is a curve that relates to concentration (as there is to learning and also to forgetting), and the curve drops sharply after about fifteen minutes. So you should change the activity at least as often as that. As with the revisiting curve above, changes of activity in fact will keep the learning/concentration curve rising or steady.

ACTIVITY 5

Concentration curves

In Figure 2, the concentration curve (a) indicates a general tendency for concentration to fall away after about fifteen minutes. Curve (b) shows the effects of changes of activity every fifteen minutes or so.

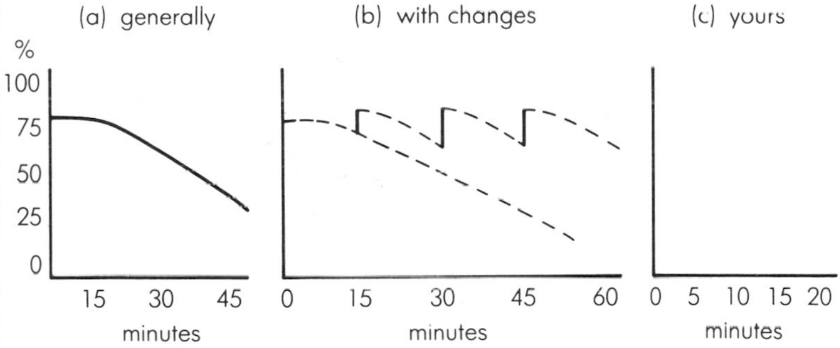

Fig. 2   Concentration curves

You can find out how you compare with the general pattern – discover what works for you.

1 Find a book that requires concentration. Make sure that you have suitable conditions for study. Note the time when you start reading, and the time at which you stop 'taking in' what is on the page in front of you. Sketch your concentration curve on the axes (c).
2 Now experiment with breaks or changes of activity, such as making notes, to see how your ability to maintain concentration is affected.

10 Communication

In Task 9 you evaluated the effectiveness of your lesson plan in a teaching context. In Task 10, we look at a particular aspect: communication.

TASK 10:   Communication skills

In evaluating your teaching in Task 9:
1 Consider how effective your communication skills were.
2 Use the criteria below to assess what needs improving.
3 What do you need to do? How can you do it?
4 What difficulties are you experiencing in communication?

PERFORMANCE CRITERIA
3.1   Interactions between individuals and groups are observed.
3.2   Groups as they form are noted. There is control.
3.3   A class group identity is established that supports members of the class in their learning activity.
3.4   Learning difficulties of individuals receive help/support.
3.5   The teacher responds to student feedback.
3.6   There is sensitivity to problems students have in grasping information and instructions.
3.7   The teacher uses appropriate vocabulary and delivery.
3.8   Learning materials and aids take account of student readiness and ability in language, and are effective in promoting the intended learning.
3.9   Visual materials are well designed and distraction removed.
3.10 The teacher watches carefully and observes what happens.
3.11 The teacher makes use of feedback and evaluates honestly.

Messages

Communicating is not just about transmitting messages. No amount of improvement in transmission will help if the radio receiver is switched off. How will you switch it on?

Are you, as a teacher, switched on to receive the messages from your students? You can be sure that when they arrive in your class they will come with all kinds of expectations: about you, what they will be doing, what the other students will be like, what it is all for.

As they explore the new experience, they will take messages from the room and the furniture, from the behaviour and language of the teacher and of other students. They will tend to form groups, create 'territories' and 'private space', and do things to try to feel comfortable there.

You will need to watch this behaviour carefully, alert to the messages it carries. Sometimes worrying patterns of behaviour develop, such as hostility between groups and individuals. You will need to interfere, perhaps to take control fairly early on, so as to ensure that a network of co-operative relationships develops.

You will probably notice that students choose a particular place to sit where they will establish 'my' chair or desk. They will tend to return to their own 'territory' and stay with the friends they first make. This may be defensive behaviour – they need to feel safe. Try to ensure that small groups do not become too well established, and regularly create new groupings for groupwork. Groups and behaviour, once firmly established, will resist change. A stranger who joins an established group will find it hard to become a member. You will probably notice also how your group identifies itself as different from other classes, other groups of students.

Be alert to how it looks and feels to them. Try to manipulate the situation to the advantage of the group as a whole, rather than just let things happen. Try to think of ways in which you could get your class to talk openly to each other, remove the barriers we all have when we are in a new social group. Just talking is usually ineffective. They need to have a specific job to do, something to give it focus.

For example, Lesson plan 1 (page 52) attempts a deliberate structuring of group behaviour, in which students are asked to interview each other in pairs and then introduce their partner to the class. This works well and becomes light-hearted fun; it also allows you to be open and honest with them, telling them about you, your interests and what you have done in the past. It establishes a bridge.

Can they do that if they are sitting in rows? How will you have to organise the room so that they feel able to talk easily? This activity may not be appropriate in other situations, but you should be able to invent something that will serve the same purpose.

Once you have broken the ice, once they know each other and there are smiles, how will you maintain the momentum? It will help if they have other things to share. Perhaps they might be asked to agree in larger groups on their expectations and needs, which can lead on to agreement of learning goals. Or they might begin work on a small-scale project.

Your messages

Look carefully at the messages in your own behaviour. As people come into a new experience they explore it: they look for the messages that tell them what kind of a place it is, and what are the patterns of behaviour, dress and relationships there – what role the teacher intends to adopt, and what their role is to be. It is your behaviour rather than your language that tells them how you feel about them.

Watch your students too, and observe their behaviour. Are you creating barriers? Are you creating distance between you and them? Most of what we 'say' to people is transmitted in body language – the closeness or distance we create, the things we do, the things we get them to do or allow them to do, the way in which they see our value system. How are they reacting to what you do?

Your tone of voice matters greatly. Listen to someone dealing with a dog in a park. Notice how the dog is controlled by and responds to the tone of voice, not to the words. Unconsciously, we do that with our students too.

Look at what you do, and ask: why do I do that? Some teachers like to have a large desk between themselves and their students, or to create distance in other ways. Some teachers seem to be trapped at the front of the class and do not move to get closer to students.

REMEMBER!
. . . We have to show a genuine interest in students' needs and problems if we want them to respond well to us.

CASE STUDY 12

Gillian taught computing in a college in the United Kingdom. Most computing classes took place in a computing room, but a theory class was in another classroom. She had thought carefully about what she was going to do and how.

The room had been set out in an open square to encourage the students to interact with each other as well as with the teacher. Gillian had prepared well. She was showing them how computing techniques had developed, and had things for students to handle such as a large magnetic tape and perforated paper rolls.

The class, however, had divided itself into three distinct groups, each with its own territory. A group of girls, age 17+, sat along one arm of the square, out of direct eye-contact with Gillian. The boys, of much the same age, sat along the opposite arm (except two who made a home for themselves in a corner). In front of Gillian sat about eight mature students, women of 30–40 years.

The girls and boys took no part in the lesson. They gave the impression of disliking each other and the class. The women were eager and had got close to Gillian, who was of their own age. They held her attention and things went very well there.

Afterwards, her mentor who watched the class asked Gillian what she felt about the lesson. She was sure it had gone well, that the students were keen and interested. Her perception of what had happened and his as observer were far apart. She had been unaware that the class had divided into three groups, two of which had taken no part in the lesson.

This characteristic of student behaviour in the class was important: she needed to change her approach in order to deal with it. Her chosen method had been highly successful with the mature students. Why did it not work for the younger ones?

She needed to find some way of integrating the three groups. She had in fact been doing most of the work in the class. Most of the students had been idle, not participating and not learning. The students had to be given learning activities. She agreed to try putting them into sets of three, one from each divided group. There would no doubt be opposition because people dislike change once groups have formed so strongly. But in practice it worked quite well.

1 Why do you think the behaviour of the mature women and youngsters was so different? Have you observed this yourself?
2 What activities do you think they could do in sets of three that would help to bring the divided groups together?
3 Why might there be opposition to this happening?
4 What is the best way to take control of group behaviour?

COMMENT

It is easy to fail to see what is actually happening in your own class. This is why it is important to observe other classes; micro-lessons are especially useful here. This is also why you need an educated eye, a mentor to share your class.

Models

Your most important task is to establish a sense of belonging and co-operation within the class as a group, to include you too if possible. Help them to feel comfortable with the group and with you. They need to agree purposes and goals and a method of working together and with you. Good management is partly setting targets and then motivating people to achieve them. This is much easier if there is a good team spirit and supportive behaviour.

Getting to know one another and having social contact is essential. Lesson plan 1 deliberately includes a coffee break after they have introduced them-selves. It may be helpful too if they are prepared to ring each other up when they are having difficulty with some learning task – so they need to know each other's telephone numbers.

Your approach, the way you come across matters. Your behaviour, warmth, enthusiasm, interest in them, energy, even your health and your value system, are communicated in many different ways. The clothes you wear say a great deal about you. Students will be looking to see what is acceptable. You cannot help being some kind of model. Everything about you will be studied by students, since you will be the focus of attention – but don't worry.

People will, of course, adopt a pattern of behaviour, language, style of dress or whatever that belongs to the group rather than to any one individual. It is fascinating to watch what they choose to do and to learn from it.

77

CASE STUDY 13

An assessor visited a course of teacher training in a college in the United Kingdom. There were two male tutors and twenty-four mature students from a wide range of backgrounds. The assessor wanted to find out if the tutors saw themselves as models for their student teachers.

The two tutors were rather worried by the idea of being models. They felt that teachers had to develop their own personal style: the teachers must be themselves, since they taught in so many different contexts. And this of course was true.

But when the assessor asked the student teachers the question the answer was different. 'When Ray comes to watch us teach, we do as he does. We have it all neat and tidy. We have a structured lesson plan, time things carefully, all our visual aids set out – have it all organised. When John comes, we don't bother. It's all thinking on your feet and letting it develop – jollying it along, seeing what happens.'

They reflected back to each tutor his behaviour in class, which they thought he would probably want to see.

1 Consider your own use of models. How did they affect what you do?
2 Where did your model of 'the teacher' come from?
3 What kind of role model would you consider appropriate for your students to see? Would that worry you?

COMMENT

We cannot avoid using models. Sometimes they are not helpful. Many people come to teaching with models of 'the teacher' and 'what teachers and students do' that are barriers to understanding.

Don't imagine that as a teacher you can avoid being seen by the students as a model. An important aspect of teaching is to ensure that the model you present is one you would like the students to adopt. You project a pattern of behaviour. For example, if you adopt careless or even dangerous practices in a workshop or laboratory, it is no good telling the students they must do things the 'safe' way.

This makes clear the nature of communication. We want to belong, to be accepted as part of our group. To do that we have to adopt the behaviour, language, style and so on that identifies us as a member of this group. You will be able, I am sure, to think of groups that exhibit quite bizarre special clothes or language or behaviour to identify 'belonging'.

And what about the groups you belong to? since we all belong to more than one in different aspects of our lives. Do you change your language style, clothes or behaviour as you move from group to group? Think carefully about that. How do you categorise people?

The student teachers in Case Study 13 had two models to compare and took a delight in the comparison. That was no doubt good learning.

Energy

Communicating is not one-way transmission, nor is it most of the time consciously done. Most important messages are unconscious, contained perhaps in the tone of voice or body language.

Most of the energy has to come from the receiver, who has to be actively seeking to find out. Humans are exploratory animals. Unless the brain is actively processing information, no change will occur in perception or understanding. Consider what you are doing now. These words simply sit on the page. The energy has to come from you to make them mean anything. In this book I, as author, must try to present what you, as reader, think is important for you to read, do, think about. I have to try to be interesting; I have chosen to do that partly by using case studies of real situations. But you have first to want to know.

Convictions

There is the problem of mind-set. People come with fixed mental images and models, so that they cannot see what we want them to see – just as I walked past the Adult Centre I was looking for because my mental image of it was wrong. We tend to select what we find easy or familiar and reject the rest. This happens if a new teacher has a fixed image of teaching behaviour.

We resist challenges to our accepted images, especially if they are part of our value system or deeply held convictions. If the evidence is all against us, we just shout louder to drown it out. You must know people who do that. Some teachers do that with students who challenge them.

Many people prefer to walk away from things rather than to face a possibility of challenge to their self-image or of failure. One of the most accurate measures of motivation is the readiness to come back from failure and try again. It is most clearly seen in individual sports. I gave up trying to ice-skate since I could not deal with the damage to me and my self-image when I performed badly. But if people are determined to succeed, nothing will stop them.

Barriers

REMEMBER!
. . . We have to be genuinely interested in problems that our students have in learning.

Often, people bring a history of painful learning experiences of the past, like mine in the skating rink. I have known graduates of famous universities declare, 'I am hopeless at maths.' What do they mean? Why should they believe it?

Such a strong conviction about oneself is usually a result of past failure or, quite often, of poor teaching or the absence of any attempt to discover what the learning problem really was. People like this present some of the strongest barriers to learning.

If you are to succeed, you have to believe there is at least some possibility of learning. Obviously, it is even better if you think you will learn if you try hard enough. As the teacher, you will need to recognise the barriers that individual students present and help them to look at them objectively and ask: is it really so?

The things we want students to do must be do-able. I take the view that if I want students to do something, I had better do it myself to find out how hard it is. Whenever I set a task I do it too; it's the only way I can find out what is involved. It helps me to assess their level of success properly, and if necessary to provide a model. How else will I know what problems they have to solve to be successful?

It is important that students do not set about trying to learn things with the wrong idea of what kind of a thing it is. They are bound to fail if they don't know what they are trying to do. Equally, they have to know beforehand what criteria will be used to judge their success. One clear advantage of stating criteria is to give the students means of assessing their own success and what they still need to learn.

If we are all learning together, there is excitement and energy in the system. As with a map, you have to explore the area so as to understand the map fully. Group and individual learning projects are exactly like that. Everyone has to be involved in learning.

They must know what they are trying to learn and, by reflecting on the experience, focus the learning for themselves so as to make it part of their learning structure.

ACTIVITY 6

Your learning barriers

Look at your own learning barriers.

1 What are the things you find particularly hard to do or to learn?
2 Can you list them? Do you know what they are?
3 Why is that? Can you think of the circumstances that led to it?
4 If students turn up in your class with such barriers, what can you do to help them?

Variety and pace

It may be that even in group activities only some are actively involved, while the others are just there. All classes should have a variety of activities that involve everyone to maintain attention. Classes need changes of pace too, including periods of high energy and periods of rest.

Language

Do we share a common language? All groups develop shared language that helps to bind them, and separates them from other groups. It is the same with academic subjects: special vocabulary has to be learned that allows specialists to communicate. This is as true of pottery and flower-arranging as it is of computing, say; I have been amazed at some of the vocabulary to be learned in a class on horse-management.

If this book is too full of jargon, or perhaps if my sentences are too complex, we will not communicate. We have to think about the readiness of students to work with these words, and of how they can link them to their own experience. Without such linking the words will not make sense. It is not a matter of intelligence, it is where we are, you and I, or you and your students.

If I were talking to you, instead of writing, you could use the expressions on my face, my gestures, my tone of voice and so on to help you to share what I am saying. Equally, I could use how you respond to what I say, what you feed back to me, to shape what I say next. More importantly, you could question me, have me repeat things in other words, or reframe them with you into your words. We can't do these things through the printed page.

But you can and must do them with your class. **Feedback matters**.

Attention

Questions are an important way of presenting challenges. And using questions to involve the group with you is also a valuable technique. Unfortunately, many teachers use the technique very badly.

One good way to improve its use is to name the person you want to answer. A general question fired into the air will usually not challenge most of the students directly enough to make them attend and concentrate. As the teacher, you lose control of what is happening.

The answers the students give must be treated as valuable, worth exploring and developing. Students soon know if you're playing the game of 'spot the teacher's right answer'. They have to make progress in their thinking from where they are.

If you want to talk or to engage in class discussion and you want them to listen, make sure they are ready to listen, not distracted or still absorbed in what was happening before.

An experienced teacher arranges the class so that, when necessary, eye-contact can be established with every student. The power of eye-contact is well known. Communication is not just words, but the whole behaviour pattern that the words are part of. We communicate in a multitude of ways. If a student is not looking at you, held by your gaze sometimes at least, what you want to share with him or her is lost. Listening usually depends on looking too.

A group of students staged a rather adventurous production of Christopher Marlowe's *Doctor Faustus*, with an ambitious set and a lot of mysterious lighting.

They invited a very famous actor to come and see the play and to give them some comments. His verdict was: 'Everything was going for the play, the set was really good for creating the right feeling. The main trouble was in the lighting. The curse of the theatre is inaudibility. And I find if you can't see it, you can't hear it.'

In discussions, in groupwork, when people have to work together they must be able to look at each other, establish eye-contact, get close enough to establish group space rather than individual space. They need to have a group territory in which they work.

REMEMBER!

... If we want people to 'hear' what we say, we have to establish contact with them first. Eye-contact is important. Physical contact may be necessary: touching, holding, even grabbing in extreme cases such as protecting someone from danger.

Students with special learning difficulties respond much better to touch than to words. A whole range of human relationships is determined by the level of contact that is made. Think about it.

Ask yourself at intervals:

- Have I lost them?
- What should happen now to restore their attention?
- Is this the time to change the activity or the focus?

Obviously, it is far better to change the activity, to involve them, to engage them actively in the learning process again.

Visual aids

The major purpose of visual aids is to create a change of focus. They help to create attention. If the class has to focus on the teacher all the time, the pressure on the teacher to perform is acute. And we all have distracting mannerisms – some teachers cultivate them deliberately.

If you switch on an OHP or a slide projector (or indeed a sound source), attention switches away from your face to the screen. This is helpful in dealing with attention span and gives variety. But it becomes self-defeating if the OHP is then left on all the time. You must switch it off again when you want the students to concentrate on something else; otherwise it becomes a distraction.

Since we experience 70 per cent of what we learn by using sight, visual images and presentation are very powerful aids to learning. They are usually more effective than sound alone. Most people's seeing skills are much more highly developed than their listening skills. But this also presents a problem. What we want is attention, and so we should attempt to control the visual images to ensure that we get it. Most rooms are full of visual images. Many of these will divert attention and distract people.

Most teachers use a chalkboard at some time or other. What does it have on it? Its purpose is the same as any other visual aid: it helps to focus attention and to present information visually. If anything on the board is irrelevant, clean it off. And try to ensure that work on the board is easy to absorb and to follow, that it has some structure. Don't use it as a jotting pad with no attempt to organise what you write.

Take control of the visual stimuli in the room, and make them work for you.

INFORMATION

Try to present a great deal of information visually. To make it effective you need to eliminate unnecessary and possibly confusing detail. A picture is worth a thousand words, but not if it is a poor one or if it is too hard to grasp. We can only absorb and make sense of a limited amount of information.

For instance, suppose you wanted to present the ideas in our earlier discussion of competence and performance criteria (Chapter 8) in a lesson. You could use a visual form, but what you use as a visual focus would not be the same as I am using here as written material in a book, or what you would have on some handout I might use in support. The handout can carry more information and detail because a student has time to study it (although it must still have a clear structure). You could use the format of Tasks 8 and 9, with performance criteria attached.

You might try using this on an OHP transparency. But there is too much information – in the wrong form – here for it to be usable in this way. The information is too wordy. The visual aid is intended to focus attention, not present *all* the information. You are to talk about it, to amplify and explain it. So what you want is a structure of key-words the students can learn quickly and remember.

The OHP might be designed to look more like this. It might even be better as several OHPs, with even less on each to talk about. It could be improved even more by the use of colour. But the important thing is not how 'clever' it is. The question is: how easy is it to read and take in as a whole? to see links between the ideas? to grasp and to understand?

KEY-WORDS
observe — interactions
recognise — needs/difficulties
respond — feedback
appropriate language
effective teaching aids
skills
confidence — understanding — sensitivity
honesty — evaluating

TASK 11:   Designing a visual aid

In designing anything to present visually, whether it is an OHP transparency or work on the chalkboard or a handout, ask critically:

How much information is there on here?
How much of that actually makes it harder to understand?
How much can I get rid of without changing what it says?
What is the least that I need to have on here?
Will one word do? and an arrow? or a simple structure?
How do I help them to see the structure? relationships?
What do I want them to take away?

11 Control of the Environment

In Task 9 you evaluated the effectiveness of a lesson plan in a teaching context, and in Task 10 you looked at the communication that was taking place. Let us now consider another important aspect: environmental factors.

Control of the environment is so important in enabling the intended pattern of learning (and teaching) to happen that I have chosen to deal with it separately here. Nevertheless, it must be seen as an integral part of the communication process, receiving due attention in your preparation for teaching.

TASK 12: Control of the environment

In completing Tasks 9 and 10, were you able to meet the performance criteria below?

PERFORMANCE CRITERIA
4.1 As far as possible the environment is made suitable for the intended learning activities. It is properly equipped.
4.2 The effect of environmental factors on learning is noted.
4.3 Learning areas are set out to support the planned learning activities and are structured to facilitate them.
4.4 Effort is made to optimise the use of the environment.
4.5 A safe working environment is created.

There is nothing particularly difficult to understand here. You know how you react to colour, light, darkness, being too hot or not having enough oxygen in a room. You get depressed when it is always dull and raining – a winter of eternal grey. How cheering it is to see bulbs coming through on a lovely spring day! You've noticed children becoming excited and noisy in a high wind. You have gone to sleep in the cinema or in a lecture. You have felt the atmosphere of railway stations and airports, the pressure of tunnels and the thrill of bridges.

Our surroundings have a marked effect on our feelings and our behaviour. Some people seem to be particularly conscious of the effect of colour – some even choose a car because of its colour. These things do not happen at a conscious level normally.

But there is an extraordinary lack of apparent concern about this kind of thing when it comes to classrooms. They are painted (or not) in rather depressing colours, and workshops and other such places are even worse. They are poorly designed for the activity that is to happen there. Quite often they are badly lit and badly ventilated – they are too hot or too cold. Both have a bad effect on the students' ability to work: in airless rooms they simply go to sleep. Unfortunately, teachers fail to see the cause.

CASE STUDY 14

David visited a high school in Florida to talk to the students. He was asked to compare British schools with those in Florida. He started by asking them if they liked living in caves.

Every public building he visited there, he said, was built without windows. People worked in artificial light and artificial air. The reason was simple. If you have windows you suffer from solar gain: the sun makes the room uncomfortably hot and air conditioning is made even more expensive.

In the more northerly states of the USA and in Europe we try to bring the outside inside with large windows where we can. In Florida, however, they hid from it. It makes for a rather strange experience when you come to it for the first time: you feel chilled to the bone as you walk from a humid street at 90°F into the cool, dry atmosphere of a room at a temperature of only 70°.

Of course, the students had not noticed the absence of windows: they took windowless rooms for granted. Almost anything can be 'normal' if that is all we know.

1 What do you consider to be 'normal' in classrooms here? Given the opportunity to start from first principles, should they really be like that?
2 If you look closely at the environment your students have to work in, how do you think they react to it? What is it saying to your students, not only about the credibility of the teacher who is expecting them to do certain things there, but also about how they are valued as people?
3 What are the effects of the environment on what is supposed to happen there? Is it supportive? suitable?
4 What improvements should be made to make learning easier?

Problems

There are many problems that may be caused by an environment that is hostile to the learning activity and attitudinal changes you wish to encourage. Look carefully at your teaching situation, and try to ensure that it provides an appropriate model of behaviour.

In a typing room there may be broken chairs or scanty work-space for the students to get themselves properly organised to work. The typist is expected to learn about the importance of posture and organisation, of having a ship-shape office.

Is a room saying 'do as I say, not as I do'? This will handicap both student and teacher. Where is credibility in the learning?

Usually, the problems are more routine. When you observe classes, ask yourself: what are the messages in this room? how is it controlling what happens here? what kind of learning or teaching behaviour does it assume? how much distraction is there? does it make it hard for students to concentrate? how noisy is it? what are the acoustics like?

Again, how much effort is required to get the things the teacher may need? an OHP or a tape-recorder or even a piece of chalk? Or to have any photocopying done? Teachers may stop trying to do more interesting things with their students if it is just too much hard work to get things ready.

Taking control

REMEMBER!

. . . It is your responsibility to ensure that the environment supports as far as possible what students have to do in order to learn.

When students arrive in a new environment, they explore it; they look for clues as to how to behave there, as to what is expected of them. The messages are easily, and quite unconsciously, read. They come to it with 'models in the head'.

If they see desks in a row facing a teacher's desk, they know it means: sit down, listen, be quiet. Could they reasonably be expected to engage in groupwork, or even to share ideas in discussion? They can only react with the teacher. Eye-contact is possible with no one else: they only see the backs of other students' heads. We need to see people's faces to talk to them, to watch their expressions, to look for the subtle ways in which we communicate: 'how did I know you intended to be funny?'

So move the furniture. Set it up to do what you want to do.

What if there are no desks, but comfortable chairs in a circle? What does that say? Or a large table with chairs around it – a committee meeting? What if there is gentle background music playing? What if coffee is set out ready on the table in the corner? What if there are pictures on the wall, and a carpet?

You can create your own environment with a little ingenuity. You are in charge, not the caretaker (though the caretaker is someone you should make friends with). You could plan it with a group of other teachers.

You may need to be quite forceful. How many teachers will have the courage or confidence to say, 'Hey! this isn't good enough for my students. If you want them to learn, help me to make it possible.' But you may be surprised how much co-operation you do get if you make enough noise – in a nice way – about it.

There are, of course, many simple things you can do. Open the windows. Make sure there is enough light. Move chairs and tables around. Put up posters and learning materials. Plan the situations you want to create. Create space and territories.

Overcoming obstacles

Quite often teachers fail to see the potential in the environment, or what can be done with a little imagination. Students may be more inventive than you are, so enlist their thinking too. Encourage them to take control of their group territory if you want them to do certain things, so long as their suggestions are not silly or destructive. They are often less inhibited than you are.

If you know in advance what you want to get hold of and plan well ahead, it is not too hard to ensure that you have the things you want. You can find out where things are, what the system is – or isn't. You can work with the technicians and AVA personnel.

REMEMBER!
. . . Most problems arise because people do not think ahead.

Safety

REMEMBER!
. . . Your principal responsibility is to ensure the health and safety of your students at all times.

If you see dangers, report them. If possible, take remedial action. Refuse to go on working in an unsafe environment, whether it be a workshop, laboratory or theatre. Management must take action.

Make sure you know where fire exits are and the fire drill. Get a copy of the safety booklet and read it. Make sure students know what to do. They must know and keep to the rules in the workshops and laboratories and when working in any hazardous places. You must also be a model to them of how to behave, what to wear, how to avoid injury.

If they behave stupidly and take idiotic risks, exclude them from the class without compunction. You must be absolutely adamant.

They must wear suitable clothing and shoes. You are responsible if they are injured, even if it is their silly fault – for example, if a student suffers an eye injury after failing to wear the goggles that have been provided.

This is a legal requirement.

Institutions and work-places have safety rules and regulations. You *must* know what they are and ensure your students know them.

12 Assessment

Here, I deal with basic concepts and ideas; we shall explore the complexities of educational examining later in Part 2 of the book. Here we are concerned with feedback, and in assessing learning to facilitate it.

TASK 13: Assessment

Use feedback and assessment in your planned lesson to promote the intended learning of your students. Evaluate your success in meeting the criteria below.

PERFORMANCE CRITERIA
5.1 The teacher notes carefully interaction between individuals, with the teacher and in groups.
5.2 Learning difficulties are noted: support and help is given.
5.3 There is clear evidence of sensitivity to the problems the students experience and willingness to use feedback.
5.4 Individuals are encouraged to take responsibility for their own learning and progress.
5.5 Assessment methods are identified in the lesson plans.
5.6 The assessment that is planned and used is appropriate for the intended learning and will provide good feedback.
5.7 Learning is assessed by students and teacher.
5.8 Learning is consolidated.
5.9 The session and outcomes are evaluated.

Feedback

Feedback enables learning to take place. How does it work?

The simplest example of feedback in a closed system is a thermostat to control a heating system and to keep the temperature constant. It feeds back information about the temperature to the boiler. When the desired temperature is reached the thermostat cuts out the boiler. When the temperature drops it re-ignites it.

But learning is not a closed system. It is dynamic and changes with time and experience. Feedback here requires not only some way of monitoring change from inside, but additional input from outside. We need a mirror to reflect back to us an image of what we are doing, or what we are not – some means of judging how well we do whatever we are trying to achieve.

When we work with other people, they provide that mirror. To use the mirror effectively, we have to know what we are looking for, the kind of responses we want – or don't want. Then we change what we do accordingly, to get the desired response.

Everybody knows how to do that. We do it all the time in our normal daily affairs. Otherwise, social groupings and social interaction would be impossible. It is the way we learn.

In formal education and learning, however, we need to invent very complex systems of feeding back information. The learning activities we engage in are complex, so that is hardly surprising.

The learning activities themselves usually provide the feedback that we need. If I am trying to learn to skate, I know whether I am being successful or not! When we attempt sophisticated tasks, when we set up learning as a series of targets with performance criteria, we need to find more complex ways of measuring success. Usually another person's perception is then crucially important.

Evidence

We have to have some evidence and we must decide what kind of evidence; then we have to make judgements about the evidence, and about what it demonstrates.

What really matters in assessment is the nature of the evidence. If we look for evidence, we must be sure that it is valid – that it actually relates to what we are trying to observe or to measure.

For instance, does it make sense to try to measure how much more skill I have acquired in playing tennis by having me write an essay about it? Yet there is a strongly held view that exams are what matter, and 'an exam is writing essays, isn't it?' What in fact will my ability to write such an essay demonstrate? That I can write the essay, of course, but that is not what I want to find out.

If I want to show that I can write a good essay, however, the only proper evidence I can provide is essays I have written. It is unlikely that I shall succeed in writing a good essay at the first attempt. By using feedback, my own assessment of what I have done maybe and what other people think about it, it is to be expected that my next essay will approximate more closely to a model of what a good essay is. I may also read essays that are said to be good models and try to imitate them. I have to build up a mental picture of what a good essay is like if I am to be able to create a fair approximation of one. It may take me many attempts before I am happy with it.

In education, we can attempt to measure change or achievement. A practical example: as a swimmer, I want to be proficient in life-saving. How shall I achieve that? How shall I know when I am acceptably proficient? How shall I demonstrate it to others?

What I have to do to demonstrate that I am proficient is the same as what I do to learn in order to achieve it. The difference between the two lies in the judgements that are made about what I do. My standard of performance is judged against criteria.

In this case, I might actually be required at some point to save someone from drowning. Proficiency cannot simply be arbitrary judgements made by a judge: either I save someone from drowning or I don't. This is the case with most important learning that we do. The test that matters comes when we have to do it 'for real'.

All learning systems require proper feedback. We must try to see the purpose of assessment as principally to improve the learning. There is a view that assessment is the same as testing. Tests do come in many forms these days and they certainly have value. They are not restricted by any means to essay-writing. But their use in providing feedback is limited. They usually attempt to show some numerical score which may not be helpful in identifying what it is students need to improve or need still to learn.

We need to know this: what we still have to learn, in what way we must improve. In trying to find this kind of evidence we have to look at what students have to do in order to learn. There are usually skills to be learned, and quite often products that can be evaluated. The essay above is a product; so is the pot I have turned on the wheel, or a flower arrangement, or a properly presented typed document.

These products are tangible evidence of achievement. They can be compared with previous attempts by this student and compared with those of others, to try to identify some agreed criteria on which we can focus our attention and thinking. We can probably identify what has changed between one attempt and another, and we can try to establish criteria for excellence.

Criteria

Clearly I will progress more quickly if I do not have to guess by what criteria my success or lack of it will be judged. In most things in life we learn by trial and error, gradually teasing out an idea of what we have to do to be successful. Often this can be a painful experience. We may ask: what are teachers for?

Unfortunately, teachers frequently fail to tell students what they have to achieve: what they must do to succeed rather than fail. What can the learner learn? Do the teachers know what the criteria are? or is it just a feeling they have?

External examinations, set and marked by examining boards, are of course designed to provide summative assessments (see Chapter 23) against which an award may or may not be made. You should seek to provide feedback to your students at every opportunity, however, and to obtain every scrap of information that will assist both you and your students to enhance your performance. Most examination boards do provide feedback; seek it out, and use it to modify and improve your teaching programme.

As we learn, we change in so many inter-related ways: knowledge and skills, perception and insight, attitudinal development. Very little of this can be measured statistically. Most of it is not accessible to the kinds of test that produce scores.

If, as many teachers are, you are required to use tests as part of your teaching programme, please look at the discussion of tests in Chapter 23.

Progression

The kind of criteria I have devised for this book are to be viewed as signposts, pointing a direction to establish good practice. They define the roads down which to travel, rather than points of arrival beyond which we do not need to go. A teacher who is fully satisfied with a personal performance in any aspect of teaching ceases to ask important questions.

As with the professional painter or musician, each product, each performance, provides a critical evaluation so that the next one can be more mature, more fully formed and more impressive. No artist is ever satisfied: every performance is a learning experience that helps the performer to improve. Your professional judgement will change with experience, insight and knowledge. Progress depends on using experience, reflecting on it to change your perception of what you are about.

It is the same with your students. They have to be fully engaged in the process of learning, and that means also in the process of assessment. They need to reflect on their learning experiences, on what they achieve, in order to improve. So your criteria for them are also signposts rather than goalposts.

When to assess

Surely, at the end of each learning experience. We need to know what we have learned, whether we have achieved the learning goals and how well: what we need to do *now*.

In designing learning experiences, we must have a clear idea of what students are setting out to learn and how we, and they, will know how far they have progressed towards mastery of it.

There are long-term goals and short-term goals. Each lesson has its short-term goals. They should be perceived as part of those longer-term goals towards which they contribute.

Much of the assessment must take place 'on the wing', as it is happening. The feedback must be as close as possible to the learning for it to have any useful effect. It is not much use knowing that we need to do something differently once the point of need has passed – a week later may seem a very long time. If I am to improve my golf-swing, I need help on the course. Much of the most useful help and feedback a teacher can provide is when students are coming up against difficulties in doing things.

TASK 14: Evidence and criteria

1 In your own area of teaching, identify what evidence you would look for to measure the progress of your students.
2 How would you get your students to produce that evidence?
3 What kind of learning would you consider it would measure?
4 In relation to the learning goals, try to identify criteria that you think the activity, or the product of the activity, could achieve if it was well done. Make the criteria as simple and clear as you can.
5 Can you share these criteria with your students before they set out to undertake the activity?
6 How will you provide feedback to your students? Will it be through discussion or in a more formal way?

Self-evaluation

At the end of any learning experience we need to evaluate, take stock of what has happened, where we are now, decide where we go from here. What have you discovered so far? What decisions do you need to make?

ACTIVITY 7

Try to answer the following questions as honestly as you can. There is no need to be highly self-critical. Use your reflective diary to try to see what has happened, what has changed and, perhaps, why.

Where you can, try to identify the evidence for your statement that you might show your mentor for comment or discussion.

1 Lesson plannning: how have you rethought your approaches, and why?
2 Communication: what do you now understand? or what has now come into focus?
3 Environment: what do you now have the confidence to do?
4 Observation: what have you observed?
5 Teaching: look again at the performance criteria. How far do you match up to them? What still needs work?
6 Attitudes: do you feel you can relate better with students? How confident are you? Can you explore various methods? How flexible are you, and how adaptable?

Part 2

Developing the Learning Programme

Introduction

While Part 1 focused on preparing and teaching individual lessons, Part 2 is concerned with designing and implementing a programme.

Relying on learning from experience for your further growth simply takes too long. To accelerate the process, you need much more information, ideas and practical advice. This is what Part 2 provides. There is a range of approaches, methods and strategies with analysis of the attendant skills and how to develop them. It is not intended, however, that you attempt to try out all the methods: you must select those that are appropriate to the learning. Select also those Activities that meet your requirements, addressing the material with your own questions related to your perception of what you need. All the Tasks are important, however, and should be undertaken in the order set out.

You will need feedback. We all do in order to learn. You also need to be able to articulate your feelings and your discovery. Ideally you will be able to use this material in a context where you can receive such support. It is feasible to do it on your own, of course, but it is so much better with a mentor and/or colleagues too.

13 A Case Study Approach

You have already become familiar with case studies. It is normal for us to deal with problems by reference to what happened on other occasions, usually anecdotally ('I remember when . . . ').

Case studies are different in that we try to impose some discipline on them. We give them shape and form so that we can learn from them by interrogating 'the experience' with questions. We can then apply that learning to find a solution either to a present case or to future cases. Or we may compare several case studies, to look for similarities and differences.

The case study

When you carry out the Tasks associated with Part 2 you will be making an extended case study of your own learning as you design, prepare, implement and evaluate a teaching/learning programme for a group of students in your own context. Your principal responsibility is clearly to your students, but you are also a student in the classroom or wherever it is you are teaching, and you will be exploring your own learning. The case study should enable you to focus on what occurs so as to monitor growth and change throughout the experience.

In Part 1, I adopted a linear approach to designing assignments and supporting ideas and activities. There is a sequence within which good practice in teaching must operate. You cannot plan in a vacuum; you need sufficient information of the right kind.

In designing your case study in Part 2 the same sequencing will be required, for exactly the same reasons. A case study develops over time and within a context. Tasks have to be undertaken in order. You cannot implement what you have not designed, nor evaluate it until after it has occurred.

The National Curriculum for Design and Technology in the United Kingdom suggests the following structure for any design project (a teaching programme is such a design project):

In order to design a programme you have to discover and attempt to answer questions. 'Explore' invites you to discover questions and structure them into a useful, practicable approach.

Strategy

One area of exploration is to look at alternative strategies for the teaching/learning programme. You need to have some view of the curriculum model you wish to use. To help you, think about a design project you are familiar with – making a dress, a menu for a dinner party, a holiday programme.

There are appropriate and inappropriate ways of setting about doing these things. There is a very wide range of alternative ways of setting about learning. You must choose one that is appropriate for what you want your students to learn: far too often, students and teachers choose unhelpful methods of learning because they have not thought the matter through.

Once you have a clear over-view of what you and your students are supposed to be about, you can formulate it into an action plan. You can then design the programme and all its parts.

All this has to be done before the teaching/learning can begin. The case study, however, starts with this thinking and planning, even if the bulk of it is reflection on what actually happens in your teaching. You could usefully start with:

- Who are the students, and what do they need to learn?
- What do they have to do? What do they have to know?
- How will they know what they have to learn?
- How are they going to learn? Where and when? What is the time-scale?
- How quickly can they learn?
- What do they need in order to achieve this learning?
- Are they going to do it alone or with other students?
- What support do they need?
- How will they know when they have learned it?
- How is learning to be demonstrated and tested?
- What standard should it be set at?
- Under what conditions?

Once you have made a list of questions and structured them you will know where to look for answers, and what helpful answers might look like. You can then make decisions.

The strategy chosen here is that of experiential learning. You have now considerable experience to build upon. In order to learn through experience, you have to be able to stand back from what happens to reflect upon it. It will help greatly if you share that reflection with others, if they can provide you with a mirror.

TASK 15: Student group

The first requirement is a more detailed study of your students. If they do not form a coherent group meeting for a programme of study, that is a pity, but it does not invalidate the exercise. You have to design and plan for students as they really are.

If at all possible, discuss various ways of setting about this with your peers and/or your mentor. Agree the form it should take, and the time by which you need to have it ready – of course, the sooner the better in relation to planning, but many teachers have to do preliminary planning work before they first meet the students.

There are many ways of setting about it. One is to create a short questionnaire for yourself or students to complete, perhaps at an enrolment or pre-course meeting.

What matters is that you actually use the information. Students may not be too happy if they are asked and then ignored.

Bear in mind that the purpose of this information is to assist you in designing the learning programme. Don't overwhelm yourself with so much information that you cannot use it effectively. Decide what is relevant and useful, what you really need to know. Identify the information that, though interesting, is not particularly useful, and decide whether it is worth having.

Set down clearly for yourself what you need to know. Validate it with your mentor and your peers. Then you can decide how you are to discover the information. Again, the experience of what you did in Part 1 should help you.

14 Identifying Needs

Considerable emphasis has been put so far on identifying needs. It will by now be clear that this is not a simple matter. Students' needs are complex and largely unknown to them; often there are feelings that are hard for them to express. Even though what they say is not a safe guide as to what is really important for them, they should always be encouraged to articulate their perception of need.

Adults require to be consulted, to agree to what the goals are and what is to be learned, what their roles and responsibilities in the learning process are to be. Students ultimately must be responsible for what happens. This may be affected by:

- bad feelings between individuals (or with the teacher)
- a failure for the group or working groups to 'gel'
- poor working conditions that do not value them as people
- pace of work, time of day, tiredness
- lack of comprehension of the teacher or of what they are to do
- lack of commitment if the work seems boring or pointless
- demands that are too heavy or that fail to stimulate or challenge
- lack of relevance to their perception of what the learning is for.

This list is merely a guide to help to shape your thinking about what needs might look like, and most of it is, or could be, within the control of the teacher.

In identifying needs, it is necessary to carry the students with us. But it requires sensitivity on your part, as the teacher, to see it from the point of view of the students. You need to experience what it is like for them. To do that you must watch, observe carefully what happens, how students respond to what they are asked to do, and how the social context of the group develops.

When a class goes well it develops its own momentum. If it dies, you have to know and try to discover what is not going well. The students may feel under-valued or badly treated; individuals or the group may exhibit withdrawal behaviour.

You, as teacher, have to make decisions on behalf of the group. You have to win commitment to a programme, establish common goals and good working relationships to achieve them. You must create supportive conditions for learning activity. To do that you must know what it is for, what is the purpose of the whole enterprise.

Asking students what they want to learn may be ineffective: they will have come expecting you to know and to tell them. You must have your own programme to present to them. Negotiation needs a baseline. To arrive with a blank piece of paper and say, 'well, what shall we do this week, this term?' will usually cause dismay.

Learning goals

Consolidation and assessment both require that learning goals are stated and agreed. Learning goals need to be stated simply, in terms it is easy for the students to comprehend and agree to, and which make it easy for them to assess in terms of progress and achievement.

Any negotiation of goals must begin from the teacher's statement of learning goals and a programme to achieve them. You need to have a rationale for your choice of programme. You should also make it clear how flexible you are prepared to be to meet your students' perception of what they need to learn. They will trust you so long as they see what they are asked to do as stimulating and interesting, and they feel they are making progress in the learning.

The better organised the teacher, and the easier it is for students to do the things planned as learning activities, the more success there will be within the programme as a whole.

Personal needs

Almost all of us, as social human beings, have personal needs. Most of us are usually shy of telling people about these, although some have no such inhibitions. Encounter groups in both the United Kingdom and America encourage people to express their anxieties and needs.

Many people come to adult/community education as a way of satisfying some of these deeply felt needs. Every student is dealing with a host of conflicting emotions and pressures. Teachers should not attempt to be counsellors or try to deal with students' personal problems, however, though the relationship with individuals may allow some of that to happen. Nevertheless, they need to be sensitive to what individuals bring to the class. Much of the behaviour relates to such feelings.

All of us need to maintain a self-image we are happy with, self-esteem and a sense of achievement. We all need success and find failure damaging. We need social contacts and friendships. Many people come to our classes looking for these things. Others feel themselves constantly under pressure from the demands of others, and are trying to identify goals or interests peculiarly their own.

There are extrinsic pressures too, such as the need for qualifications and to get or keep a job. Students may feel threatened by change in their working environment and the need to keep up with it.

It is easier to deal with personal needs as part of a learning programme through individual (or even small group) tutorials (see Chapter 17). The progress, or lack of it, in learning activities may be because of personal factors that students cannot express in front of the large group, or even in a small group they work well with.

What students (or employers) pay for in teaching sessions is time, and the effective use of time is what planning of programmes is mostly about. It is impossible to do everything in class time. Whatever programme is set up, much learning has to take place outside class time with students working on their own or in groups.

In designing teaching/learning programmes, teachers will need to cost the use of time in some way. To be effective, students must take an active part in the learning process. Setting the learning up as individual and group learning activities should release time that can be used for individual tutorial support. They require opportunities for individual feedback and support.

Motivation: tasks

Herzberg, in *The Motivation to Work*, saw 'motivators' as largely arising from tasks: what the individual or group was expected to do. Many women, for instance, complain of the menial quality of much of what they have to do, and how this defines their role. Such feelings tend to demotivate.

Our perception of our role and the tasks we have to do can give rise to satisfaction, excitement and stimulation, or to hostility and even despair. Bear this in mind as you identify roles in group learning, and as you design tasks for your students to do.

What roles do the students perceive? How does it look to them? For example, what effect will it have on apprentices who are expected to take dictated notes in class for three hours and practise for hours in a workshop things they do every day at work, if they are then told by the boss, 'You can forget that – we don't do it that way'? Things like this do happen.

Motivation has been studied intensively. What makes people want to do things? to put in effort? to overcome pain? Most people find they do much better, keep going against the odds, if they have the support and challenge of others with them. There are so many examples. It explains the enormous growth of clubs for slimmers, cyclists, those trying to give up alcohol or people rebuilding their lives after emotional trauma. We all need others to share what we do, the pain and the thrills. It is so hard to keep going on your own. We need competition as well as support.

From this stems the importance of groupwork and group tasks. Individuals will often achieve a great deal more through peer group support. But peer group pressure may level down as well as up, so that the teacher needs to monitor carefully what actually happens.

Success breeds success, failure demotivates. Ensure that the tasks and the learning programme you set up are likely to be achievable by your students. If they are too hard (equally if they are not challenging enough) or incomprehensible or seem to have little to do with what the students feel they are actually trying to learn, little real effort will be put into them.

In designing learning programmes, designing the learning tasks will be the most important part of the preparation.

The cost of failure

Much motivation can be calculated by the cost of failure and how well people are prepared to come back from failure.

Perception of the cost of failure to achieve goals set by oneself, by parents, by employers or by one's peer group, is vitally important in what people are prepared to do. In some societies, the cost is very great – it can lead to high suicide rates. Elsewhere it may lead to people playing very safe, and being unwilling to take risks or personal responsibility.

In other societies, individuals are encouraged to take risks when failure is tolerated or there is always a second chance to do it. When failure is over-indulged and all pressures are removed, the tendency is to drop out and take it easy.

This is why it is so important to establish clearly the rules and expectations within the learning group. Teachers can use the natural competitiveness of groups to good effect here. Peer group pressure not to let the group down is a powerful motivator. But individuals also need to know what is expected of them in regard to their personal learning programme. They need an action plan and time schedules. These should be monitored through tutorials.

15 Devising a Learning/Teaching Strategy

If you are to build a sound strategy, you must have a clear sense of purpose. It cannot be good enough just to set off with a half-thought-out plan of what you are going to do, how your teaching will link to students' learning. As we have said before, there has to be some rationale for what we do both as learners and as teachers.

It is not enough for teachers to adopt teaching strategies without thinking in terms of the learning methods they envisage for students, or the likely success or otherwise of those strategies. They should have an over-view of the changes in the students that the teaching programme they are designing seeks to promote, of how the changes will occur, and how they are to be managed and assessed. Any course or programme may be judged on

- the **cognitive changes** it is intended to facilitate
- the **behavioural changes** that will be observed
- the **enrichment** it provides through learning experiences and
- its **effectiveness** in achieving this learning (obviously).

Cognitive and behavioural changes are the easiest of these to assess and it is usual to devise courses with emphasis on one or the other.

Enrichment is most important, since attitudinal change is usually a prerequisite of other learning, and is the result of the nature of the learning experiences. Often sharing with colleagues, teams and groups is effective; so too is facing and overcoming challenge. The appropriate way forward is for you to identify:

- what your students are setting out to learn
- what learning behaviour is likely to succeed best.

You can then plan a teaching strategy to facilitate the learning.

Many teachers will say that the strategy is decided for them by examining board *diktat* or requirements of other bodies, including the employers. I am talking here about matters intrinsic to the learning process, not about instrumental questions such as method of assessment of the outcomes of learning.

Any strategy, yours or the students', may be more or less successful. People do not usually decide consciously how they are going to learn, they just set off. Frequently they run into trouble because their chosen learning strategy is inappropriate to the intended outcomes. Observe students in your classes who have not grasped what the task is they are asked to do. If they thought about it they could do it more efficiently. The important questions about a learning strategy are:

- Does it work? Will it work?
- Is it the most effective way of learning this?
- Is it efficient in the expenditure of time and effort?
- Are there other strategies? Would they be more effective?

Murder Game (bottom-up/top-down)

Play the Murder Game to see learning strategies in action.

There always seems to be the same pattern of behaviour when a group plays this game. Obviously, it won't work for you since you will have read this description first!

THE MURDER GAME

The purpose of the game is to extract the information about a murder in a country house (a cliché, of course). All the 'clues' and information are printed on individual cards. The cards are shuffled and dealt out to the participants so that each has a fairly even number of clues.

It is a leaderless game: this is important. Everyone in the group has equal responsibility for solving the mystery and the methodology for doing so. No information is given that is not on the cards. No instructions are given. The group has to make up its own rules of play.

Two observers make notes on what occurs – what individuals and the group decide and do, how the mystery is solved. The debrief is concerned with the strategies of learning they chose.

People usually try a 'bottom-up' approach first: 'Let's have everyone read out what's on their cards, I'll start.' 'Let's put the cards on the table so we can see the information.' This soon becomes impossible; there is too much to take in and no shape or order to it. There is a moment of hilarity or panic.

Someone will probably suggest that they should look for patterns. 'I've got something about a knife on the floor. Has anyone got anything to add to that?' This looks and feels more promising. Confidence begins to rise.

Eventually, someone is likely to suggest they write down specific questions and see who has information to answer them: for example, who was killed? when? where? what with? any red herrings? This begins to look and feel like business.

It will be successful if they identify the right questions. This is called a 'top-down' strategy: it aims to ask who has got any information about the weapon, the room, the time and so on. It imposes some logic and structure and pattern on the proceedings which pays off immediately. It is pro-active. Soon, all is revealed.

In the debrief, it is important to ensure that people talk about their feelings as well as their lack of comprehension. How did it feel to be frustrated? to be baffled? to be overwhelmed with information you could not use or make sense of? How did it feel when light began to dawn? How did they eventually reach the result? Was it by little steps, or did it suddenly all fall into place?

The game is experiential, about 'feeling it'. We have to feel these things if we are to know how it frequently is for students.

Case Study 5 in Part 1 used the Table Game, which provides another valuable way to gain insight into learning strategies. How do people attempt to learn the contents of the table? What strategies do they use?

Those who try to memorise a jumble of disconnected ideas fail. Those who can relate things in terms of categories or structures succeed better. How often we choose the first way in so many things we try to learn! How often teachers impose this on students too! Why do they do that?

First find the questions. I strongly advocate the 'top-down' approach.

Other strategies

This is only one example of learning strategies. Here are a few more that you will observe students – and teachers – using. There are many more, of course, and you should try to add to the list as you observe what your students, peers and colleagues do.

TRAVELLING HOPEFULLY

This is the strategy most people use most of the time: it turns out to be mainly trial and error learning. It is how we deal with life, of course – a Micawberish optimism that 'something will turn up' – and it is often painful and ineffective, an inefficient way of learning. What are teachers for? It is impossible to avoid such learning in most things, and particularly in acquiring skills. It is much easier when given a structure and made more effective by proper use of feedback in relation to identified goals.

INDOCTRINATION

Some teachers may wish to avoid risks altogether, making all the decisions themselves and avoiding challenge or thinking. Where the importance of demonstrably high standards of performance weighs heavily, with strong emphasis on using the 'right' techniques, it may lead to repetitive practice and rote-learning without understanding.

Many forms of training have used such strategies, but they are less effective than involving the students more actively in decisions about their learning, to give them some ownership.

'CRAM IT ALL IN'

Students faced with examinations frequently adopt the strategy, of 'memorise it, don't try to understand it – that will come later.' Teachers also succumb to it in despair at the size of syllabuses they and the students have to cover.

COMPETING GROUPS

This strategy is frequently used in business, on playing fields or even on the factory floor. Many games are used in education and training programmes. Properly managed, they may generate motivation and energy; when badly handled they can destroy good working relationships.

INTERACTIVE AND GROUP-BASED PROJECTS

I have advocated the use of this strategy for the enrichment of the learning experience and the interpersonal skills that can be developed. Humans are social animals and produce better results when they work effectively in groups. There is a richness in the resources available from the experience and expertise within the group and from generating ideas and tackling problems together.

In the survey of learning theories in Part 3, I explore arguments for adopting particular approaches. Behaviourists have closed programmes: teacher-centred, with predicted outcomes and structured processes to achieve them. Cognitive philosophers advocate open, dynamic, student-centred learning: their outcomes are unpredictable and the processes dynamic, changing with time.

Deductive approaches to learning/teaching are closed strategies. In these, rules and concepts are stated that lead to predictable outcomes. There is little room for creativity even in student-centred programmes. Learning mathematics for most students, even in maths workshops, is getting right answers by correct methods. Inductive strategies on the other hand are open: 'we're going to mess about in this area for a bit to see what we can discover.' They are about generating questions and problem-solving.

Strategies may be more or less open, allow more or less control of goals and processes. Travelling hopefully is an open strategy. It is unpredictable in both its processes and its outcomes.

Indoctrination is a closed strategy. All the decisions have been made by the teacher; everything is to be predicted, process and outcomes alike. Some strategies employ 'conditioning' as a deliberate means of controlling/shaping learning; these derive from the theory of learning known as behaviourism.

TASK 16:   Strategy and learning programme

You must develop some over-view of what you and your students are about – what the relationship is between your activity as teacher and theirs as learners.

1 Try to clarify to yourself what you consider the responsibilities and roles to be, both theirs and yours. How far are you willing to involve them in the decision-making? What are the constraints?

2 How will you communicate with them to share such thinking?

3 What kind of learning/teaching strategy is most likely to help them achieve the learning goals you have in mind for them? How would you justify your choice of that particular strategy?

Design a learning/teaching programme for your student group.

This programme will clearly develop and change, since it covers a series of sessions over time. The strategy you devise will give it overall shape. Within that there has to be a variety of learning experiences that match the learning needs and goals.

The performance criteria below are intended to outline what is good practice in such a design. The statements build on those in Part 1, but are to be understood as implying greater depth. The feedback from reflecting on your experience of using various approaches and methods will ensure there will be development both of the strategy and the methodology through the programme.

Lesson plans and evaluations with consequent rethinking, getting together of materials and resources cumulate into the case study.

PERFORMANCE CRITERIA FOR PREPARATION/DESIGN

1 Students within the group are known in relation to their educational and/or employment background, personal learning goals and motivation.

2 There is shared perception of learning goals in the group and with the teacher, both overall and within each lesson.

3 Teaching sessions are planned and sequenced to meet specified and/or negotiated goals clearly known to all. Links are clear; the students understand how the activities and sessions are intended to progress towards achievement of the overall learning goals.

4 There are clear links with prior learning in the process.

5 Where appropriate, the learning is consistent with requirements of external examining bodies with suitable assessment.

6 Teaching methods/learning activities planned are relevant and appropriate to promote the intended learning and for the students in terms of their background and ability.

7 Sessions will engage students in learning through activities consistent with their readiness to learn and undertake them.

8 Sufficient flexibility will allow for different pace/styles of learning for individual students.

9 The learning materials and aids designed/selected will be effective for the intended learning and of a presentable standard.

10 Assessment of the learning is clearly identified in planning sessions and activities, and there is evidence of critical evaluation of the effectiveness of the materials, the activities and the learning programme.

TASK 17: Designing tasks

Analyse carefully what it is you are asking your students to do. What is their role? What is your role? How much is required of individuals and how much full participation by the group?

What level of difficulty and challenge do you perceive? How will they see it? Have you thought through what is required to achieve the task? What are the criteria for success? How will they know?

What level of preparation and guidance is there? What resources will you provide and what must they devise?

What are the learning goals? Have the students agreed them? Is it clear what the task is for – how it contributes to the learning? How will the learning be demonstrated and assessed?

It is essential that *before they begin* students know clearly what they have to do individually and together, what it is for, where it is going, how to get there and how it will all be assessed.

TASK 18: Designing and implementing individual lessons/sessions

The good practice established in Part 1 should inform what you do. Each learning session will require a lesson plan and teaching/learning activities and materials. The links should be clear, and what is planned should be relevant and stimulating.

Since you will be using these sessions as the main substance of your case study, use a variety of methods and approaches. The criterion must be that they make sense to students in what they feel they are about.

You should also be able to evaluate sessions with your mentor to match your views of what happens and to make your own assessment of progress towards satisfying the performance criteria set out below. There should, therefore, be evidence of this in the way your thinking and teaching develop through this programme. To summarise:

- plan and use a variety of approaches and methods
- evaluate what happens thoroughly and honestly.

PERFORMANCE CRITERIA FOR INDIVIDUAL SESSIONS

1 Each session addresses specified learning goals.

2 Teaching methods and techniques are appropriate/relevant to these goals and the characteristics of the students.

3 Sufficient skill is demonstrated in using the chosen methods.

4 The duration, sequence, structure and content of each session is effective and properly controlled.

5 Where appropriate, the teaching/learning content and methods are consistent with examining board requirements.

6 Learning problems and opportunities for further learning are identified during the session and the programme adapted.

7 Learning and teaching aids are used skilfully and effectively.

8 Individuals and groups are managed effectively. Control of the session and the learning is maintained. The health and safety of the students are assured.

9 Learning is linked, consolidated and assessed.

10 Each session is properly evaluated.

16 Teaching Methods – Teaching Skills

Control and management

The methodology from which teachers may choose ranges through a continuum, from total control by the teacher to total control by the individual student of his or her own learning. Where over the range you, as teacher, choose methodology in relation to retaining control depends on many factors, not least your confidence in yourself and in how far you feel able to trust your students. The table summarises the teacher control/student control continuum.

Teacher control		Lecture
		Demonstration
		Discussion – structured
	Less control	Discussion – unstructured
		Seminar
		Tutorial
	Shared control	Practical
		Simulation and games
		Role play
		Resource-based learning
		Films/TV programmes
		Visits
	Student control	Distance learning/Flexistudy
		Discovery projects/research
Least control		Real-life experience

Who makes the decisions? Who chooses the content or sequence, the learning materials, learning goals or interactions? Who controls pace, assessment procedures and criteria for success? Is it the teacher or the students? It depends on so many things:

- the teacher's ability to cope with demands students may make if decisions are left to them
- their ability to cope with the responsibility of choice
- their motivation, and the commitment they have to the learning
- their expectations of roles and responsibilities in relation to learning
- their sense of ownership of decisions that are made
- whether they are used to a totally passive role and, if so, whether they can cope with a greater degree of control – will they know how to learn?

Teachers and students have to learn to use the chosen methods effectively. Choice depends on the following:

- knowing enough about the alternatives available
- having confidence to use the appropriate choice
- having sufficient skill to be effective
- ensuring that it works – feedback/evaluation.

Effectiveness involves:

- suitability of methods for promoting the intended learning
- variety, both within learning sessions and in a programme
- economy of effort relative to learning benefit
- human factors
- proper planning and resourcing within constraints of time
- proper control and management of the learning process
- sufficient skill in using methodology (both teacher and students)
- proper use of feedback, monitoring and flexibility
- assessment of learning, and evaluating process and outcomes.

Competence

All learning by teachers is experiential. Competence in the use of any methodology involves being able to choose intelligently, with the knowledge, experience and skill to make chosen methods work effectively. This can only be acquired by experience, which requires confidence, risk-taking and reflection on what happens.

The appropriateness of chosen methods of teaching or learning, as noted with regard to overall strategy, is vital. Frequently, the method is hardly 'chosen' at all: teachers and students go for a familiar behaviour pattern without thinking it through. 'Old and tried' usually means 'easiest, least bother'. Ask, 'what are we/they setting out to learn?' and 'what is the best way to do that?'

Methods of teaching and learning need to be matched to what is to be learned, but the conditions and constraints under which learning is to take place will affect both decisions and outcomes.

It is hard, therefore, to specify too closely what the performance criteria should be for success in the use of any method. The measure of success is always how far the students achieve their learning goals rather than the performance of the teacher. Nor is it easy to match one to the other: all sorts of factors that are not within the control of the teacher affect success.

Any method can be made more effective. Decisions about which you use and what then happens must be carefully evaluated. A mentor to share the experience, to provide a mirror, matters. So too do your students' views. Learning requires controlled risk-taking.

Lectures

This is a general term covering a range of activities. Some lectures are very formal, given in spacious lecture theatres to large audiences at a safe distance, even requiring use of a microphone.

Lecture-style is used with ordinary classes, too. Micro-lessons may turn into mini-lectures – the skills involved do need practice. All teachers use a didactic style some of the time, even in informal classes and programmes. All lessons have input, even if it is brief (as it should be). This does need to be done well.

Many teachers will point to the advantages of lecturing. It is economic in time and teacher costs. Teachers can deal with large amounts of content relatively quickly and efficiently, possibly with many students. Lecturing allows the efficient transmission of accurate and up-to-date information.

Lectures may be effective not only in ensuring students acquire information, but also in stimulating them to want to find out more about a topic, to become active, enthusiastic learners rather than passive listeners. How can we ensure that happens?

PREPARATION

Know your stuff. You cannot teach what you do not know.

Leave nothing to chance. Prepare AVA materials, set them up beforehand and test the equipment. You don't want to have to change a fuse at the start of your lecture. (All the same, I carry a small screwdriver, just in case. Spare bulbs, too.)

Test also for visibility and acoustics. Have things such as handouts and acetate slides to hand, in order and sequence. It is important to control the learning conditions. Practise.

Appear – and be – organised. Impressions count. Take control.

STRUCTURE

Give your students a handout with a key-word structure. It should state your learning goals and your method of assessing the learning, if appropriate. Tell them whether they are to take notes, and in what form: you may decide to provide a summary note-structure for them, leaving space for their own notes. (Note-taking is discussed on pages 147–8.)

Bear in mind their attention span – about fifteen minutes, or less if things become physically uncomfortable. Change the focus frequently with visual stimuli. And think two-way. Use opportunities for feedback at intervals, such as taking questions; this is often done at the end of the session, but I find it better to take questions as they arise. Or consolidate by recapping and making a link to the next section. This removes strain and gives students confidence that they do understand the information. Use the key-word structure to check you are not straying.

Another approach is to take questions at the beginning. If a group comes to a lecture properly alert they will have their own questions. This is a good way of knowing where they are starting from, their mind-set, that can help you to direct your input more accurately to their needs. It is very easy for teachers to 'miss' students completely. Your alerting structure must address questions, yours and theirs.

Leave time at the end for a final consolidation. Link your input to what they are to do to ensure they use it effectively.

HUMAN FACTORS

Watch and check that you can be heard, and that your visual aids can be seen. Ask the people at the back – tell them to keep you up to the mark if they can't hear you. Pitch your voice low, but think of talking only to the person furthest away. Talk slowly. Leave gaps for them to think about what you have said. Watch! If you see attention drifting, consolidate and recap. Consider 'noise' and distractions – don't just ignore them and hope.

PERSONAL CONTACT AND FEEDBACK

Language register and use of symbols and/or vocabulary must be at a level of shared experience with the audience; if not, you must explain them. A good strong image is useful to grab attention. Use personal names if at all possible. Humour helps too! Get your audience on your side.

Try to establish eye-contact with members of the group. Don't get trapped by the situation in the lecture-hall. Move around when you can, or even go behind them to teach from the back, especially if you want them to concentrate on the visual material you are showing – you can then see it as they do.

Enter a closer space zone. Become part of the group, discussing what is being shown, so that you can understand how it is for them, and be aware of any difficulties particular students may be having. Ask individuals (by name) to explain things – to give you feedback, a two-way exchange. 'Distance' matters.

Lecturing can create barriers. What is your posture saying to them? What are your signals about personal space and physical distance? behind a desk? on a rostrum? What is the message about roles and relationships?

ASSESSMENT/FOLLOW-UP

What have they learned? How will you know? How will they? You need to consider what is appropriate in terms of assessing learning from input however it happens. They need to do something with it. They need a means of revisiting the learning too. What will they take away in order to do this? Consider that carefully in your planning.

Unless your lecture is a one-off occasion, it should have an effect on the learning process you have devised overall. What part? How does it link to other input or other activity? What is to happen after the input/lecture, however short or long? What do the students need to enable them to use the new material effectively?

EVALUATION

All this forms part of the evaluation of the lecture/input. But if all that is evaluated is the teacher's performance, what has that to do with student learning? What should the evaluation be about?

This is a most important question. The answer includes the factors above, clearly. But was it effective for its major purpose? How did it affect or accelerate learning?

The performance criteria for competence in using the lecture method are not essentially different from those for other approaches and are those set out in Task 18: Designing and Implementing Individual Sessions, above.

Demonstrations

All teachers are role-models. We inevitably demonstrate to our students what we truly believe to be appropriate behaviour, whatever we are doing, wherever we are working. Bear this in mind, especially if you are working in areas of danger or where good practice in working should be a matter of habit. It is too easy to signal 'do as I say, not as I do!' – if it is unsafe, you *must* not do it. The teacher's over-riding, inescapable responsibility is the students' health and safety. In that sense everything we do is a demonstration.

More particularly, we need to consider the formal demonstrations of a skill or a technique, if only how to structure notes.

PREPARATION

Much more time is required for the preparation than for the actual demonstration. You have to think it through. Remember that, to be effective, a demonstration has to be short and highly focused. If the students are to attempt to master them afterwards, you can only demonstrate small-scale skills/ techniques. Students cannot take in the whole of a long presentation from one exposure. So they have to select what they think they need or what they are alert to. Plan on providing the essentials – never mind the frills.

MODELS

Support the learning with an additional model in the form of written instructions (set out clearly and sequentially as 'do this' statements), possibly supplemented with a diagram or a flow-chart.

Think about models. If they know where they are going, what the finished product should look like, say, they will have a model in the head to work towards. Whether the model is a gâteau or a machined part, a step in ballet or a passage on the piano, it had better be a good one. Arthur Cranmer, in his book *The Art of Singing*, tells how Sir Thomas Beecham did not like the way a singer sang a particular phrase. 'Not like this . . . ,' he said, and made an awful noise. 'Like this . . . '. He made the same awful noise!

THE WHOLE AND THE BITS

If you plan to give your demonstration only once, it will be hard for the students to grasp unless it is very short and/or immediately followed by their doing it.

One way of overcoming the problem is to have what you do recorded on video. This is not to replace the actuality of demonstrating in an appropriate context with the group observing you. That is necessary, but a video-recording of the same demonstration has advantages:

- you do it at normal speed, using your practised skill
- you can watch with them and explain things clearly
- you can replay the video at half-speed (it is very hard for a skilled person to actually do things at half-speed)
- you can put the video-tape on 'hold' to look at details and take questions
- the students can always replay the model.

This last is vital. Learning is most effective at a point of need. You cannot know what you have failed to see or need to grasp until you find you 'can't remember how to do this bit'.

In practice, when the students' turn comes round, they will go through the experience a bit at a time. It is easy for the teacher's demonstration either to ignore the bits or to fail to present the whole properly. It is important to analyse the various steps and skills needed – the tricks of the trade – to show clearly how each is done. But they are to be seen as part of the whole conception, like phrasing in music or brush-strokes on canvas.

HOW AND WHY

Although you demonstrate 'how', you are in fact telling the students 'why' this rather than that: your demonstration is about knowledge as well as about skill. So you must explain clearly, as well as show, the skills or techniques they are to learn. This is the part that is easy to ignore or do badly. Make sure you understand what it is they need to know. How will you ensure they know it?

It is much more effective to make the theory part of the 'doing', rather than a separate input session: even if you choose to teach it separately, the link can only be made in a practical context.

Again, the video helps, since you can pause and repeat and so involve the group in question and answer to ensure they understand *why* as well as *how*.

WHERE

The environment should be properly designed for the activity. You are modelling good practice, so everything must be right. Set up everything to hand

and in order. You can't be hunting for something at a critical moment. Check equipment is working and is what it should be – improvising is wrong. If you are using knives, say, which knife? is it sharp?

Wear the right clothes too. Do things need to be sterile? Are special safety precautions involved? Students must see them used.

HUMAN FACTORS

Nor can the students learn if they cannot hear or see the demonstration. Later, it is important for them to explore the experience with all the senses, and only then will they fully grasp it – the weight of the knife, the pressure to exert and so on. But in your part, you can get them to handle a piece of the equipment or feel the texture of, say, clay, or a fabric, as long as it serves to concentrate attention rather than to distract.

How can you ensure every student can see? This can be a major problem if more than ten are trying to crowd around you. Practical work is often done on flat surfaces, and uses small hand movements rather than large gestures. What angle of view do they need? Even in the round, how can a group of nurses crowd around a bed and all see the same thing? Or apprentices around a lathe, or caterers around a bench?

Some cookery rooms have large mirrors over the bench. Most teachers have to solve the problem in other ways. One way is to show the skill/technique repetitively to four or five students at a time. This is excellent use of personal space, but what will the others do meanwhile? Plan an activity for them – otherwise, boredom.

A video camera may be the only practical solution (you need a technician too). It lets you focus to cut out distracting detail, and can let the students see things exactly as the demonstrator sees them. You can view things from odd angles – from vertically above, say. This can overcome the problem of trying to talk to students through the back of your head too – if you are working at a lathe, say. How can they possibly hear your explanation? Do you talk as you do? talk first? or do, then talk about it? You can't maintain eye-contact so you have no feedback, while the group may neither see nor hear properly.

TIME-MANAGEMENT

You need to plan how much time to allow for the various activities. Where do you need to put the emphasis, on what they see or what they do? Indeed, what are they to do while you demonstrate? Time needed relates to the content and complexity of what you and they are setting out to do. Since doing it well has to be properly planned, that needs costing in time too.

STRUCTURE

Structure is concerned with sequencing within a time-plan. The students need to practise themselves, as soon as possible after a demonstration, so that your part and theirs become linked into the learning process. In order to plan properly you must know what the students are going to do to acquire the skill/technique and make it part of their competence.

SPEED AND DEXTERITY

You find it easy. Try to remember when it was hard. That is where they are now, and where you need to start from. Their newly acquired ability will be the measure of your success.

A skilled performance is characterised by its speed and dexterity, by not having to think about it, by the memory in the muscles. This doesn't just happen: it comes from doing it many times successfully. It is true of all skills, at whatever level.

It is very hard to teach something slowly that you don't think about at all when you do it normally. Thinking about what you are doing can make you clumsy. If you try to think how you ride a bike you can fall off! If you try to analyse how you balance going down every step of the stairs, or how you hit a ball with a racket, you will see how complex these actions are. It requires practice to do them slowly and to be aware of each step. Practise doing your demonstration slowly – but not in front of students.

Skill in the end is about what it feels like to do something well. It is an internal experience that leads to externally observable behaviour. The teacher provides the mirror to enable a student to do it well, and how it feels to do it well.

EVALUATION

You need feedback from your students. It is not enough for you to feel good about it. Did it help them to gain insight? Do they understand what is involved, and why, as well as how to do it?

Lecture–demonstrations

Lecture theatres and science laboratories are often equipped with demonstration benches, designed to enable lecturers to demonstrate practical applications of principles they are teaching. In science, the teacher may demonstrate an experiment that students will then also do on their benches. This is an advance on what used to happen in many science classes when the students' activity was confined to taking notes.

The main purpose is to enhance transmission of information to the group by the use of tangible, sometimes sizeable and sophisticated equipment. It is better to see real things actually working than to be told about it. But the ergonomics of seeing from any considerable distance or as a group around a bench are the same as in any other demonstration. Lecturers often need to ask, 'Can you see what happens when I do this? or how this part works?' The answer almost equally often is 'no'.

When teachers wish to use such demonstrations as part of lecture presentation of information, they must consider such factors seriously. No visual material is much good if students cannot see it. Nor is there much advantage in having tangible objects, as against perhaps a video presentation, if students cannot touch them.

Film or video may be much more successful where presentation is to be made to a large group. The ability to focus attention, or to enlarge the image of small parts, or to stop and repeat, adding to the explanation or using two-way discussion, will ensure that what is presented is seen and understood. For small groups there may be greater advantage in the tangible experiment.

Enhancement of the images using a video set-up in the ways described on page 117 may be even better. The group can see both the experiment or equipment on the bench and the person getting it to work, while the camera can focus, enlarge and so on to ensure that everyone gets a first-class view. If the demonstration is also recorded, the re-run can be used along with previous recordings.

Skills practice

The essence of a practical is 'getting the feel of it'. I feel the weight of a knife in my hand, the danger of cutting my finger off, or the wetness and smell of the clay, the near-impossibility of drawing it up off a wheel. 'Why won't it do it for me when the teacher seemed to do it so easily?' 'Why does my cake sag in the middle?'

Handling a practical is handling frustration for teacher and student. Oh! the temptation to be able to take it out of their hands and just show them again how easy it is! Why is it they can't understand? It's individualised, resource-based learning: all the 'good' words. What can we do to make it easier and more rewarding for them and for us?

We can improve performance once a minimum competence is achieved by a better understanding of what happens and why. No amount of knowledge about balance or moments or forward velocity will help you to ride a bike until you have mastered the ability to stay on it. You must know what it feels like to pedal, steer and balance, to go much faster on the bike than you expect to without panicking.

BARRIERS

The teacher cannot be totally in charge of what happens, even if the class 'do it by numbers', army training style. Individuals adopt their own learning pattern and strategy, and bring attitudes and learning barriers to the experience as well as acquired skill.

Clearly, they have to believe they *can* do it. If a demonstration makes it look too magical and amazingly perfect, it may convince some people that they never will. We have to deal with the confidence of students: success breeds success. At what level of difficulty is this skill/technique? What level of skill do they need before they can even attempt it? A positive attitude is essential.

The learners may have learned behaviour that needs unlearning. It is so hard to unlearn! Established patterns of movement may not help in what they should be doing. A teacher may need to analyse what is getting in the way. Some students have problems anyway with vision or hearing or balance, particularly if they have to wear protection such as goggles. Some may seem clumsy in everything they do, not very skilful at anything: they may need help to develop eye–hand co-ordination.

PREPARATION

Students must come properly prepared. To do that they need to be clearly informed of what is required: clothing, what materials they have to provide and so on.

Tasks must be agreed and set out on work-sheets, which also need to show equipment they are to use and their responsibilities.

Performance criteria for successful achievement of each task should be agreed and stated, so that everyone knows what they are. It is hard to find you failed to do something in a way that was expected but which no one told you about until afterwards!

Equipment and materials must be properly organised, in good working order and of the right quality and quantity. Thought must be given to establishing good working practice.

RULES AND SAFETY

It is vital that students establish quickly the right ways of setting about the task. Unlearning is so hard. Rules must be framed accordingly. The students cannot be allowed to work without proper equipment and clothing. They must take responsibility for an organised work-station.

The environment must support the learning activity. This may require planning, particularly if person–machine ergonomics are involved. Teachers dealing with machines should read a good book on person–machine ergonomics; Oborne's *Ergonomics of Work* (1982) can be recommended.

Again, students must know what the rules are, for three reasons:

- we are about establishing good practice
- we must ensure that risk-taking does not lead to danger
- disorganisation is costly and inefficient.

PLATEAUX AND READINESS

A practical following a demonstration only makes sense as a part of a longer programme of skills development. Research into skills learning found that learning curves generally rise quickly, and then flatten into plateaux for a period of embedding and consolidation. Teachers need to look for challenges to shorten this waiting time.

Readiness to take on further challenges and greater tests is for teacher and learner to judge. The teacher may be able to recognise and use rhythms in an individual's learning. Certainly, much learning is cyclical. There is a need to build up the whole together and the teacher can take part by creating more interesting tasks for the learner to undertake. Too big a challenge too soon undermines confidence; too little will demotivate.

ACTION PLANS: ATTENTION, FREQUENCY AND PRACTICE

Attention is also a real problem. Because skills learning is so repetitive, it can easily become tedious. But students need to concentrate and be alert in order to learn. So more practice, if it is highly monotonous, will not necessarily give a significantly improved skill. Tasks have to be designed that give purpose and demonstrable outcomes from the learning activity while demanding improved levels of skill. Concentration on achieving the task will give meaning and direction to the skill.

For example, this is clearly what happens in learning to play the piano. A learner attempts more and more difficult piano pieces. While developing the technical skills to play them, he or she is also attempting to recreate a musical performance. But it is no good someone turning up for a piano lesson once a week and never touching a piano in between lessons. There has to be a pattern involving frequency of practice.

Teacher and learner have to agree a learning programme, an action plan that identifies frequency of practice and study – a kind of contract that identifies responsibility, goals and schedules. Skills are best learned by practice involving plenty of variety. In devising learning tasks, the teacher must identify the skills and how they are to be developed and demonstrated.

And without feedback, one-off practicals make little sense. Skills have to be seen as meaningful by students in their context and important to them. Tangible products, cakes or pots or whatever else they may be, assist assessment and evaluation and maintain motivation.

PERCEPTION AND INSIGHT

For most students problems lie in the complexity of what they are attempting to do. People learn skills experientially, and do so better when they have role-models as well as clear 'models in the head'. Knowledge, belief and attitude are the basis for skill. In the early stages of skill development, learners have to be aware (sometimes painfully) of what they do, and take conscious control of their actions.

We cannot begin to be inventive until skills are so embedded that we can think of other things. This implies that skills may be at different levels of conscious control. Once the brain has set up a pattern of behaviour, the skill itself takes less and less attention, less conscious control. Eventually, and as soon as possible, thought can be concentrated on what that skill is intended to allow us to achieve. For example, a driver can concentrate on the road ahead, rather than on how to co-ordinate clutch, gear change and accelerator.

Skill is a means to an end, not an end in itself. Unfortunately, much skills teaching has focused simply on learning the skill rather than on using it. More recently, the demands of examinations have shifted away from skill-testing to using the skill effectively, with the criteria for success defined in terms of the context and the product.

Hence, skills learning must be related to individual needs; tasks must be designed as programmes. The students determine their own pace and readiness by feedback from the teacher, using the performance criteria agreed for the tasks. Action plans need frequent renegotiation.

Knowledge becomes increasingly important. The increase in ability in athletics followed extensive research into what makes for a better performance – as much science as art. But theory has to make sense in relation to what it is for.

HUMAN FACTORS

Students cannot learn without proper well-maintained equipment. Each student needs to 'own' a working territory, although there is advantage in experiencing a variety of similar machines, for example in word-processing or engineering. Work simulation, which practicals ought to aim at, requires the right materials to work with too.

What of supervision? How many students can work safely in a workshop or a craftroom or a kitchen supervised, let alone tutored, by only one teacher? How must the room be designed or set out to enable the teacher to see the students, either to spot where help is required or to intervene if necessary? In some situations teachers just cannot see what students are doing: who takes the responsibility then?

MONITORING

The purpose is to ensure that all students achieve mastery as defined by the performance criteria. The teacher's main role in the practical, therefore, is monitoring progress of individuals, insisting on repetition or finding new ways to tackle something if there is a blockage, intervening where the student is in difficulty or getting it wrong, or to avoid disaster of some kind, and adjusting or renegotiating action plans.

The main teaching skills required are observation, listening and the ability to communicate one-to-one while keeping an eye on what others are doing. Monitoring may be seen as an on-going tutorial function and depends on established relationships.

ASSESSMENT

The purpose is mastery, so assessment is based on achievement of performance criteria for each task. This is more complex than it sounds. No progress will be made without cognitive and attitudinal change. It is easy to observe 'can do', but 'can't do' requires analysis of what is wrong and appropriate remedial action – which may be dealing with problems of knowledge or lack of confidence, or removing barriers to learning.

DESIGNING THE PERFORMANCE CRITERIA

Performance criteria should state clearly what you believe to be good practice. Achieving the criteria identifies to what extent that good practice has become a matter of habit.

Group practicals

Practicals are about individuals learning, but in some situations group practicals are essential – for example, in drama, music, languages and sports. Here the skills and insight of individuals need development but relate also to a context where a group of people are working together to achieve agreed and shared learning goals. Group projects (to put on a play or a concert, to perform together, to create a winning team, or simply to share a learning experience – all languages operate in social contexts) are essential to promote these learning goals.

The whole is much greater than the sum of the parts. Individuals as part of successful teams learn quite different skills, insight and behaviour than when learning alone. Here, role and responsibility, commitment to the team and to team goals become even more important. An orchestra consisting only of soloists will make a poor showing in a symphony. This is a major problem in drama training and in the development of sports teams.

As a teacher, your role cannot be largely didactic. You will have to lead, to shape, to manage and inspire. You will need excellent skills of organisation and management, and the ability to win people over. You will provide the 'model in the head' and often the role-model of what the group is to achieve. You must ensure this is communicated clearly, that the sharing to bind the group together happens.

Practical activities are the means by which this happens. One major teaching activity is evaluating carefully with the group what happens and what they need to do as a group and as individuals so as to progress towards agreed goals. In practical situations, when the students are working together, the skill is in observing and analysing what is happening and why, and what needs to happen next and how – to match the model in the head with what actually occurs and to communicate that understanding and insight with the group.

At the beginning of this chapter we discussed the continuum that ranges from teacher control to student control of decision-making/learning activity. How far along that continuum you progress depends on the extent to which the team develops its own momentum and on where the sense of ownership resides. There is no short cut here. You will have to learn how to work with such groups, not only to get the best out of them, to set standards and to ensure they achieve them, but also to avoid teacher-dependence. In the end, the team has to play the game without the coach.

Nor should you attempt to be a one-man orchestra playing all the parts. It is a team effort. Individuals must agree to take on roles, be responsible, make sure things happen when and how they should. Occasionally, you will have to intervene or take over to ensure it happens, but should do so reluctantly. It is your role to provide the over-view to maintain proper control.

Performance criteria and assessment are concerned with how far the team achieves its goals as a team. It is hard to identify how individuals are to be assessed in relation to such activity.

Discussion

In general, discussion is handled least well of all teaching methodology. It seems to come so naturally that there appears no need to intervene. But it is the one area where you, as the teacher, have to be at your most skilful and where you can most easily lose control of the learning.

In teaching, discussion has to be deliberately organised. Since it is one of the most common of human activities this is hard to do. The level of heat in the process depends on context, personalities or passions involved. Discussions can be very unproductive: they can turn into arguments, or even shouting matches or fights. But if well-managed, they can solve problems, promote co-ordinated activity and generate enthusiasm and commitment. They can be used to clarify thinking and ideas, tackle misconceptions and bring to the surface deeply held convictions that may be the cause of misunderstanding.

When we say that communication within a social unit has broken down, we usually mean that the parties (boss and union, husband and wife, parent and child) cannot discuss their differences, but are isolated in their own positions. So learning the skills of discussion must be something education should promote: it rarely does. Why? Mainly because teachers tend to lack the skills themselves.

Sharing is two-way communication. Teachers have to listen. They must create the right conditions for such communication.

AGREE THE PURPOSE

'Gee, Mr Stravinsky,' said a New York socialite, 'how do you know when to stop?' The maestro replied, 'Before I begin, madam.'

Generally we can tell the beginning, middle and end of some activity. Not so with discussions, which often appear to have none of these. Why is that? They lack shape because they lack a sense of purpose – they appear to be going nowhere.

However much pulsing energy and forward drive there may be in any discussion, students need to know where they are supposed to be going and why they are doing it, before they begin. Only then can teachers hope to control the interactions of people, to monitor what happens, intervene, shape or stop or whatever. Students and teacher alike must know the direction of travel, so that when the discussion starts to stray the teacher can bring it back on course. They must also agree together the rules that govern what happens.

Student satisfaction or frustration depends critically on this, since most adults are impatient of time-wasting, of a feeling of getting nowhere. They want to feel there is progress. People who know where they are going are more likely to arrive there and to have some sense of arriving.

Nor can teachers revisit rambling discussions that have no shape or pattern, or consolidate learning from them. The brain works with patterns and rules; we must assist the process. There has to be some perceived structure and agreed rules.

Committee meetings have agendas, so as to make minute-writing possible. This model is a most useful one. You need to recognise that no one comes to discussion without an agenda. Usually there are as many agendas as there are persons involved, and this is the problem. Misunderstandings are avoided if the agenda is agreed, overt and purposeful, if the rules are understood and if someone takes the chair.

The best discussion has purposeful outcomes, such as action plans involving groups and individuals. People know what it is for: it is to clarify ideas and make decisions. Committees that meet simply to meet are wasting time. We all need to be clear: 'what happens next? as a result of our discussing it here, what is supposed to happen?'

On the other hand, discussion that has no purpose is best avoided. General social discussion as the glue for binding the group can happen in coffee breaks; class time has to be seen to be used purposefully.

STRUCTURE: THE TEACHER'S ROLE

Students expect you to take charge. This does not mean that it is always you who takes the chair. You can set up whole class or group discussions, sometimes without leaders, so long as the students have a clear agenda and will know where they are going and when they have arrived.

But 'how do I know what I think till I hear what I say?' or what others say? You will have to encourage openness, a willingness to explore issues, bring out emotions and deeply held beliefs as well as helping the students to restructure their ideas and their thinking by sharing with others. This may be the opportunity to break out of mind-set, to be ready to listen, to look at things from a new angle, to reconstruct a value-system.

The structure, therefore, is more to do with purpose and process than with content. Discussion of closed questions or where the outcomes have already been determined ('the chairman had the minutes in his pocket when he arrived') are soon exposed. The views of all students must be seen to be valued and taken into account in whatever decisions are made.

All group activities involve group dynamics. These are not predictable even from one class to another. The clearer the structure and goal-setting, the easier it is to maintain control. All groups exhibit patterns of dominance and/or withdrawal. Try to involve all the students, and inhibit those who seek to dominate or use things for their own purposes – to pursue a personal agenda.

You will make the structure loose or tight, you will establish more or less teacher control, in the way you set it up. You can give the group(s) specific questions with guidance as to the kind of answers you will accept, or you can set out a series of structured (but still open) questions, intended to lead discussion down particular paths almost to a predetermined conclusion.

The students should all have a copy of your lesson plan. It should state clearly when and how discussion is to occur, the time constraints and the intended outcomes – what it is supposed to achieve and where it fits with other learning activity. The clearer the guidance the better: preparation matters.

CHAIRING

You may appoint a chairperson for the discussion, to keep it going along the right path. You could make it rather like a committee meeting, perhaps, with a secretary to report back. If you want to be more in control, chair it yourself.

Who chairs the group discussion matters greatly. Some will let discussions ramble; others keep speakers to the point, inhibit interruption and defuse conflict, emphasising issues and trying to avoid personal or emotive interactions. Teachers in the chair often seem to have the minutes already in their pockets. It is really another lecture in disguise.

REPORTING BACK

The discipline of reporting back is important. It concentrates the group's thinking if there is a need to report, to explain to others what conclusions and decisions about actions have been arrived at. The reporting method should be agreed.

One excellent way is to supply each group with OHP acetates and ask them to make a key-word structure for the reporter to talk to. This puts additional discipline on to the discussion; the students have to agree on words and structure and create it – it all takes time, but it concentrates attention on the need for demonstrable outcomes. A composite can easily be made, and comparison with other groups is also simple. If this technique is used in an inductive discussion with the whole class, a student should fill in the OHP rather than the teacher.

Students can take away the structured reports. If they have also specified action, they know what to do and who is to do it. This also serves to consolidate the learning.

The minutes of the effective committees have a strong structure, with minimum reporting of the discussion but very clearly stated outcomes and 'action points' with individual responsibilities clearly defined.

HUMAN FACTORS

People unconsciously take messages from the arrangement of furniture, and are annoyed by messages that are contradictory or confusing. People sitting in rows, talking to the backs of each other's heads, miss subtleties of communication – facial expressions, eye-contact, humour.

An expectation of committee behaviour is expressed by chairs around a central table. We know immediately what is to happen. But this is only one possibility. We can think about how to manipulate messages, or how to create group space/territory to get people to work more closely together, to identify with each other and break down barriers.

We have to think about sound and vision: groups competing at 'shouting' levels in the same room, for instance. How will they identify their space and their equipment? If there are seminar rooms, use them.

Plan ahead. Define spaces and equip them for what you want the groups to do. For example, some teachers favour the use of flip-charts as against OHP, but to the same purpose: to present key-word structures to the other groups. The sheets can be put up around the walls for others to walk around and compare with their own.

Set up chairs, tables, screens, OHP, flip-charts. Give each group the tools for the job. Make it easy for them. Be businesslike.

ASSESSMENT/EVALUATION

Did the students achieve the goals and the intended outcomes? Are they practicable ideas? Does it make good sense? What will they now do with the new structure they have created?

Discussion is not about new information but is a restructuring of the information we have already, making it group-orientated and usable. In the end it affects attitudes and behaviour and leads to action.

Seminars

No discussion makes progress unless it is informed discussion: a shared and sound basis of information prevents the rehearsing and arguing *ad nauseam* of unfounded but often passionately held opinions. Addition of new information may change suddenly the direction of argument, which may then hasten agreement (or throw things into confusion).

The means of adding information varies. Sometimes a lecture, film or video will be the starting point, sometimes reading matter that the students will be expected to digest beforehand. If the input is complex, it is necessary to revisit it somehow. A seminar's purpose may be to revisit and clarify earlier input and ensure that it is fully understood, to provide fresh input. Seminars should be used to provide or consolidate an information base the group can then work on. Many go much further and generate creative thinking.

Often, someone is invited to lead the seminar, and to make a short introduction to supply a basis and questions for the group to address. A preliminary paper with information and a working paper (with questions and key-words) will help to give shape to the seminar – maybe as 'challenge' and 'defence' as in a debate.

There are advantages in someone producing a draft paper which the group then modifies and improves to present as a group paper. It hastens things along and helps to give shape and direction – it is, incidentally, the best way to arrive at clear action plans in committee.

If the purpose is to encourage all members of the seminar group to research the topic and then share what they discover (and if each is clear as to his or her specific contribution), this can rapidly increase the information available. This technique is valuable when the content of a syllabus seems extremely large and the teacher is faced with problems of covering *some* of it *somehow*!

PURPOSE AND STRUCTURE

To be effective seminars must be pretty tightly structured with clear time constraints and schedules. If someone is to produce a paper, it must be available to be read beforehand. Any input must be punchy and short, and discussion must be focused and to the point: it is its narrowness of focus that makes the session a seminar.

A seminar is strongly goal-orientated. Goals must be clear and agreed, and the group must be committed to them. Where action is required it must happen. Everyone carries equal responsibility for process and outcomes, for success.

COMPETITION

It is not unusual for seminar groups to become competitive. This may be deliberately arranged. 'Games' as tools for learning are based on such groups, which frequently become very tightly knit as a result – with both benefits and costs.

The tasks the groups are given to do determine what happens. Watch carefully how such groups interact and come together. If they are to produce an agreed view to present to others there will be less energy than if they are asked to come up with solutions to a problem, and to discover the best solution, either for kudos or for a prize(!). Many projects run like this. Tremendously energetic seminar groupwork frequently happens.

EXAMPLE 1

An elaborate seminar game was used at a weekend Department of Trade and Industry conference. Seminar groups were set the task of designing a science kit that would enable any learner in any country in the world (and without creating language barriers) to learn and understand a principle in science. There were certain constraints: it had to work with minimum technology available anywhere (it must not need electricity); it had to pack flat but be possible to assemble using diagrams as instructions. Similarly, learning had to be experiential, using the kit and diagrams.

To achieve this goal, each group had to decide on a specific principle and then on how the learners would learn it, what they had to do and what equipment they would need and, finally, how to overcome the constraints above.

Each group had a seminar room with OHP, flip-chart, whiteboard, pens, paper and so on: a group territory properly equipped. There was also a workshop with craft materials to make the kit and to ensure it worked. Each group was required to demonstrate a working model to the other groups, and explain how it would be used.

Initially each group had to formulate ideas and a design plan, and explain it to the others: this was to share thinking and ideas and to get feedback. At a later time the final demonstration was required.

One group set out to facilitate learning about kinetic and potential energy. They agreed everyone would have water. Water has potential energy if it is stored at a height. If the water falls its energy is converted into kinetic energy, which can be demonstrated with a turbine. This in turn could be converted into electrical energy and used to light a bulb. The only remaining requirement was energy input to raise the water. If the learners had to put in their own energy they could learn about work. The important thing was that the system had to be a closed one: no extra energy had to be added other than the pupils' own work.

A kit was designed, and then built out of simple craft materials, to raise the water and store it in a tank. A tube with a tap led the water to turn a turbine (slats in a spindle) and so a simple dynamo to light a bulb. The water was collected in a lower tank to be returned to the upper tank by energy supplied by the learner, using a shadoof to raise the water: this energy was the only thing to be added to the system.

The whole thing could pack flat for assembly on site. Instructions for building the kit and running it were given in diagrams. The group wanted to use the old 'flickbook' technique here – flicking the edges of a series of photographs so that the images appeared to move.

This inventiveness resulted from having to compete against others and within tight constraints and parameters.

Simulation, games, role play

Teachers sometimes confuse these activities. They are different.

SIMULATION

Here the teacher attempts to simulate a real situation. The students learn skills and confidence to deal with reality in a controlled environment and context. The constraints can be carefully chosen, and pressures such as the consequences of failure can be removed.

The closer the simulation is to reality, the better. Rules that apply to real encounters apply in simulations. To set up a workshop simulation may involve scaling things down – to what will fit into a booth rather than into a house, say, if we are dealing with plumbing or wiring. But the system has to work in exactly the same way. A simulated committee meeting has a proper agenda and clearly identified roles. We can play roles, but constraints of money, time, production targets, or whatever the committee is about, have to be real. The group is learning to run a committee effectively and purposively.

Simulations involve time-scales. We need to be able to reflect on the experience, to look at the process and the outcomes. This is easier if the experience is relatively short. But there are many long simulations, such as caterers in a training kitchen and restaurant, or a production team simulation for apprentices to undertake a project in design and construction. In all cases, what is to be assessed is not simply the quality of products or other tangible outcomes but changes in attitudes, insights and skills.

The advantages of simulation are:

- the removal of consequences of failure, leading to a greater willingness to take risks
- opportunity to experience roles and responsibilities which are not one's own, but normally those of more senior people
- elimination of arbitrary problems and control of constraints
- feedback and reflection on the experience; the flexibility to change the constraints, goals, time-schedules and so forth
- simplification of outcomes and criteria for assessment.

Real-life experiential learning can be painful, slow and confusing. There are many risks manager and learner deliberately avoid. Much of what is going on is missed because of limitations in sensory perception and the attention we can give it. Teachers in simulations can help learners to see much that they would otherwise miss. And since learners can never acquire all the necessary skills together at once, the learning of skills is easier if they are practised under controlled conditions.

But teachers can also make simulations closed or open. Catering training tends to be closed, almost rehearsing a script with very strongly defined role-models and procedures to follow; invention comes later. Other simulations are deliberately left to develop. A design project requires creativity within constraints. Teachers have to trust the students and monitor what happens closely.

In the end the learning has to be tested in the fire. Most fail to match pressures in the employment base. Other factors beside skills and insights come into play very forcefully. Much carefully trained and desirable behaviour has to be set aside; that may lead to mismatch and disillusionment. This also happens all too often when teachers go away for training courses.

IMPROVING SIMULATION

Ensure that the match with real world experience is close. Unless the learning is transferable it will soon be lost. It is transferability of skills and insight (attitudes too) to real contexts that matters most.

This has implications for the resourcing and organisation of the simulation, and for the methods of assessment. You can only learn good working practice in appropriately equipped environments. In this sense much vocational training may be seen as simulating real world working conditions. Much of this kind of learning is caught rather than taught.

EXAMPLE 2

Some fire officers on a teacher training course redesigned a course for training firemen to deal with accidents on a motorway. They had available a most sophisticated simulation. An old airfield had been converted into a training ground with mock-ups of ships, tower blocks, railways, motorways and many other structures. Fire could be set, or accidents staged, in any of these. There were also lavishly equipped lecture theatres.

Once they had designed the course making full use of the above, they evaluated it against the agreed criteria. One problem was how to assess the learning. They looked for methods of assessing it *as a course*. It was, however, a simulation with some input lecture style, using video-playback and so on.

They agreed that the only sensible way to assess the learning was to watch the firemen in action. The acid test was whether the trainees, under pressure of the real situation, perform more effectively or not. It was the transferability of the learning that mattered.

GAMES

In games the important thing is the pressure of competition. Look at Example 1 above. Games have rules which may be arbitrary and are meant to even out the odds, to eliminate certain aspects of reality to concentrate on the insights the students are intended to learn.

The skills required are not necessarily the same as those that they would need in real situations. The rules can be changed, the situation manipulated. It is the arbitrary nature of games that makes them unlike simulations.

Nor is it intended that what is learned should be practised in any real context. The learning is about insight into human behaviour, how things happen, the factors involved in decision-making, working as a team, competing with others, problem-solving, winning!

Games like Monopoly are played using boards and rules. Others are very physical, involving problem-solving in the round (the Army uses such games to select 'officer potential'). They can be 'intellectual power games', or playing the stock exchange, being Wellington at Waterloo, or solving murders. So many kinds!

To use a game, first think through carefully what is involved and what it is for.

Games are dangerous if handled badly. They can take over, gain their own momentum and become extremely 'noisy' in the ergonomic sense, so that it becomes very hard to know what is being learned. It is easy to lose control of the game once it is set going.

All the same, students love such things and they can be great fun – which learning should undoubtedly be much of the time. But the students know they are playing, it's not real, and the rules are arbitrary. It can still become very serious, raise emotional pressures and anxieties and take over. Students in a losing team can become angry or demoralised.

Students and teacher must agree what the game is for, and what they are setting out to learn. They cannot begin to focus on that while the game is in progress. It has to happen as reflection on the experience. There must be plenty of time to do that or there will be little learning – merely a glow.

Equally, the teacher must intervene if things are really not going in the intended direction or if emotional factors are likely to create negative outcomes.

EVALUATING AND LEARNING

Simulations and games bring us increasingly up against ourselves. What we learn is not simply how to do something, or even insight into the way the thing works, but most importantly what it feels like to be there, to be under pressure making decisions, taking responsibility, making things happen. 'Can I cope?' 'Is this really me?'

We are faced with the challenge of performance. We adopt roles, take on responsibility: we cannot avoid it. We learn what it means to try to work in a team, relying on others and they on us. With any luck, we find a good team and lots of support, but this doesn't always happen. Some people may be badly hurt, their self-esteem and self-image damaged not improved. That is what real life does to people!

To draw benefit from simulations and games, students have to focus on the positive learning that comes from the experience, both for them personally and for the team. Tutor support is essential if they are to gain fully from these learning activities.

It is difficult to define learning goals as specific, demonstrable outcomes in activities where much of what will occur is unpredictable – deliberately so. It is possible, though, and in some cases, such as the catering simulation mentioned above, is desirable to make the outcomes 'closed' and quite specific as learning goals to be assessed.

To consolidate the learning, students need to agree what learning occurred as a result of the activity, as a process of reflection on it. To assist that process, it is helpful to agree a statement of intended learning, what the activity is for, before they undertake it. As an example only, the list might include:

- to understand the value of teamwork and planning
- to gain insight into roles and responsibilities
- to discover what my strengths and weaknesses are
- to discover how to work effectively in a team
- to discover how to tackle problems systematically
- to discover how to deal with frustration and stress
- to discover skills such as [...]
- to gain confidence and coping skills.

Knowing what you are trying to learn before you set out will help you to identify questions to address to the experience when it is over.

It is obviously difficult to specify clear learning goals in such activities since much of what occurs is unpredictable, unless it is 'closed' like the catering simulation mentioned above. It is necessary, however, to have agreed learning goals that can be assessed and evaluated by both teacher and students at the end. Otherwise, consolidation becomes impossible.

ROLE PLAY

Many simulations involve taking on roles. Sometimes, as we have seen, there is a script (actual or implied) that controls what is allowed of the characters. Often, specific characters are needed to make the simulation more real: in a committee, for example, those who are eager to get things done, those who want to block things, those who are pursuing a personal agenda, those whose personalities clash. Teachers can deliberately identify such personalities.

When exploring roles takes precedence over other factors the exercise becomes role play. When someone goes into role, they must adopt a level of belief about themselves and the person they have become. There is a liberation in role play you must watch: 'There are a hundred different me's trying to get out,' said one student.

Since it is not 'me', the usual constraints on my behaviour may be relaxed. This is great, if that is what we want to happen. Many students can only get past their own inhibitions this way, and this can be most important in learning languages, or in learning to deal with people in social situations. Here, such methods can be used with excellent results.

In most contexts, role play should be used with great care. It is a very powerful tool, and teachers can use it effectively or dangerously. It may be largely discovering feelings, emotions, images, stereotypes, values and so on that lie hidden in our subconscious and are released by the role play. Both adults and youngsters can be quite startled by what they do, since they are not consciously in control. The most hilariously funny things I have seen anywhere have occurred during role play; so have some of the most traumatic. We are asking people to discover things about themselves, about relationships with others, perhaps about deeply held values too.

Taking on a role may uncover one of the 'hundreds of me's trying to get out'. It may release inhibitions and barriers that make it difficult for people to talk about things rationally. Relationships, like sex and space, are hard to talk about. Acted out, we may discover what we really feel and truly believe, even if we may wish to deny these feelings and beliefs. It may be best to avoid role play which explores suppressed strong emotions such as anger or fear or jealousy.

To use role play as a learning tool the teacher must maintain control, be fully in charge, in an activity where it is impossible to predict what is going to happen, and be ready to intervene if things take off in ways that are not helpful to the intended learning.

Be prepared for participants to use stereotyping they hardly know they have, even when roles are incidental to simulations: union negotiator, manager/boss, wife or husband, mother-in-law, customer and so forth. They are exploring their image of such persons. You will need to evaluate such images with students and help them to talk through where they have come from, and what effect such stereotyping has on their own behaviour.

Use role as a way of getting at aspects of learning that students find difficult because of attitudinal problems or inhibitions. There are so many examples: speaking a foreign language is a good one. Another is to get students to negotiate a price for a catering buffet, or for a product they want to sell.

GUIDANCE

There is no value in going into a role play without clear guidance to everyone concerned as to what role they are to play and what is to be discovered from the exercise. It is not always easy to set out guidance since people will only see what they expect to see. They usually just look at the name on the label and not the contents of the bottle. It is the same with any information. So ensure that there is a preliminary session in which things are carefully explored and explained.

Get them each to tell you what their role is so that you can share perceptions of it all before they begin. This will help the evaluation at the end, of course.

As part of your course design, consider the place of any of these methods within your lessons. A lesson is itself a mini-strategy. It is important to build in as much sensible variety as you can.

To learn you must tackle them systematically and look carefully at what happens and why afterwards. You will discover where you are lacking in skill and understanding so that the next time you will be better prepared and tackle that method more effectively.

17 Resource-based Learning

As the continuum of teaching methodology becomes more student-centred and controlled, the discussion takes on new dimensions. New factors are involved.

Using resources

The teacher is an important resource for students, but not the only one they may use. Some teachers put intolerable burdens on themselves to deliver because they feel all learning must be funnelled through them. But the emphasis has changed. Increasingly, teachers must become managers of learning that uses all manner of resources, not least those the students bring with them.

Teachers need different skills to become such managers. They are handing over much of the responsibility for learning and control to the students. Teachers need confidence and trust in students and their own ability to cope. 'I want them where I can see them,' cries the insecure teacher who finds it hard to let go in case the class gets out of control.

Much resource-based learning happens under strict control. A workshop is a major resource: individualised programmes with the students using lathes and work-sheets is exactly that. So is reading an English literature text quietly and discussing it in groups, or writing an essay to show insight into the writer's style under supervision. There is hardly anything revolutionary here.

What is intended is a total change in methodology, with different roles and responsibilities for teacher and students. There are to be teaching teams to concentrate on designing learning as whole programmes. They will plan how students will learn, what they will need in order to learn, where they will learn, what materials they will use, and what guidance and equipment they will need. How progress will be managed, possibly framing action plans, individual programmes of study and tutorial support. Development of materials, organisation, supervision, monitoring, assessment and handling feedback will be major functions. So will setting targets and schedules and performance criteria, and assessing achievement, all things that are very familiar to the reader of this book.

The responsibility for the learning is firmly with the students. The teacher is to manage the resources and the programme, ensuring that students have access to what is needed, and controlling the process.

All this requires redefinition of teaching time and scheduling. Decisions have to be made about input sessions and group activities. Do they happen regularly week by week or as needed to maintain progress? Since programmes are individualised, there has to be time for tutorials. How is it to be paid for?

Costing of programmes becomes important. The cost of making the materials is offset against the freedom teachers then have to do other things that are perhaps more effective than regular classroom teaching. Preparation pays off, but setting it up is expensive. The time and effort to design and create useful, valid resources will have to be paid for out of whole budget planning.

Resource-based learning works well if:

- learning structure and design are carefully thought through
- tasks and assignments are well designed and well presented
- the learning is interesting, stimulating and relevant
- there is clear understanding of 'activity' and criteria for successful achievement/completion of the tasks
- there is sufficient finance and good support facilities
- students are taught how to organise their own learning
- feedback is immediate at a point of need, and is supportive and positive – preferably in a tutorial context
- there is flexibility and adaptability to individual need
- record-keeping and profiling of achievement is maintained
- there is a team and resource-base for developing materials.

TASK DESIGN

This is the essential skill. Patterns help. Establish a format that is understood. Ask yourself what the students need in the way of information and guidance in order to do the task. Provide an over-view of how this task fits into the whole. In setting out to do it, they need to know clearly what they are setting out to learn, what they have to do and why, what they will use in order to do it and where it is to be found, how they will get hold of the resources they will use.

If the task is to achieve a product they must know the form it should take, and/or the criteria for success. They must understand what the assessment process will be, and how it will be handled, how the achievement will be recorded and profiled. It must therefore be clear to them what successful achievement of each task contributes to achievement of major learning goals.

The tasks need to be appraised for the demands they make on the students. Pace, readiness, ability to meet a challenge have to be thought about. Is there sufficient flexibility in the guidance and criteria to allow for variations in individual ability to cope with the demands, and/or to interpret the tasks to meet their personal learning needs?

Above all, clarity and simplicity in the guidance matter.

PROCESS

The students will do tasks in some sequence: how will that be known and who will make the decisions? How will targets be set? What time constraints are there, what 'complete by' dates? How much of all this is negotiable – or renegotiable – with the tutor?

They may need to be walked through early tasks, finding out where they can get help and additional resources, how to use the library or other resource areas, how to deal with equipment. If a programme involves seeking help, information or exploring major resources elsewhere, they must be shown how.

Some tasks deal with people more than with books or things. Especially if the learning is concerned with developing social skills and ability to work with others, students may need help in dealing with people, perhaps interviewing them or conducting negotiations or a survey. None of this can be taken for granted: it is courting disaster just to ask students to do such things and hope it will be all right.

Teachers will not know what is involved, how hard it is or what difficulties will occur unless they experience it themselves. All tasks therefore need validating by experience.

ASSESSMENT

The process of assessment and the process of learning are closely linked. One feeds back to the other. It is possible to treat each task as separate for the purposes of assessment, with its own criteria. But this is to lose the process completely and to concentrate entirely on outcomes. The tasks become a series of coconuts in a shy.

This will have an unfortunate effect on motivation. Tutoring must be concerned with overall learning goals and progress towards their achievement. The tasks identify the process by which progress is made. To develop an action plan with a student the tutor has to monitor what is learned or achieved by completion of any of the tasks and what has been identified as learning need. That is what assessment is for.

This requires a profiling approach to recording achievement and progress – not in the sense of ticking off boxes, but as a developing learning map which the student perceives and owns. Performance criteria are not once for all, but to be seen as signposts to greater, more mature achievement.

The nature of the profile and ways of developing it with the student need to be clearly established from the outset.

EVALUATION

Programmes of this kind need constant review. All aspects of the process need revision in the light of experience. Each task must be evaluated for its level of difficulty, the way in which students coped with it, its effectiveness in promoting the intended learning. The same is true of resources, guidance, support and so on. The aim must be to make the programme as effective as possible. It could be argued that if students fail to learn the fault is with the programme, either its design or its operation, or perhaps the nature of the tasks or the assessment process: it is not necessarily the inability of the students to achieve the learning goals that we are measuring or addressing.

Evaluation therefore is team-based and should lead to teams revising their programmes, techniques and action plans.

Tutorials

Tutorials serve many purposes. They are necessary for progress-chasing and support. They may also act as small-scale seminars to clarify ideas or create action plans. But they are expensive of time and teaching cost, usually one-to-one or at most one-to-three.

An easy-going tutor is of no benefit to students. Tutorials must be cost-effective: contract-based and strongly goal-orientated. Student and tutor are both responsible for achieving the goals. The major skill required is in handling this relationship.

There must be two-way exchange – a tutorial is certainly not a lecture! Tutors have to listen, indeed to act as a mirror. The agenda must be agreed, not imposed. Students must feel able to control the agenda to meet needs they perceive if they are to trust the tutor and be open in discussion. It is their learning programme, their action plan.

Tutorials provide feedback in both directions. The students need to know how they are progressing relative to agreed performance criteria. The teacher needs to know whether the tasks the group has been set to do make sense to each student, and whether each can cope: how to make progress or whether to renegotiate the programme in some way, or to put in additional learning activity or support.

Progress-chasing is vital. Schedules matter: they are targets agreed and to be met. But there has to be flexibility, since individuals learn at their own pace and bring their own barriers and problems. The major purpose of assessing is to advance the learning, not to put a mark on it as a grade. Tutorials are an important part of this assessment/learning process, to shape individual learning paths.

The frequency of tutorials relates to the way the programme has been designed. They support individual learning through agreed action plans based on assignments. For time to be available for tutorials, less time has to be used in full class teaching. The programme should be sustained by student learning activity, group and individual tasks.

HANDLING TUTORIALS

Choose a suitable environment. Set it up to give the right messages. Appear organised and serious. It is terrible if the student feels the tutorial is simply a formality. You have to listen. Eliminate 'noise': make sure you won't be interrupted by the telephone or by other people. The tutorial needs your full attention as well as that of the student. Come prepared, too. Know about this student: what he or she is doing and what has happened already.

Think about personal space. Chairs should preferably be soft or at least comfortable. Avoid obstructions like desks that create distance. Chairs should be close but not confrontational: they are better set at an angle so that eye-contact can be made and broken easily – looking away must not be a problem.

Timing matters. Start on time. Students need to learn how to handle time effectively, to say things clearly but succinctly. More time does not mean better. You need to do this too.

Listen carefully, and wait for the student to say it. Teachers tend to be impatient. One of the skills you need to develop (and with class interactions) is how to be patient and wait. Jumping in to fill a silence too soon stops important things from happening. When teachers do this as a matter of habit, students just let them get on with it. Things need space and time in order to happen, as in the theatre. Encourage, but don't take over.

To listen is to show concern. How hard it is to find someone who actually wants to listen to you, who will find the time to do it! You are a mirror. Try to see it from where they sit so that you reflect back accurately what they say and do, then to match it against the agreed criteria – where we are going.

Students mainly need support and reassurance. If they are slipping in terms of targets, they have to perceive the need to achieve them. Tutorials are about feedback, enabling them to see things more clearly themselves. They do not usually need bullying. Target-setting, keeping to schedule, yes. Most students want to succeed. Matching the programme to individual needs is the tutor's responsibility.

Keep records of tutorials, with a copy for the student. The negotiation of the learning programme and action plans for individuals (and the revisions) need documenting. Targets or progress need monitoring and recording. Be businesslike.

Films and television

There are good and bad ways of using films and television programmes. All these are by their nature 'verbose': they contain far too much information and visual imagery for students to make sense of, certainly if they see it only once. Their main purpose is to entertain, or to stimulate interest. Where they set out to inform, they have to assume some general audience they are addressing. Students will find it hard to select what they need. Even instructional films may not be particularly easy to digest. Most information is selected out by the lack of attention we can give to it – and usually, too, the dimly lit and comfortable environment is not conducive to giving attention. Only the strongest of images will be remembered.

USING FILMS AND TELEVISION WELL

You must see the material first (simple advice, but often ignored). Analyse the film into structure to see how it is put together – after all, someone planned it. Provide students with this structure (as key-words) to help them grasp the parts in relation to the whole.

Alert students for what they can learn, what to look out for – pinpoint the questions the film addresses; otherwise they will not know what to look or listen for, and will certainly miss most of it. And it's no good asking them afterwards, 'did you notice . . . ?'

Even better, select those, possibly short, parts of the film or programme that contain what you want students to learn, and show only those. This has the added advantage that you can show these parts more than once.

Using this technique:

1 Prepare the students with questions and structure.
2 Show them relevant and important extracts from the whole.
3 Revisit these with the questions to elicit answers – or maybe more searching questions.
4 Reshow the extracts to consolidate the learning and link it to other learning experiences.
5 Evaluate the learning with them.

If this technique is used with video-recordings, the students can have material available as part of a data-bank (for example, in a library) to consult when they need to revise.

Electronic mail and interactive video

New technology will have a great impact on the kind of things a student will do as resource-based learning. There is a tendency for teachers to think mainly in terms of paper-based materials – a great pity, since there are many exciting ways of learning as well as reading for information. Libraries already use electronic data-bases that can search and find information from a vast range of sources. Using these, learners can immediately access exactly what they want.

The same technology allows teachers and students to work with others hundreds of miles away on joint projects using electronic mail. This links computers through the telephone system and allows people to share computer-based materials. Consult your librarian, and familiarise yourself with these new and fascinating approaches to learning.

Another innovation of increasing importance is interactive video, which combines computer and video technology. Immense amounts of information, stimulus and interest material can be made available on a video disc. The Domesday Project is a good example. Using a suitably written computer program, learners address questions to ('interrogate') the disc-recorded materials. The technology searches the disc and replays the appropriate video material.

The problem, as we have seen with television material, is the sheer volume of information. Its very richness makes it hard to use. But this richness should be exploited, not ignored. Teachers can interrogate the data-base for their students, or help them make their own searches. But it is arbitrary and cannot focus on individual needs.

In order to use such technology really well, teachers may need to learn some simple computer programming, to construct 'menus' of questions. The learning programme is individualised by students selecting questions from a range of menus in the computer and so plotting their own learning path through the material. There are feedback loops and checks that ensure mastery of material where it is used to provide a structured training programme.

The computer can also, of course, test the learning, respond in many other ways, allow for access to other data-base materials in word-processor form, and print out material as required. So the same technology can be used, say, in careers advice or anywhere else a student needs accurate and up-to-date information.

Training in using the technology is straightforward for both the teachers and the learners. If there is also the possibility of recording one's own material, much that is presently in paper form can be stored on disc, either in the computer or in the video machine. Students will then simply print off what they need on paper (maybe even using internal electronic mail), and teachers can develop visual and computer material specifically for their own teaching programmes.

Like a map, this brief description of a new technology will not come fully to life for you until you actually see and/or use the equipment for yourself.

Visits

Films and television are ways of bringing the world into the classroom. Often, but not always, it is useful to take the class to the real world. Apart from the logistics of doing it and the time it consumes, the benefits can be great.

EFFECTIVE USE OF VISITS

The students may be faced with an overwhelming amount of information to try to take in. Again, they will select. They are visiting 'foreign' territory.

How can we help them to make sense of it? What are they in fact trying to learn? Do they know? How does it fit in to learning on their programme? What are they going to do to reflect on the experience? How will they use the learning? All this needs clarifying and agreeing beforehand. As with other methods: alerting, structuring, revisiting.

A video presentation beforehand showing them what they are going to see, with clear explanation, makes it familiar, less foreign, when they arrive. This can then be treated in the same way as the television material discussed above.

They will take a set of structured questions to address. It may be no bad thing to set it up competitively in terms of what they can report back. This provides incentive: the level of motivation is important.

Younger students need to know exactly what rules they are to keep to, the constraints on their actions.

There are always rules. What dress do they need? It's not a good idea to go down a coal-mine in a mini-skirt. What do they need to take to make notes, to record information and so on? Have it all clearly stated on a handout well in advance.

There must be time for reflection after the experience. The learning has to be properly focused and consolidated. They must do something with it to make sure it has 'value'.

Real life/discovery learning

Students' learning from films and television at home, and in places where they work or visit, is not within the control of teachers. The learning they provide is largely unconscious, but it is too important to ignore. Students need to focus that learning somehow and so integrate it with the learning that is controlled. This has come to be known as 'prior learning'. It is the intention that full credit should be given for this learning in certificating skills, which require that it is so integrated. Without a process that makes sense of all learning and builds it together into a whole structure, much of it remains unhelpful – unusable.

The richness of this resource is immense, but usually it is left untapped. A major problem with using it is its lack of structure. How does one select what is good, relevant and valuable? After all, no one said there would be a test. Clearly, many occasions will arise when the learning can be tapped. If there is shared experience it can be used in groupwork. Students should constantly be asked to match what they learn against their own experience in life.

There is increasing pressure for teachers to work closely with employers to integrate 'real life imperatives' – those felt by employers and the community – with what teachers feel important.

Assessment of competence is to be work-based, with the pressures and constraints felt face-to-face with production or the customer rather than in workshop simulations. Liaison is essential. Teaching cannot remain isolated from the reality it is preparing students to deal with.

Teachers have to develop skills, not only in working with students, but with those who also have important relationships with them at work and elsewhere. They will have joint responsibility for the programmes students undertake and they need to ensure their coherence.

Distance learning/Flexistudy

Flexibility of response by educational institutions is required to tackle the difficulties so many adult students have in getting at training and education opportunities. Programmes of study and training have to be devised that allow learners (or employers, or whoever requires the service) to negotiate how the learning is to be achieved.

This may take any pattern. It may (or may not) involve attendance at the educational institution, either on a regular basis or as a negotiated provision, perhaps related to the needs of the employer. It may involve sessions on other premises. It may be based only on tasks and assignments, supported by input through reading and other materials designed as a distance learning programme. The teacher is tutor to individuals, and may be contacted for consultation in a variety of ways. There may be blocks of time when groups of students can come together (Saturdays, weekends, maybe even a residential week along Open University lines).

In the future, teachers will need to adopt so many new roles that require also training in novel skills and techniques. For a new teacher, it is enough for the present to know that these possibilities exist.

18 Developing Study Skills

It cannot be assumed that students can cope with learning on their own. Most people have poorly developed study skills; your own may well need further development. In this chapter you will find some ideas and activities that should help you and your students to improve the ability to learn.

Targets and short-term goals

All skill development depends on practice. As long as you understand what you are trying to do and set yourself targets, then if you use the skill often enough and it becomes habitual, you will do it.

There is the difficulty of motivation. Long-term goals seem to take so long and get no nearer – they even become disincentives. You need short-term goals and targets attainable within days or weeks, and these can then build towards the longer-term goals. This is also true of your students.

Think of useful things. Set yourself attainable tasks:

I will master the Dewey Decimal System in the library.
I will make a list of books and materials in my field.
I will learn how to use the microfiche catalogue.
I will find out about TTNS and other electronic mail.
I will learn how to use Ceefax and other television data-bases.
I will learn to use a word-processor.
I will discipline myself to use no more than 500 words in whatever communications I send to colleagues.
I will make sure the structure of my communications is clear, easy to follow.
I will increase my reading speed by searching documents/book and other material for answers to my questions.

All this sort of activity will encourage you to work closely with staff in resource centres and libraries, who will support you. It is essential to develop these skills so as to create or gather a bank of resource material that your students may learn from, as well as to be a creative member of a team with your colleagues.

ACTIVITY 10

Learning from lectures

To be followable the lecture must have a structure. Properly handled lectures make the structure plain, with a structure plan employing key-words. The listeners can add notes of their own.

The worst kind of notes are verbatim scribble. Listening, watching and addressing questions to the lecturer are more important than getting down everything that is said. You cannot do both.

If you listen carefully a pattern will emerge, with 'alerting' words about the links, or 'now I want . . .' statements, or rhetorical questions. Key-words are usually not too hard to pick up if you listen out for them.

This skeleton, or pattern, is what you need to take away. You will need to look at it again, revisit as soon as possible afterwards, and reorganise the structure so that it makes sense to you. This allows you to clarify it as you review it. Look again at my advice in Part 1. Approach a lecture like this:

1 What are you hoping to learn? Are you ready and alert?
2 Be ready. Create your working space.
3 Listen to the preamble. If the lecture is part of a series, there should be a recap and links to previous learning. Note the links. There should be a 'map' of what is to come, even a plan which will help you to know where you are – in case you or the lecturer wanders, as lecturers are prone to do.
4 Listen for key-words, structural statements and recap statements – to consolidate as it goes along – opportunities for feedback, voice inflections, gestures and so forth that show important points.
5 Watch: if there are OHP presentations, they should offer key-words or patterns you can note down.
6 Use key-words only. You have to listen, not write.
7 If you lose track, if the lecturer wanders, or if you do not understand, *ask*. The lecturer knows it already, but cannot know your difficulty unless you say so – you are trying to learn. The lecture is not intended to be a sermon in church.
8 Listen to any summary/consolidation and check your notes.
9 **Review soon**. Within twenty-four hours you will have lost 70 per cent of it.

Learning from written materials

You can employ similar techniques to written materials such as this book. It is important to identify clearly the structure the author uses, and how parts relate to the whole. Your needs are not the same as those of other readers, nor are you starting from where the author is. Approach the material with your own questions as well as those the author seems to address.

You should certainly make structure notes. In Part 1 I discussed the problem of 'forgetting' and the need for revisiting. This is made much easier to tackle if you make notes and review them whenever you come back to them.

In any case, you will change and your perception will change with a fuller understanding of the author's intentions and growing experience to make comparisons of your own. Be proactive.

All books have maps – use them. Take charge of your learning.

Making notes

Why make notes at all?

- to be attentive, proactive learners. Humans are exploratory animals and need to be 'searching' in order to learn
- to get at the structure in order to see the whole and how it all fits together
- to produce a pattern we can absorb, match with our knowledge and experience
- to avoid the necessity of constantly rereading everything
- to enable us to revisit and review and so consolidate: it is important that we learn it 'right', for unlearning is harder than learning
- to challenge and restructure our own understanding.

ACTIVITY 11

Using television advertisements

How to practise? You need short, repetitive activity. Television advertisements provide the shortest, most accessible and punchiest means. These are highly efficient in the use of time in getting the message across. Within about thirty seconds, they grab attention and hold it. They convey a message (of some kind). They have to make it memorable, not necessarily simple in meaning but effective for the purpose of the advertisement. They may appeal to us in quite subtle ways, which it is interesting to analyse and explore. They are very efficient in the use of words and compelling images.

One advertisement will usually be repeated several times, so that you can check what you do. Be proactive: address questions to the experience. Once you have the skill, you can apply it to any experience, including this book. Write down the questions; revise them as new ideas occur to you.

Try to see the script behind words and images. Visualise the script into camera shots, which hardly ever last more than a few seconds. Then add the words. It is unusual for sound and vision to be recorded together.

You are trying to get behind the presentation to the structure to see how the thing has been put together and how it works. Nothing happens without a great deal of design-work first. Find the questions the designers posed to themselves:

How many camera shots? how long for each shot? why choose those?
What is the message? how is it built up, conveyed?
What are the words? how do they work with the images?
What is the advertisement appealing to? and to whom?
Is it effective? What makes is so? If not, why not?

STRUCTURES

Patterning and sequencing

Notes are not verbatim reports. They are for you. To be useful they must provide:

- triggers to facilitate recall
- a means of showing links, patterns of ideas that make a whole.

You will develop your own pattern for notes. Some people prefer to make linear structures, to see a spine of argument developing. Others prefer to start with a central idea, and then to use links by key-words to related but not necessarily sequential ideas, forming what has been named a 'coral' structure (after the branching coral). Figure 3 illustrates these two different types.

Both rely on key-words as triggers. Other clues to structure and relationships can be added: you can draw circles and boxes to enclose related ideas/words, and arrows to show direction and connections. You must develop your own methodology of making sense of the information.

Once you have something that works well for you, you can use it to get the message across effectively to others on hand-outs or OHP transparencies or on the chalkboard.

Experiment with different structures of notes. See which one is the most useful, the most meaningful for you. Remember, students will have their own way of visualising and dealing with information you present. Some will respond to linear structures, others to patterning. Do not assume that what works for you works for everyone.

Brain behaviour

Brain behaviour appears to use pattern-making and rule-making. It seems this may be to do with the ways in which the two halves of the brain prefer to work:

A. Linear style

COMMUNICATION

Individuals	Channels	Groups
barriers	signals	sharing
self-image	messages	boundaries
attitude	interference	identifying
mind-set	noise	signals
emotions	redundancy	measures
prior learning	(radio/TV)	rules
experience		bonding
knowledge		common goals
skills		teams
convictions		support
messages		individuals
reading		personal needs
interpreting		common language
sending		concepts/group
concepts		experience
formal thinking		leadership
vocabulary		roles
		decisions
		action plans

B. Linking pattern

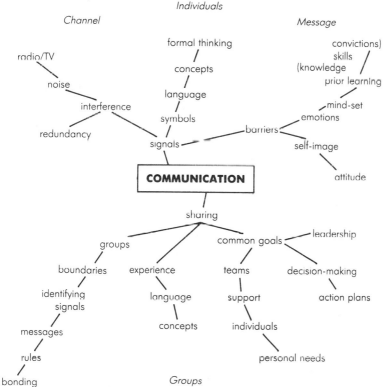

Fig. 3 Patterns of ideas

the left and right hemispheres appear to be different. In the 1970s Dr Roger Sperry did pioneering research that led to conceptions of dominance in brain behaviour. Studying brain electrical pulses of people doing different activities, he and his colleagues found that each hemisphere appeared to be involved in one kind rather than another. They 'specialise'. Studies of people who have suffered brain damage, or whose brain hemispheres have been physically divided, show this differentiated behaviour.

The left hemisphere is responsible for logical thought, language and mathematical processes, reasoning and analysis. Left brain dominance leads to goal-seeking, logical and linear thinking, a preference for analytical behaviour. It seems to be concerned with rule-making and linear structuring. Centres for language, reading and writing are located there (see Figure 4).

The right hemisphere deals with rhythm, colour, spatial concepts, imagination and synthesis. Right brain dominance is characterised by patterns and 'wholes', rather than by analysis. It facilitates the rather mysterious insights and 'leaps in the dark' that all of us experience. It seems to allow us to respond intuitively, emotionally, sensitively. It works with images and pictures, internal representations, models and patterns. It tends to work also on numerous parallel paths, matching and hypothesising to produce new structures.

It is a simplification to say all this is to do simply with the different hemispheres of the brain. But it is a fact that we do exhibit these quite different ways of behaving in the way we think about and deal with the world and social life.

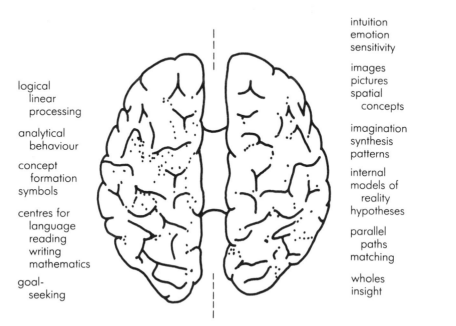

logical
  linear
   processing

analytical
  behaviour

concept
  formation
symbols

centres for
  language
  reading
  writing
  mathematics

goal-
  seeking

intuition
emotion
sensitivity

images
pictures
spatial
  concepts

imagination
synthesis
patterns

internal
models of
  reality
hypotheses

parallel
  paths
matching

wholes
insight

Fig. 4 Hemispheres of the brain (derived from a paper presented at the Industrial Society, 1989)

They are clearly different kinds of activity. One promotes more creativity, essential in order to go about problem-solving and exploring alternatives. The other is essential for planning, getting things done, organising and communicating in a logical fashion.

It is an unfortunate feature of modern education that emphasis is put so heavily on left brain behaviour. At school and at work it is left brain behaviour that is valued, considered 'clever'. The creativity and imagination of students are not rewarded with high marks in examinations which more easily test memory, logic and so on. Consequently, we tend to try to do everything logically. There is a preference for linear structures. We cannot analyse our own thinking: we cannot watch ourselves think. But we can have a view of our preferred patterns and seek to exploit those fully, while ensuring that we improve where we need to those activities that we personally find less attractive.

STUDYING

Studying requires us to be able to handle both pattern-making and rule-making. We have to be able to grasp the whole in order to see how the parts make sense. But we also need to see the structure. We do need to follow the logic of argument and to analyse the validity of the evidence, but we also need to match it with experience and insight gained elsewhere so as to construct our own picture of it all.

In setting about studying, you need to be aware of how you perform best in order to maximise the benefit. Establish for yourself what you find the most effective procedures for you.

19 Ergonomics

Ergonomics (called 'human factors' in the United States) can be defined as 'managing work'. It is a study of the interaction of human beings with things they use and environments where they work. It is concerned with the amount of effort it costs to do something, and what can be done to make it more human, less inefficient in the way it affects the people concerned. All objects, or whole environments, intended for human use should be designed to take account of the human users, of what is supposed to happen and what is to be done there.

How often do teachers have to battle with badly designed rooms or workshops? How many are expected to teach in environments 'designed' on assumptions about what is going to happen as learning activity which are no longer valid? How hard is it for them to get things they need, or to do adequate preparation? How hard is it for the students too? How can you maintain motivation if it is too hard?

Certainly, industrialisation has forced workers into desperately uncomfortable, exhausting environments: noisy, machine-dominated, production-orientated and inhuman. Think of the early cotton-mills; imagine what it was like to drive and stoke great steam engines on the railway, where a man had to shovel six tons of coal between Leeds and London while the engine bounced around at high speed. Until quite recently, factories survived where riveters had to work inside huge boilers with the result that they became deaf.

It is all grossly inefficient. The cost of the human has to be measured in with the cost of machines and buildings. As teachers we can try to ensure that factors under our control support what we ask the students to do rather than get in the way.

Risk-taking

Studies of road accidents show that the compulsory wearing of seat-belts has not brought about any reduction in deaths in the UK. Why? We need arousal to keep our perception of risk and sense of danger in balance, so we have risk-compensation to keep our arousal at an acceptable level. Straightening roads merely makes people go faster. With the security of the seat-belt we drive faster and brake later. It is risk-taking in all human activity that leads to progress.

Teachers must take risks. You cannot learn by playing safe. I wonder if children know this somehow. The development of adventure playgrounds on bomb-sites after the war was a response to what children actually did in play. It is risk-taking in every human activity that leads to progress. It is clearly risky to share decision-making with students, to experiment with new (to you) methods of teaching/learning, or let go control in some measure over what occurs, maybe to send out a group to do a survey or field research or to use resource bases, rather than to keep them where you can see them. Controlled risk-taking is absolutely essential. Growth as a teacher involves also the growing confidence to let go, to involve students and so give them 'ownership' of their learning processes.

But you have responsibility for safety. If the environment has hazards that are avoidable, you must take action. You are also a role-model. Risk-taking is necessary, but it must be under control and with purpose, organisation and direction. The right kind of risks must be taken to bring about the most profitable kind of arousal.

Personal space

Personal space is felt as an area surrounding a person's body in which there are boundaries for interactions with other people. It is defined by zones of social contact. The types of possible interaction vary with distance, which is shaped by the context and environment.

A study by Hall simplified this into concentric circles. He identified four zones: intimate, personal, social and public distances from the centre (see Figure 5, overleaf). The behaviour of a person whose space is violated may change considerably if the 'wrong' person enters a zone or if 'wrong' interactions are attempted there.

Closeness increases the effect of one person on another. There is increased sensory stimulation; smell and sound are added to sight. And the amounts of physical contact allowed between individuals varies in different cultures: for example, it seems greater among the French and Italians than the English, who like to keep each other at arm's length (a distance confirmed by research). Middle-class people seem to be more likely to hug and kiss each other than are the working class, and women more so than men – except on the football field, perhaps.

People who work together tend to use close social distance, while business is conducted more distantly. It has to do with seeing the whole person: with the enlargement and importance of the head as people approach, and with maintaining eye-contact. This distance is important also in screening out other people. Public distance is well outside a circle of social involvement, and at this distance other communication problems occur.

Establishing right relationships relates to identifying appropriate zones for social contacts. To be intimate in behaviour, one has to be close and to be comfortable there. Men and women behave differently in this zone. Invasion may seem threatening: there may be tension, discomfort or even flight. Drama training uses techniques to overcome such barriers to physical contact, and they

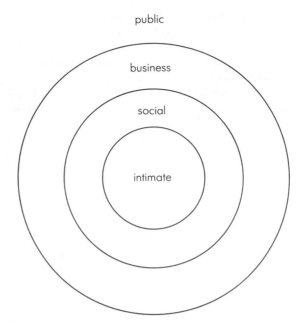

Fig. 5   Personal space (derived from *Silent Language* by E. T. Hall, Fawcett, 1959)

are also broken down in sports like rugby. Working together in a physical way requires contact; indeed, team behaviour requires a redefining of everyone's personal space zones, perhaps creating group space instead.

A typical reaction to invasion of personal space is to face away, avoid eye-contact, become stiff, pull in the shoulders – leave! Defensive behaviour is typified by lack of verbal response, or by abusiveness. Hall says, 'We treat space as we do sex. It is there, but we don't talk about it.'

Studies of crowding and empty space on trains identified a stress chemical in the urine of passengers who had travelled in crowded carriages. Invasion created responses that were complex, but intended to distance the intruder from the victim: leaning away, turning, or more simply withdrawing into oneself. In crowded trains people shrink their private space and control their discomfort by staring at the floor or into space: their body language projects non-relating to non-persons.

Territoriality

Concepts such as personal space and territoriality are borrowed from behavioural analyses of animals to explain how such factors may affect performance. You will have watched a dog mark out his territory. Most male animals seem to have some means of doing it, so why not humans? And is it only males?

Like personal space, territoriality is a concept that has social, unwritten rules of space behaviour. Infringing these rules will cause discomfort and often hostility. Territoriality differs from personal space in that territories are fixed locations, and do not move around with the people who define them. The boundaries are sensory, marked by stimuli such as scent in animals, and visible cues such as coats and bags with humans. You will see students mark out their territories in this way. Why do people feel more comfortable if they always use the same seat or table?

We all know the rules that govern territory. We can all distinguish that which is 'mine', such as a house or flat which can be controlled even when 'I' am not there, from that which is for everyone like a park, and from that which becomes semi-private – claimed by someone on a temporary basis, such as a seat on a train.

Behaviour related to semi-private territory is of importance to teachers. It appears when students reserve seats and mark seat boundaries in a class with 'ownership' of equipment. Studies in trains showed there was little verbal exchange; passengers had territory markers like bags and coats on the adjacent seat. Students use bags and books. An invader is forced to ask for a marker to be removed – 'is this seat taken?' Removing it oneself breaks the social code.

Well-designed teaching spaces need to take into account not only the more obvious things (often ignored, though), such as acoustics, noise levels, temperature control and ventilation, but also the spaces that are occupied for particular purposes. Teaching spaces may be rendered ineffective if seating arrangements are such that students are unable to mark territories (they can't spread out), or if they feel impelled to withdraw into themselves to preserve their need for personal space. Density and crowding are threatening both to personal space and territoriality. Having too many students in a class also makes social grouping difficult.

Teachers need to control the spaces students occupy. They should try to define group territories where they want group activities. Having students sitting in rows merely defines the teacher's space.

Activity has to be planned in relation to physical distance, eye-contact, territorial identification of working groups and their resources. It needs to be restructured frequently to prevent the fixing of small cliques, and to ensure that space is right for each particular learning activity. Variety is important.

TASK 19: Environment, space and territories

Make a detailed study of the environment where you teach.

What factors influenced the design? What was assumed to happen as learning and teaching activities? Is that still appropriate?

What would you consider to be the right conditions, taking into account all factors involved in achieving your learning goals?

What action and by whom is necessary to create these conditions?

Look carefully at use of space and territory in your class.

1 Do you mark out your territory? How? Some teachers have a desk with their papers in between themselves and their students, perhaps as a protection. What signals do you use?
2 How close do you get to students, or let them get to you? Where would you place the socially acceptable zones around yourself? How do you indicate those to the students? (Remember that they will take you as a role-model.)
3 How do individuals define their personal space or territory? What if this creates difficulties? What should you do?
4 Has the class broken up into more than one group? Are they defining group territory or group space and behaviour?
5 How can you ensure that there is positive use of space?

It is up to you, as teacher, to take control, to establish the rules for group behaviour, to define territories if need be by moving people around, to set up different groupings for varied activity. And whatever you do, do not let groups settle into one fixed pattern.

20 Barriers to Communication

In order to make progress in engaging students in the learning process, we must ensure that we and they recognise the barriers to learning they bring with them. We, as teachers, should be able to recognise specific problems students create for themselves or behavioural characteristics. It is not easy for us to see our own.

Mind-set and emotion

Emotional or attitudinal barriers result from cultural conditioning or response to past experience. We all have a mind-set about things that relate to us, a self-image that inhibits our willingness to believe we can do certain things, attitudes and beliefs we defend against overwhelming evidence.

Perhaps you know someone who is a banker. What image does that word conjure up for him or her, and for you? 'There are certain things bankers do, wear, enjoy, don't do, don't wear, don't enjoy, aren't there? I couldn't possibly . . . ' and this will inhibit certain kinds of behaviour. Some girls (or their parents) still reject the idea of engineering as a career: 'Do women actually enjoy engineering or science or maths? Isn't that what men do, not women?' Some men sincerely believe it is not their role to wash up and they do it very badly. Where do such attitudes come from?

They clearly relate to our perception of ourselves, a powerful self-image we have developed as a result of our experience. Many, such as that of the banker, we derive from models around us. It is not unusual to meet students who genuinely see themselves as 'thick', not 'clever like these other people'. It may be a result of painful experiences in education in the past, or a defensive posture to protect them from possible failure.

We have our needs for personal space and territory. Our value-system, our likes and dislikes, are often firmly embedded: they are inextricable from 'me – who I am' and exhibited both in words and in body language. We can all read such body signals easily.

Someone who has a mind-set that says 'I can't do maths' is not going to succeed in maths, however hard the teacher tries, unless that mould can somehow be broken. This learner has had past experience of maths learning, perhaps reinforced with some role-model that has established a conviction that it is not worth trying. The same happens in most areas of learning. Ball games defeat some people utterly; some are all thumbs in craftwork; some are word-blind; some cannot draw a straight line. You will have heard people say these things. They are self-fulfilling prophecies.

It is far from easy to tackle such attitudinal barriers. Equally, when someone discovers a way through such a barrier, the effect on their self-image and on their lives can be quite dramatic. The discussion above on motivation (page 103) may suggest ways forward.

Information theory

In 1949, the Shannon–Weaver mathematical theory of communication was published. These workers made a distinction between 'information' and 'informational channels': between what the information is about and the way it is transmitted, person to person. Shannon and Weaver were concerned to improve radar and radio transmission: 'we want to maintain a high-fidelity transmission so that messages don't get garbled on the way. We also want a lot of redundancy and clarity: we don't want noise interfering with the transmission.'

'Noise' and 'redundancy' are technical terms. Noise in radio is the jumble of background sound that may prevent us hearing what we are trying to listen to. We have all had the frustration of noise when we try to hear a concert or a talk on the radio; it can be even worse when television pictures break up, develop strange images or disappear. It is often referred to as interference. Redundancy refers to an excess deliberately put into the signal to ensure that something of the message gets through. The theory is about effectiveness in sending and receiving signals.

We are dealing here in metaphors, so this account is not to be taken too literally. Problems in classrooms that affect information transmission, whatever the kind of signal, increase with distance. The further people are away, the harder it is for them to read our signals, for us to read theirs. So much of what we wish to share is to be read in the way we say or demonstrate it. Subtleties and nuances are lost.

Distraction in the classroom is one kind of 'noise'. For example, I was running a discussion with a group of teachers. A colleague who was with me said at the end that he had had great difficulty in concentrating on what I was saying because a woman sitting opposite him had such 'noisy legs'. After another session a group of students told me they found the design of the sweatshirt I was wearing so fascinating they simply couldn't follow my arguments.

Conflicting messages, emotional stress, aggressive behaviour may also act as 'noise'. The problem relates to the learner's 'attention'. Learners need to concentrate on what is to be learned, but so much can get in the way. Anything that interferes with attention is noise.

But so is lack of clarity in the signals and messages we wish to convey. The means of transmission – the tone of voice, perhaps, the words we speak or the visual materials used – all need to be clear and easy to understand. Monotony of delivery will become 'noisy'. Rooms with difficult acoustics, rooms that are too hot, lighting conditions that prevent proper vision, seats that are too hard (or soft) can all get in the way of the message. Try to experience it as students do.

Redundancy implies that a message is so strong that it overcomes any noise likely to be around. A tale may be so absorbing that listeners ignore everything else; people can 'lose themselves' in a computer program, a book or a film. Most people are actually quite good at doing this.

Chaotic presentation of information with little or no structure will produce a great deal of noise. Ask yourself: How hard is this for students to understand? What exactly do I want them to take away? What can I get rid of so that they can grasp essentials presented?

It is notoriously difficult to write instruction manuals. Here again, structure is all-important. There has to be a clear learning path and action plan. Often a simplified diagram helps. And a correctly sequenced structure is vital. In one jet aircraft, the instructions to the pilot to eject were set out on the pilot's canopy: the first instruction was 'Eject the canopy'. Think about it.

AMBIGUITY

'Crematorium Pedestrians Only' reads the sign.

I remember writing a memo to a colleague telling her to arrange a week's leave with her team leader: 'Do you think Corfu would be nice?' she said.

Sometimes ambiguity can be dangerous. Which switch? when? in what sequence? 'I didn't mean you to plug it in there!' Whose fault is it if there is an explosion? It is essential to get a third party to validate any set of instructions, to ensure there is no ambiguity.

SELECTION

The brain selects from experience. However hard we seem to be concentrating, we will select some things and ignore others. Teachers who recognise this can try to ensure that the important things do not get selected out. Repetition and redundancy, as already mentioned, are important here: hence the need for revisiting and consolidation.

A reasonably effective way of doing this is to get students to explain what they understand or what they have to do – what the thing is about or how it works. In trying to explain it to someone else there is not only an alerting of the brain, but also processing of what has been learned into the student's personal knowledge structure.

Repetition of material, revisiting, presentation of information in several different forms (OHPs, discussions, handouts) may be useful redundancy. It is very hard for students to grasp something they are only exposed to once.

VERBOSITY

Sheer volume of information is noisy. An overloaded channel or receiver obviously cannot cope. Have a look at the OHP transparencies you use. How much of the information can possibly get through, and how much is noise? What about the learning materials you use? Are they clear? Could you simplify it, make it easier to grasp? Could you structure it more clearly? How much is essential?

You need to be constantly alert to problems of distraction and the need for clarity. *Less* may actually mean *better*. It is so easy to believe that the more that is said, the clearer it will be. Frequently, the opposite is true. Teachers tend to be verbose, to put too many words and symbols into OHP acetates or into instructions. Structure and key-words matter more than the information they contain. The message is: simplify it.

INCOMPLETE INFORMATION

The opposite problem can arise, however. Sometimes students are not given all the information they need by the teacher or the instruction card or the work-sheet or other task guidance. It is easy to make unjustified assumptions about what the learner knows already or will bring to the activity, or to fail to think through what it is that they need to know.

Using jargon can also lead to incompleteness. The purpose of jargon is to share understanding, to be unambiguous. It fails if the student does not know the words or the symbols.

TASK 20: Noise

Before you start a teaching session, remove distractions. Check for 'noise'.

Use a minimum of information in materials you present but ensure that it is structured as a learning path, or where appropriate an action plan. Use key-words and indicate direction clearly.

Sequence your instructions, and ensure they are complete.

Validate your materials for ambiguity and omission.

Be positive, not negative (the Ten Commandments fail this test).

Familiar words (watch out for jargon), short sentences and active verbs ('do this . . .', not 'It is best to . . .') are the easiest to grasp.

Use a variety of presentation to ensure useful redundancy.

---

21 Teaching and Learning Aids: Overcoming Barriers

TASK 21: Teaching/learning aids

Design, produce and use a variety of teaching/learning aids.

For each session, the activities planned for students and teacher should be clearly identified within the lesson plan. Aids and materials to support that activity should be designed or selected to be appropriate and effective. Where they are produced it is expected that they will be of a presentable standard.

All these aids and materials need careful evaluation after use. They will accumulate to create a resource file which you should frequently edit, organise and keep up to date.

PERFORMANCE CRITERIA FOR TEACHING/LEARNING MATERIALS AND AIDS
1 Learning materials are designed to stimulate and challenge while building links and structures to earlier learning.
2 Learning materials use symbols and language and require the students to undertake activities appropriate to their needs.
3 Learning materials are easy to understand and clear in what they say. They are well produced and sequence learning in a sensible and supportive way.
4 Teaching aids are well designed for their purpose, and of a presentable quality.
5 Teaching aids are simple, taking account of known difficulty students have in comprehension. They show an understanding of the principles of designing such aids.
6 Teaching aids and learning materials are used skilfully and effectively in the session and are adapted sensitively to student needs as they arise.
7 All are evaluated for effectiveness or redesigned as needed.

Audio-visual aids

The major purpose of audio-visual aids in the classroom is to focus attention. If you switch on an OHP, attention moves from your face to the screen. This helps by providing variety and regenerating interest – attention span is normally no more than fifteen minutes – but is obviously self-defeating if the OHP is then just left on. Use it only as needed; otherwise, it becomes 'noise'. Students need to concentrate on you when you wish to engage them in two-way exchange.

Visual stimuli are in the control of the teacher and should be used effectively. Clear the chalkboard and the walls of distracting material, including work from previous classes. And don't inflict your material on others.

Visual images

Since we learn 70 per cent of our information by seeing, visual stimuli are particularly powerful. They should be chosen or designed with care. A picture can be worth a thousand words, but not if it is a bad picture or misleading or irrelevant or difficult to interpret.

Pictures are extremely rich in information, and simplifed diagrams are often much clearer and simpler to grasp. They let you eliminate everything except what you want to show. You can also build up the structure using overlay techniques on an OHP, for example. Focus on essentials, and select out noisy detail.

In choosing a visual stimulus, you must appraise it for what you want to achieve by using it. How effective is it for the specific purpose you intend? It may be to show how the parts relate to the whole, or to concentrate attention on fine detail. Both are necessary to understanding and good diagrams or pictures can make understanding very much easier. But they are a means to an end. Support them if possible by physical exploration of the reality.

In constructing images, certain factors improve effectiveness:

- **simplicity**: the brain simplifies – searches for patterns; to help we too should simplify our images where we can
- **closure**: we like to perceive things as 'wholes' rather than in bits; we should ensure that the whole is clear even when we want to concentrate on details
- **clarity**: the brain tests hypotheses about figures and will try different ones; avoid ambiguity or lack of clarity
- **boundary**: to see we must differentiate things; clear boundaries will help, and the use of colour can also be effective.

A good example to visualise is a child's wooden train. Think of the simplification of the complex engine into horizontal and vertical cylinders, cubes and circles, especially if these are differentiated by being painted in bright contrasting colours.

Audibility and visibility

Consider the acoustics of the room and the lighting conditions. Do not assume that people can hear or see. The screen may be masked for some students by others, or by the OHP. Even the greatest visual aid is useless if it can't be seen. Always ask the people furthest away or at the widest angle if they are having difficulty. When possible test it out yourself – walk around to see. In particular, check any material you have put up on the chalkboard for its legibility and structure, preferably from the furthest point. This has the added advantage that you can make personal contact with students and experience it from their point of view. It is easy to remain rather fixed at the front when using AVA.

Think about the personalities involved. Are there any in the group with poor eyesight? (They may be too embarrassed to put on their spectacles – this quite frequently happens!) Is anyone there colour-blind (6 per cent of males are)? Maybe colour differentiation is important. Some people cannot distinguish lines that are too fine or present narrow angles. Ask people to move if it might help. Think about brightness of illumination or contrast with general brightness in the room. Draw the curtains or switch off lights. There may be angles at which reflections make it hard to see. Experiment; move the screen (or the class). Take control.

Deafness tends to be more embarrassing and more difficult, and people are often less aware of the onset of deafness than they are of failing vision. Both affect people gradually, usually as they get older. A physical decline seems inevitable, though often people compensate with greater effort too. We need to be alert to problems, to clarity of diction and pace of delivery.

Listening skills

Listening skills require a great effort. We are surrounded by a cacophony of sounds. Students have been conditioned to be unhappy with silence. Some people wake up listening anxiously to silence in the middle of the night. So we routinely block out most of what we hear. Listen to a tape-recording of an hour of your life in normal circumstances. What sounds are there you do not 'hear'?

Yet teachers expect students to listen more than to do anything else, without recognising the problems involved. Students may be talked at for an hour or more. They are also often expected to take down notes at the same time. Apart from the difficulty of trying to do two things at once, there are many problems of inaccuracy, mis-hearing, misunderstanding and so on. Many teachers take a cynical view: 'As long as they've been given the information, what the hell! If they can't make use of it, it's nothing to do with me.'

All social behaviour depends on listening to others; most people are very bad at it. Teachers are also notoriously bad at listening to students. Parliament is a public display of egotists talking and no one listening. Eventually people have to scream and shout, even become social vandals, to get others to listen.

Alerting signals

If you want students to listen it is essential that you give them cues, alerting signals, questions to think about. They need to be able to follow your structure easily. Give them the pattern. It can be built up using key-words. There should also be opportunities for feedback, two-way communication, loops or links to consolidate learning at least every fifteen minutes or so.

Take stock of your delivery. How fast do you talk, and how monotonous is your voice? Inexperienced teachers tend to let their voices rise, become rather strangled or shrill. Relax, slow down. Slower pace gives you and them thinking time. Try to pitch your voice lower, and to vary its pitch; it will be nicer to listen to and will probably carry better. Try to improve your diction, too. Do you miss consonants off the ends of words? Are there difficult acoustics in the room? What do you do about that?

Listen to yourself on a tape-recorder after a class. Better than video, it can be quite revealing.

Structure

Students need to take away a pattern, a structure, in order to learn it. If they try to listen and copy out they are likely to select and distort information, and embed misunderstanding. If you are using a lecture approach, it is best to give them the structure of your lecture beforehand so that they can use it to follow what you wish to present. It may be in the form of headings with gaps for their own notes, but they need to be helped to structure them with key-words and patterns to make sense of them.

If the method you choose is inductive, you must genuinely build up on the board or OHP what they discover or suggest. But it will need to be written up into a comprehensible structure afterwards, to ensure it makes sense as a whole. Produce your own version as a handout when you make the links to the next class.

OHP: projector and screen

The OHP is a most versatile tool. It has the advantage that you can prepare material beforehand, but also add to it or adapt it in the class. You can maintain eye-contact with the students while you use it, and encourage their participation. (You have to turn your back to write on a chalkboard, and risk losing the contact.)

You can also sit to appear part of the group when appropriate, or invite them to work with you. You should, in any case, develop techniques that will not divide you from your class. Some teachers treat the screen as if it were a chalkboard and do all the explanation at the screen, so losing the advantage of the OHP.

You can point out relevant detail on the transparency, perhaps using a pen to lie as a semi-permanent pointer, moving it as needed to focus attention. You can reveal and mask parts of the structure or diagram as you want to concentrate on particular things. You can use a host of visual clues, exploiting the four basic factors set out on page 162.

All that I emphasised earlier about structure and sequence applies to the use of the OHP. Once you have a clear structure, take the students through it. Too much all at once is difficult to grasp, but they will need to see the structure as a whole by the end. Build it up gradually, revealing it a bit at a time as you elaborate the key-words or diagram. It helps to black out all the image except the bit you want to concentrate on (easily done with ordinary paper), and then gradually reveal the building blocks. Remember that the OHP is an aid for your explanation, not a subsitute for it.

Think, too, about the density of information and verbosity. It is easy to make A4 printed pages into transparencies, and teachers frequently do. But the result can be illegibility and incomprehension. An OHP transparency must be read at a distance, while a paper is held in the hand. Keep the difference in mind.

SETTING UP THE PROJECTOR AND SCREEN

Where are you going to place yourself in relation to the OHP? The OHP allows you to face your audience, maintain eye-contact and so on. You do not have to stand, presentation-style. You can use it with a group in a much more relaxed way. You can sit beside the OHP, which signals that you are part of the group. It also allows you to interact more easily with the group rather than with the screen. This kind of teaching is about sharing, not telling.

Make sure that the machine itself is not preventing students from seeing the screen. Try putting it on a low table (or even a chair) rather than obstructing the sight-line for people sitting down (see Figure 6). It helps if the screen can be tilted forward at the top.

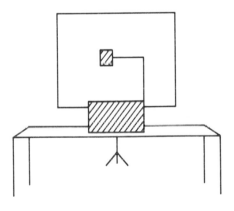

Fig. 6
(Left) *Impossible to avoid obscuring the screen for some people, and when you write or point on OHP: you could raise the screen. Also puts a table between you and the group: creates distance, formality.*

(Right) *OHP not on sight-line or dominating. Screen needs angling forward. Easier to see in most illuminations, feels comfortably closer. Barriers removed.*

BUILDING UP RESOURCES

OHP slides form part of a developing resource bank. This requires organising too to allow for order and retrieval. The slides need to be framed and covered. Using such frames, you can make slides that use several acetate sections as overlays, although this is probably only worth the effort if you intend to use them more than once. Have the acetates firmly located in their frames so that the overlays fall easily into the right place. Start with a 'stripped' diagram or structure, and add complexity using slices of acetate with the additional information or detail. Provide students with the basic figure as a 'gapped handout' on paper for them to fill out as you add information, such as labels.

Resource rooms will have appropriate cutting and pasting equipment. They should have acetate sheets in different colours, frames, a cutting board and a sharp knife. The simplest way to add colour is with felt pens, which come in different thicknesses – some colours become almost illegible when projected, however. White lettering on a coloured ground can be more effective.

Experiment. Prepare your slides beforehand, since only then can you design them properly. Make sure print is of a suitable size and density, with good colour contrast if possible. Think too of the four rules above. OHPs are about the bones of the teaching, not the flesh.

The photocopier can be used in conjunction with OHP to produce good-quality transparencies quickly. A structured lesson plan, for instance, should be in handout form, but also on OHP acetate to provide an over-view of learning goals and activities.

Boardwork

Structure matters in boardwork too. It is easy to use a board as a jotting pad; this is quite helpful to concentrate attention and move the focus, but it doesn't produce a pattern that is easy to remember. Plan your boardwork whenever you can, or at least determine some structure within which you can make notes on the board. Look at it at the end and see if the pattern makes sense for them to take away. You need a 'model in the head'. You can put up an outline before they come. White boards have the advantage you can use colours for boundary.

Write legibly. This requires practice – it's quite different from any other writing you do. Can the people at the back read it? If it is too small or the letters are poorly formed, no! Try to look at it from the back, to see it as they do.

Handouts

The most valuable, least understood resource is the photocopier. It tends to be used merely to reproduce masses of 'stuff to give the students' without thinking through what they are going to do with it, or whether it will contribute effectively to learning. As with every other aid, a handout needs careful planning. What is it for? How should it look? When do they need it? What is to be the sequence? Here are some useful examples.

1 It is most important that students read widely. It is also much better if they do this *before* a session, so that what they have read forms a basis for their work. It is easy to use material as if it were a textbook, to let it run the class. Better to see it like a committee paper circulated as a basis for discussion, to take as read – somewhere to start from.

A teacher has to assume knowledge, breadth of experience, to be able to concentrate on what can be done in class. There has to be a lot of learning elsewhere. A handout ensures that all have the same accurate and up-to-date information. (Of course, they have to read it!)

Students should be encouraged to find their own reading too. They will need access to photocopying in the library to make up a reading portfolio. They should be encouraged to adopt the approach I have set out in my advice on the development of study skills, in Chapter 2.

2 Reduce a handout to be used in class to a skeleton of key-words, which students can flesh out with their own notes. Use it to help students to grasp the structure and pattern of the whole, the flow and sequence. Wordy handouts are confusing 'noise'.

Structure and linking, alerting and outline notes, are much better than the (usually) selective and inaccurate notes that students scribble while their attention should be on listening and watching. The brain cannot be alerted with questions while the ears are trying to catch the answers.

A 'gapped handout' can assist note-taking and consolidation, by enabling students to recall accurately what was covered in class. It can also be used to test recall, words, whole sentences, labels – or whatever needs to be tested. It can be filed for revision.

3 A handout can be designed as an instruction sheet, an action plan or a working document. Guidance, drawings to complete, questions to find answers to, maps, treasure hunts – there are so many ways of using handouts creatively. But they all need design so that they are effective to their purpose. This is much better than inventing the material on the hoof and then getting the group to copy it down from the board. Distortion and misunderstanding become inevitable.

Once you have designed a handout, always get it validated by someone else for clarity, ambiguity, what it is like for someone who is coming to it fresh and possibly not already knowledgeable.

4 Use handouts to 'share'. As with OHPs for groupwork, handouts can ensure that all accumulate the same ideas – and can focus them through revisiting – and have the same richness of resources to work with.

RESOURCE BANK

A most important feature of handouts is that they accumulate as a personal resource file. They need organising: given headings and dates, and perhaps colour-coded. Using different colours for the different kinds of handouts can be extremely helpful.

Sensible use of handouts ensures a well-structured, clear, non-verbose and accurate information-base with a linking pattern. It is unhelpful for students to try to revise from material that is as wrong, incomplete, ambiguous, illusory or fictional as student notes so frequently turn out to be.

Simple learning materials are often as effective as complex ones. All AVA is expensive in time and effort. Time spent making AVA or handouts will only make sense if the products solve a real problem in learning; it is also far better if they can be used for more than one session or class. An advantage of working in a team, or with colleagues, is that you share ideas and the effort of creating resources. There should be a team resource bank to use.

Problem-solving

One good exercise is to identify the real learning problems in your field of teaching. Then with colleagues think of creative ways in which you could tackle the problems. You could use models as well as OHP presentations or slides. You could think of games or activities that require setting out as instructions.

I have seen extraordinarily inventive ideas in a wide range of disciplines from such an exercise. I gave an example in Case Study 7, in which a doll's house was used to help students who had difficulty in visualising things, and to 'see it happening' somehow.

A group (or an individual) might pose themselves a learning or a visualising problem: for example, to show how far away the nearest star is by taking the sun to be the size of a pea, and where the planets are on the same scale. Or how you might explain planetary motion. Or to convey the idea of a standing wave in physics, maybe, or the menstrual cycle or the circulation of the blood. Or dealing in stocks and shares, or decision-making in a business enterprise. Or to analyse the action of the four-stroke engine.

These have all been designed as models, charts (some with parts that move), board and card games – some were highly competitive. If a visual stimulus can be helped with action, all the better. Think of the 'sculpting' in Case Study 6.

Team-based resourcing

Teams share their expertise and creativity in building up a team resource bank of teaching/learning materials. Examining boards are demanding team approaches that integrate curriculum. Students are to learn through projects that cross subject disciplines, while teachers work as teams to produce the learning materials.

A resource base is needed where materials can be located and are accessible to the team. It needs to be equipped not only for the storage and retrieval of materials but for creative work too. This is a base where the team can generate ideas and activity-work for a whole curriculum programme. Clearly, since it consists mostly of handouts and consumables, there must be a system that tracks usage and ensures replacement. All team members carry responsibility. The production of AVA, models and so on requires work-benches, word-processing, video machines, materials such as acetates, and so forth. The control of expenditure and decision-making is important, and record-keeping must be well organised too.

In Chapter 18 I suggested ways in which teachers can prepare their own skills to contribute effectively to such work. Clearly, teachers will have to work closely with staff who are in charge of major resources such as the library, and to plan the learning programme with them. It is no good sending students to work with these resources if they are not organised in advance.

Word-processing and desk top publishing

Do learn to use a word-processor. It makes the production of good-quality handouts much easier. Handwritten ones are untidy. You can manipulate text in a word-processor to ensure that it is presented in the most effective way without the tedium of having to rewrite (or retype) things. Learn to compose, to 'invent', at the keyboard.

Those that have a range of fonts and allow the use of graphics will enable you to produce excellent OHP materials also. You can make transparencies from text produced with a word-processor.

All computers can now support desk top publishing programs that allow teachers to produce materials that look as attractive and well produced as a printed page, but at a fraction of the cost. Once the basic text and diagrams have been set up, they can be manipulated into all the ways magazines use to make them visually exciting. But you can also make them work with the way in which learners learn using all the visual techniques mentioned above – simplifying, structuring, sequencing, headlining, marking strong boundaries using lines and boxes, and integrating diagrams and other images with the text.

Poor visual presentation of teaching materials fails to stimulate, and can simply switch students off. Look at almost any commercially produced stuff, and see how it depends on visual impact for its effect. Even quite awful content can be made compelling reading. Teachers need to exploit every possible technique to the full.

22 More on Communication: Groups

Watch your class carefully as it becomes a social group, and in particular if people join the group late. What happens? Why?

What action should you take if they form not one cohesive group, but several cliques? How will you ensure they come together and agree purpose, goals, rules, patterns of sharing and working as a team together? How will you help them define their boundaries?

TASK 22: Managing groups

Demonstrate skill in managing your students and group behaviour. Consider carefully the performance criteria below.

PERFORMANCE CRITERIA IN COMMUNICATION

1 Students establish with the teacher a supportive, positive group identity: they have agreed and shared purposes.
2 Social and personal interactions are carefully observed. Groups as they form are noted, together with the behaviour of students in them.
3 Dominance patterns, effects of personalities and personal factors are noted. So too are the students' reactions to teacher language and behaviour. The teacher takes appropriate action.
4 The teacher responds to feedback. Teaching method, language and behaviour are modified to match student reaction.
5 Teacher language and stimulus material are appropriate.
6 The teacher is sensitive to learning problems and to the students' difficulty in comprehending information and instructions.
7 There is variety of pace, presentation, activity and skilful use of open and closed questions.
8 Individuals and groups are managed well.
9 The teacher is respected by students, and has established an acceptable role relationship with them and with colleagues.

Community

Human beings are social animals. Communication is 'sharing' within a community: a group with defined boundaries, shared purposes and duties, and a common language.

ACTIVITY 13 | Social groups

1 Think about the groups to which you belong. How are they defined and what are their boundaries, shared purposes and understanding?

What did you have to learn and do to become accepted as a member?

2 Consider the social group that is your class. Try to clarify:

- what you consider to be the purposes that you all share
- how those purposes are to be identified and agreed to
- what are the rules that should regulate group behaviour
- what roles you expect your students to adopt
- what role(s) you see for yourself
- how do you ensure students 'join the club'
- how you should deal with outsiders coming in.

Exploring and social behaviour

Learning is an activity on the part of learners in which teachers may play a minor role. We talk about a picture, or a building or a statue, communicating with a person. What can we mean? Clearly, pictures just hang there. The energy for anything to happen has to come from the viewer, whatever skill the artist had.

Albert Einstein invented the 'thought experiment', to explore the behaviour of objects approaching the speed of light. Here is a thought experiment for you to do, preferably with colleagues.

ACTIVITY 14 | Contexts

What can we learn about communication from the contexts below?

- visiting an art gallery alone
- listening to a classical music concert or a rock concert
- going to a foreign country for the first time
- becoming a member of a club
- practising with a sports team
- watching a television programme
- telling friends about a holiday, using slides.

The important thing is to think: what actually happens there?

With colleagues you could divide into groups of three and report what you have discovered to the whole group, to see if any principles about communicating emerge that apply to all the contexts.

Joining groups

In looking for the bases of communication, we should bear in mind the idea of the group with boundaries. Competition between groups will define boundaries more sharply. Members of each group will invent all sorts of glue and banners to proclaim 'us' against 'them'. In extremes, it can turn into secret societies with handshakes and coded signalling, but frequently it is a matter of dress or uniform and other open signals. In most societies we recognise groups that adopt pseudo-military uniform and indications of rank: the police, fire service, ambulance service, nurses and so on. When people put on a particular uniform they also adopt a behaviour pattern with it.

One hidden purpose is to ensure that 'the whole is greater than the sum of the parts'. Groups that gel – that is, that work well together – achieve much more than the same individuals would on their own. Where does this added value come from?

We can see analogies in the animal world. Some are mysterious. The ant-hill, created by termites, is a remarkable structure with a complex ventilation system including chimneys that heat up and extract stale air, so generating air currents through the tunnels. But where is the 'model in the head' that enables termites to build it? There is no possibility of the parts existing alone, so how do individual termites know in their tiny blind world what each has to do to construct the whole? Communication, we know, is by chemical pheromones excreted by the queen. In human groups too there is a mystery as to how purposes and direction arise, and how they are communicated to all involved.

Joining a sports team carries with it the competitive element. A team spirit is exhibited in dress and observation of specific rules and codes. It is derived partly from agreed purposes (goals!) and partly from perceived antagonists (other teams). Team members rely on the others, and display a commitment to the team that supersedes other social commitments. The same is true of a drama group or an orchestra. We exploit this competitive glue in setting up learning games.

Group behaviour imposes a need for individuals to discover a role in the group. This is no less true for you, as teacher, than for any other members, unless you choose to remain as an 'outsider'. To be the disruptive outsider cannot be right.

To be effective, you will have to establish that you are working with the students as part of a group while you are together – to be one of 'us'. The unhappiest experience you can have as a teacher is to find a group ganging up against you and to be fighting to establish common ground. Your own behaviour may even help to create that distance. Your first job as the teacher is to establish the class as a group with agreed goals, roles, rules of behaving and responsibilities.

We may think of an evening class as a club. Complicated things may be going on. There are rules which govern the operation of the club: what are they for? how are they arrived at? Anyone joining has to learn and observe them and has to take trouble to see what this means. People who have dealt with adult groups know that breaking into established groups is difficult and disruptive.

It is easier if the rules are stated explicitly, but important ones are usually exhibited only in the behaviour of the club members: what is considered acceptable and what is not. Peer group pressure and a desire to become, or remain, one of the group ensure that members learn rules quickly. New members arrive feeling 'foreign', but wanting to be accepted as one of 'us'. They look constantly for clues as to how to behave and are extremely sensitive to modelling and feedback: they will conform in dress and language use, even if it feels odd or wrong. They will absorb values and ways of thinking too.

Stimulating interest

Television is a visual and auditory medium. It is extremely powerful. You have to make an effort to read a paper; many are 'comics' rather than newspapers. Television is principally for leisure. As a force for change it is unparalleled.

Have you noticed how people feel out of it when they have missed a popular programme? especially if it is part of a soap opera. Others discuss it at length – they feel isolated. Television universality matters. In communication terms, viewers are totally passive and receptive. Their attention is held by careful choice of visual images and rapid change of focus, using a range of camera shots. They are also made restless, and put in constant need of fresh stimulation. You can learn a great deal about teaching methods from analysis of such techniques, especially how to maintain interest and overcome problems of limited attention span.

Television producers and editors of tabloid newspapers assume that people don't really want to know – that their attention and interest have to be captured. Even the most serious topics are treated sensationally. Otherwise, people switch off, or they don't buy the paper. Editors know about motivating people to want to read or to buy. How do they do it?

Apart from the obvious use of headlines and 'exciting' words even when the story is excruciatingly dull, they use language, length of sentences and paragraphs, attention span, visual images, change of focus and presentation; the limited attention span of the reader is always allowed for, and there is a constant regeneration of interest. They assume an increasing laziness of mind.

Listen to people discussing a news item. You will often hear a rehearsal of words used by the reporter, either on television or radio or in particular newspapers. Groups will read the same paper, so they will find themselves using the same words and the same value statements in their discussion. You might even be able to say which paper or programme gave them their words and their understanding. People read a newspaper as much to know what to say socially as to find anything out. It is part of group identification. Editors are very conscious of this in developing their 'brand image'.

The same happens with television programmes. When selling anything, you must start from where the customer is, what is likely to interest him or her, not you. Presenters of travel programmes try to avoid what happens when people show their friends their holiday slides. The producer anticipates questions of the viewer: how do I get there? how much will it cost? what is there to do? and so on. Often, a home slide show is about 'us and what we did'.

Questions

Many classes seem to operate like the holiday slide show. There is no communication, because there is little sharing. Students are excluded. It is essential that they approach the experience alert and with a questioning brain. Humans are exploratory animals, so curiosity must be an important trait. If the brain operates by pattern-making and rule-making it must be searching to find the patterns and the rules. Exploring is a trait we share with the animal kingdom. Progress requires challenge, tackling and solving problems. Much of it is inherited behaviour; how else would you explain what beavers do?

What distinguishes humans is the ability to distance ourselves from reality and to construct concepts – mental models that we describe in words. Exploratory, discovering activity is organised into concepts constructed to explain or control our experience.

It is this level of curiosity that questioning relates to. Most children are full of the word 'why?' A baby is asking a question when she puts a rattle in her mouth to explore hardness. Questions really require language, words, concepts; but would a child develop concepts without this physical exploration?

Questions have to do with alerting the brain to some new experience, idea or word-pattern that is coming and which might challenge our present understanding. Knowledge, according to Jerome Bruner in *The Process of Education* (1977), is a process of constant restructuring of concepts. It is not lumps of stuff to transmit somehow from here to there. Nor can you just hammer knowledge into your students' brains: they must be made ready to restructure, to deal with what is new. Information can only become personal knowledge when it is processed in some way. The radio must be switched on, as it were.

Without preparation the brain cannot deal with new information. It will ignore it, as it ignores most of the sensory data around us most of the time. We just do not notice it. We perceive consciously only the things we alert our brain to – the rest passes unnoticed and apparently unrecorded. That we have in fact recorded it can be shown by hypnosis, but concept formation depends on conscious alerting. What do you remember of the last twenty-four hours? Why those things and not all the rest?

Hence the importance of questions. Rote-learning, although powerful, actually has no effect on what people think or do. The learning is not part of our own structure of concepts, the way words work for us. It belongs to someone else.

LEVELS OF QUESTIONS

We can alert the brain to explore present experience or revisit past experience. Questions work at various levels:

Level 1: direct experience – focusing on what is happening now

Level 2: describing experience, to ourselves and to others; this is a second level of abstraction

Level 3: comparing and interpreting experiences (a third level of abstraction) – this involves mental models/patterns; we restructure our conceptual understanding when patterns do not match

Level 4: thinking creatively, generalising, transferring learning to new contexts, using it to solve problems.

Much brain activity is to do with processing information. We may use questioning to make the brain receptive to take the information we want it to have and to provide us with perceptions of the world, and of our internal mental ideas. We need to do this all the time to be able to deal competently with our world.

But we can set the brain actively thinking to form new concepts and abstractions from experience, patterning information into new insights. There is a social function of language that allows us to share and bond: we experience this when we try to tell others how we are perceiving this information and experience – what we now know. We can compare it with the new structures they have created, and which they in turn express in their words.

This working with other people helps us to refine our ideas, to create hypotheses about the world and people that allow us to attempt to predict what will happen or what people will do. We need to explain and to predict in order to try to control what happens. This is how technology works – and most human and social activity too. It is also how words acquire their meanings.

TEACHER'S QUESTIONS

How can teachers handle questions? What should teachers do?

These two sentences are alerting statements, pseudo-questions, rhetorical questions: all teachers use them. They are not looking for creative response, but merely aiming to alert the students' brains.

They prepare them for 'my' answers, without stimulating them to find their own. Having a student actually discover answers different from 'mine' can seem to be bad news for many teachers. They want students to remember the 'right' answer, in other words 'mine'. Great weight is given to this procedure through the examination and testing system. The level of restructuring by the student depends not so much on curiosity as on extrinsic motivating factors such as the teacher's pleasure or anger, or passing the exam, or just 'getting it right'.

It depends critically too on how easy it is for the student to link the information or concepts into what is known already. If the pace of arrival of new information (or new words or new definitions) is too fast, or if the volume of information is overwhelming, learners cannot deal with it. In any case, just being exposed to it once will not work. It has to be revisited and rethought. It has to 'arrive' – to be put into familiar language or symbols. Teachers need to pitch it at the right level and recognise the barriers to learning that all of us have.

Effectiveness depends on the students' readiness to learn and on the control exercised by the teacher, who must manage pace and volume and the form in which the information is acquired. It must match the students' readiness and receptivity.

It is easier for learners if the structure is clear, and if it leads them through identifying questions which build one from another, even if they are presented in the form of statements of key-words only. This will ensure alerting of the brain to deal with the information and assist processing.

CLOSED AND OPEN QUESTIONS

Closed questions assume the 'right' answer exists. They can often be answered yes or no. Many tests are of this kind: true/false, objective tests, computations and so on. Much of education seems to be about closed questions. Teachers often have a preference for them in many of their classroom interactions.

As an alerting exercise a closed question can be successful. But to be effective as a technique the teacher must name students who are to answer. General questions addressed to the whole group are ineffective in alerting all students, since most will leave it to clever-clogs to answer. It is realised that this is teacher's game: I don't want to play at guessing teacher's right answer. Why don't you just tell us, sir?

The teacher is not looking for competing answers, nor even for students to reframe the information into their own words. This last is vitally important and questioning can be used effectively to promote level 2 activity. The questions may still be closed. But if students are to achieve level 3 or 4, they need open questions that stimulate them to think.

Inductive methodology is the use of open questions.

EXAMPLE 3

A television programme on teaching methods showed a teacher using an inductive approach. A military sergeant was teaching cadets in a very crowded classroom. He asked questions in order to elicit a structure of ideas that could be used to formulate a problem.

He asked a series of questions. After each one, he walked halfway down the class and took the answer from one particular cadet. He then returned to the chalkboard and put up the answer. At the end, he produced an OHP transparency with the same answers ready in the same structure but neatly presented. It was rather like a committee meeting in which the chairman arrives with the minutes already typed out in his pocket.

Clearly, this was not inductive methodology. The sergeant knew which cadet would give him 'teacher's right answer'. No other answers were sought or taken, although many cadets offered. In particular, he ignored the only three girls in the class, who had sat at the front eager to learn. He walked past them every time, perhaps deliberately. It seemed the last thing he wanted was competing answers. It was a good example of closed questions.

Open questions receive unpredictable answers: 'messing about here for a bit to see what we can discover'. Indeed, their purpose is not to elicit answers at all, but to generate increasingly searching questions. Open questions are about an attitude of mind, stimulating natural curiosity to explore and find out.

They also involve openly valuing each student's answer, however improbable it might be. It is very easy to demotivate students from even trying to find answers or generate ideas. Most can experience damage to their self-esteem if they find themselves competing with others in discovery learning. The most successful approach is usually to set students up in groups to explore problems and ideas. They feel less exposed and can give mutual support.

A great deal of wasted effort is also caused by asking questions which are of the wrong kind, looking for unhelpful answers. First find the right questions and validate them to make sure they alert the students to useful activity, and they will look in the right sort of places.

Structured questions that define a linking path are better than a series of unconnected general questions, at least until students have sufficient experience to structure their own paths. But the students may still arrive at the 'wrong' answers or go off in the wrong direction. A teacher using inductive methods has to decide when to intervene, certainly if discovery learning is intended. Unlearning is much harder than learning, so students need to get it right first time. There is frustration in letting them get into a mess with it, nor should they be trying to reinvent the wheel.

The appropriateness or otherwise of discovery needs appraising. Again, it is a matter of clearly formulating what has to be done and controlling the learning activity through structure. The main purpose may be to promote group bonding rather than what they in fact discover for themselves.

ACTIVITY 15 | Your use of questions

Look at your use of questions. What level are they operating at? What level of mental activity do they demand of students? The following is intended to guide your thinking.

1 Clearly, it is important the students are awake to what is happening here and now. They need to develop the skills to see and to hear, and to deal with new information properly. Think, for example, of an experiment in science: the student needs to record accurately what happens. This is only the first level of questioning, however, and many fail even to achieve that satisfactorily.
2 It is essential they also achieve level 2, and they need questions that have been shaped to enable them to do it. We can see this as consolidation of the learning.
3 Reflection on the learning promotes thinking at level 3. Students need to be given activities that ensure processing, linking new knowledge into a properly structured whole so as to gain a proper understanding and insight. Questions that promote activity at this level are more searching.

4 Problem-solving involves also having a clear mental picture of the problem to be solved. We should not assume that most people can visualise problems, make mental models. In fact many find it almost impossible to do that. But tackling a problem may accelerate learning dramatically. Teachers can help students to frame the problem in a tractable way. This means also shaping the questions into helpful form.

Now look carefully at your use of closed and open questions.
   How do you handle class interactions using questions? Have you thought carefully about why you do what you do?
   When you use closed questions (all teachers do, frequently), what techniques do you use to ensure that they alert all the students?
   How far would the use of open questions work with your class? If you used them, what would you need to do to ensure students found them helpful rather than disruptive?

Language barriers

The cartoons in Figure 7 are taken from a refreshingly different way of helping adults to come to terms with Chinese characters. One way of trying to learn is by association of ideas. Most memory training sets great store by such techniques, which work better if they are amusing.

When a native speaker, Chinese or Japanese, reads the characters he or she not only turns them into words and sentences, but also takes the meaning that has accumulated around the symbol as part of the total meaning of the passage. Robert Graves said the poet should strive after compressed yet powerful expression. He might have approved of kanji (as the Japanese call them).

Japanese do seem to think and talk in poetry rather than prose. They often draw kanji on their hands when talking too, showing that the visual form is intimately bound up with meaning.

But all language works like this. Practically all our words have accumulated a depth of reference and meaning quite separate from their use in linear thinking and prose, with different meanings in different contexts. It is better to think of words as having uses rather than meanings as they are full of value concepts.

It is easy to fail to understand someone if their words, though familiar, carry all sorts of implications, references to values and expectations that are different from ours. We are not 'coming from the same place'.

ACTIVITY 16   Your words

Look carefully at the words you use in your teaching.
   How many of them are jargon words, part of your specialism? How do you ensure the students understand and are comfortable in using these jargon words? How much is still a foreign language to them?

Fig. 7   Fun with Chinese characters (T. H. Peng, Straits Times Collection, Federal Publications, Singapore, 1980)

How far are you aware of your use of language? When you talk, do you consciously choose words so as to ensure the students share a common level of understanding with you, and among themselves?

In your handout material and teaching aids, do you look at words and symbols carefully to ensure they are clear, unambiguous and within the comprehension of your students?

How complex do you make your sentences? Can students follow you?

23 Assessment and Testing

In Part 1, you were introduced to basic principles and practice in feedback and assessment within the learning process. A great deal of time and money is spent on education assessment, because education is a very expensive and important activity in all societies – more costly than almost anything else. It is felt that control of assessment is the most effective way of controlling the system, so that it will achieve the outcomes government, employers and society generally believe it is set up to deliver.

The expected outcomes of education change with time. So do the preferred ways of assessing learning outcomes to certificate achievement. One result is that assessing is big business. It is confused also by political pressures. Teachers in the United Kingdom will hardly need reminding of the constant large-scale revision of assessment processes in all levels and areas of education.

There is similarity in the approach taken to assessment by the National Curriculum Council and the Schools Examination and Assessment Council, and by the GCSE boards (and BTEC), but it stands in contrast to that required by the National Council for Vocational Qualifications. In the former, the emphasis has moved from outcomes to process; in the latter, from process to outcomes. (You might find it helpful to contact such organisations to obtain details of their assessment policy and any handbooks or guidance materials they make available.)

Both are important. In Part 1, I put heavy emphasis on feedback within the learning process. But we cannot ignore what students are setting out to achieve as outcomes of the process. What must be resisted is setting up assessment procedures that distort the process for the sake of the assessment.

Appraisal

The terms appraisal, evaluation and assessment are often used to describe the same activity, especially if prefixed by 'self-'.

To appraise is defined as 'to establish the provenance and set a value on a thing', such as a Georgian silver salver. An expert looks to see its age, its silver content, where it was made and by whom, what condition it is in, what is its quality or workmanship, rarity and so on. He or she compares it with other known items and estimates a price. This may be tested at auction.

Appraisal has two elements: establishing the facts and estimating value. How much is fact and how much expert opinion varies from one context to another – and we can ask for a second opinion. We have to trust the experts. It is not unusual for an appraisal to tell us more about the expert than about what is being appraised.

Companies and institutions appraise the needs of their staff with the needs of the company in mind. There may be judgements about competency and needs for training, potential for promotion, where in the organisation individuals can best be used and how they are to be prepared for their roles. All this is about the future. The evidence, of course, is in the past. The anxiety for many is how far they can trust the experts, or the objectivity of it all. It is necessary that individuals are involved in appraising their own needs in negotiation with department heads or others. So we must involve our students in self-appraisal, sharing with us the evidence and the decisions when we are trying to design learning programmes to meet their needs. We can only evaluate process and outcomes if we know what we were setting out to achieve.

It could help if we limited the meaning of appraisal to *what occurs before doing something*. It is part of the setting-up process. It is a common enough activity, but we tend to do it sub-consciously.

Every task we undertake requires appraisal: otherwise, how shall we know what it is and how to set about it? How can we tackle it if we do not know what it is? How shall we cost it?

Everyone does that, surely. You can't make a dress without first deciding just what dress you are going to make. Nor a cake, nor a go-cart. Yet there are teachers who regularly set out to teach courses of which they have no over-view:

what kind of thing it is, what it is for and so on. How can they hope to set it up as an effective course or evaluate it?

Evaluation

This can be a highly complex or a fairly straightforward activity. The Open University has published many models of evaluation. The range is wide: from comparing starting conditions with outcomes to see what has changed (and ignoring everything in between – the process) to 'goal-free' evaluation which tends to look only at the process and what happens (and to ignore intentions and goals).

It helps to see the activity properly linked to the appraisal. If we know where we are going and how we intend to get there, we can match our expectations against what actually happened. We may then learn how to do it better next time. We also learn what we have not achieved and what is still to do: a new appraisal.

But first we must be sure of the facts – be able to demonstrate to someone else the evidence for what we say has occurred. This does not mean that the evidence is about only those things that we can measure. The most important changes in learning are the least easy to measure, and are therefore sometimes ignored in assessment and evaluation.

REMEMBER!
. . . To be systematic: state the facts with the evidence
state the judgements made (with the criteria).
Emphasis will then be placed on the nature of the evidence.

Evaluation must involve matching of outcomes with intentions as set up in the appraisal. To ignore goals and intentions is to pretend that the activity is purposeless. The satisfaction for teachers and students depends on the matching achieved. But we also need to perceive clearly what happened and why (the process), if we are to learn from the evaluation. The purpose of evaluating must be the improvement of what we do.

The next class I run, or the next course, or the next cake I bake will benefit from the experience I have gained. But it will do so only if I reflect properly on what happened, and in some way focus it to learn from it. It will be much easier to do, too, if I share my perception of it with someone else who will have a different perspective – to help establish the facts at least. For maximum benefit and effect, *everything* should be evaluated.

When evaluation happens also matters. If we are too close to something we cannot see it. We need distance. But since the purpose of doing an evaluation is to make decisions about what we do 'now' (or next time), we must evaluate before we set off again.

Assessment

The evidence used in evaluation may include measurements of learning achievement. To do that we must have reliable and valid methods of assessment.

WHAT CAN WE MEASURE?

It is confusing to try to measure a large number of variables all at once. Science has made advances by discriminating carefully the variables that are to be observed and measured. Accuracy may be determined by the degree of separation: the discrimination. But discrimination in assessment is used to mean the ability to separate scores on tests, although it clearly has more important uses.

Most teachers, and society generally, are content with relatively blunt measures of achievement which do not differentiate the many kinds of behavioural change that they might be measuring. Behaviour is observable as a whole, not as bits.

We must also be clear about *why* we are assessing. There are normally two reasons: first, to check on the progress and effectiveness of the learning; second, in order to report at a particular stage of development.

Formative assessment is assessment that is being used to check progress, to ensure that the objectives are being achieved. You will need to use formative assessment frequently, either formally or informally, to make sure that your students are progressing and that such progress is towards the aims of the learning programme.

Summative assessment, on the other hand, is used to check if particular aims have been achieved. The aims may be for a course or an award where certain standards or criteria have to be achieved before success can be recorded. For example, the National Council for Vocational Qualifications accredited awards are dependent upon summative assessment made against clearly identified standards and performance criteria.

Some things are relatively easy to measure and to record as a score: accurate recall of information, simple skills, ability to solve puzzles where the 'right' answer is not in dispute. The more unambiguous a learned behaviour is, objective in the sense of being independent of someone's judgement, the easier it is to assess. The reverse is also true. Recall is more easily tested than are imagination and creativity, responses to which are by their nature subjective and therefore imprecise.

Yet sophisticated measuring devices are available, at a price, to measure more tenuous things: levels of introversion and extroversion, and anxiety states. If something is observable, it should be measurable. Orthodoxy says, 'Attitudes and values, although clearly exhibited in changes in behaviour, are not measurable and should be ignored for assessment purposes.' That is, you can only test 'can do' not 'will do'. But 'will do' is fundamentally important.

It turns out that it is not usually the measuring that is hard so much as the interpretation of the results of assessment. Can we rely on the judgements made when they are subjective?

CHOICE OF METHOD

Reliance on one form of assessment only is now a thing of the past. Now alternative strategies for assessment using a range of methods have emerged. This range includes the essay paper, but increasingly objective and short-answer tests are used with other measuring devices as continuous assessment within programmes. End-of-course examining is replaced by regular assessments to provide feedback as well as cumulative scores. The assessment is intended to match the learning, if not to be integrated with it in tasks.

Most schemes now recognise the need to integrate assessment into the learning process. The two processes are perceived as the same but viewed for different purposes. Large-scale coursework takes the form of projects and tasks that encompass and integrate many elements of learning using common criteria for success. They will provide not only the measure of success but also the evidence.

HIERARCHY OF ASSESSMENT

A typical assessment hierarchy is shown below.

Level A	Level B	Level C
Knowledge/recall; accuracy/breadth	Understanding/application to new context/situation	Analysing/synthesising; restructuring information; tackling questions and problem-solving
Skill rehearsal; competence at a routine level	Applying skills to new contexts and challenges	Creative/inventive use of skills; interpretation/ 'style'; craftsmanship
Weight 20%	Weight (20% =) 40%	Weight (60% =) 100%

In this hierarchy B includes A: C includes A and B – makes 100%

WEIGHTING

Weighting in assessment – whatever methods are used – means the adjustment of scores when the results are processed so that a specified balance is achieved between various elements. It is better if the assessments are designed already weighted. Weighting is nothing to do with the proportions of time allocated to elements of the course.

In learning programmes, valid assessment is most easily achieved by designing tasks that make specific demands of students: this means that the tasks themselves measure the students' ability to achieve the behaviour they set out to learn. The weighting above is intended to affect design of the tasks required of teachers as well as the balance overall in assessing learning.

REMEMBER!

. . . Teaching is about decision-making, managing and problem-solving, among so much else. The behaviour is principally at Level C. In designing tasks and assessment, the above balance is required.

This says nothing about the content of the programme. Textbooks that are entirely 'content' without making demands on students to use the information, however complex their language and style, do not make demands beyond Level A. Frequently, learning of them is tested by simple recall procedures. Students must apply what they learn at Level A to achieve any degree of mastery.

MASTERY

Some assessment programmes use only a sample of the standards and performance criteria, selected without the prior knowledge of the student. Programmes like these have obvious advantages in terms of cost and time, but they do not assess mastery. Mastery requires that *all* the standards and performance are achieved, and all must therefore be assessed.

Performance criteria can identify directions of travel, as well as 'final' targets. Achievement of mastery that satisfies the criteria at one level can therefore be the starting-point for more demanding challenges, tougher criteria.

Good practice demands that tasks are repeated so that mastery is redefined. A young pianist may perform a Beethoven sonata and play very well for a student, but the student who turns professional is likely to play the sonata many times. Audiences will now demand much more in technique, musical insight and a thrill in performance. The pianist will not be satisfied with any performance; there is always something to improve: new insight, nuance, phrasing. We must constantly apply more testing criteria to our own 'performances' as we work and learn with our students.

RELIABILITY AND VALIDITY

'To assess' means to sit beside a judge, giving expert advice. It came to be used in the context of taxation because tax collectors sat physically in judgement on those they taxed. The term 'assessor' is used too of an expert who estimates, say, the cost of repairing a car. We know (or believe) we can rely on the personal judgement of an assessor to calculate costs for a crime, a property, an income, a repair. Judgement relates to calculation, measurement and fairness.

The judgements are expected also to be consistent between cases. In educational assessment, consistency and fairness in relation to measurement of learning (change or achievement) are important. Assessors are concerned with interpreting standards and with ensuring comparability between measurements of achievement.

Everyone involved in assessment must be concerned with reliability and validity, but these obviously have a special importance for examining boards.

- **Reliability** requires that the same candidate would score the same on a test if he took it on another occasion. It may sound silly, but we must assume that two candidates are the same person if we are to rely on the scores they both achieve. Reliability is enhanced by careful and skilful selection of appropriate assessment methods and test construction, as well as the avoidance of bias through the use of inappropriate language.
- **Validity** requires that the assessment measures what it sets out to measure and not something else. This is most important but hard to achieve. How do we know what a method of assessment is measuring? It depends on our ability to identify all the possible variables it could measure, and to distinguish the particular ones we wish to assess. We then have to devise an appropriate way of focusing the assessment to achieve that.

    There may be a mismatch between the stated learning goals for the programme and the learning the test implicitly seems to be testing. An essay test clearly tests the ability to write essays, but is that what students set out to learn? or did they and the teacher perceive quite a different goal? to become skilful, competent teachers, perhaps.

Of course, in the real world teachers assess a whole bundle of learning behaviours together. And reasonably so, since learning is as a whole and hardly ever in identifiable bits. But there are gross mismatches which we should avoid. How far can skills be tested using objective answer tests or essay questions? What in fact are these testing apart from the ability to do the test?

Assessment is an attempt to measure change or achievement. There should be a clear understanding of what is being measured. The students also need to know why and how fair it will be. Who is it for? Is it to help them learn and progress, or to ensure that there is a record of their achievement? Who wants the record?

We need some indication of the degree of precision that is hoped for. The tendency is often to value more highly the assessments that quantify results, present results in terms of numbers. There is scepticism about the objectivity of qualitative judgements, even if criteria are clearly spelled out. The elimination of the examiner's subjectivity is seen as a proper goal.

SUBJECTIVITY AND CRITERIA

Many examinations used to be norm-referenced (and some still are): that is, the achievement of an individual is measured by its relationship to what is achieved by others taking the same (or notionally the same) assessment.

Criterion-referenced assessment avoids the problems of norm-referenced assessment. It is intended to give learners a clear view of what each personally has to achieve. Feedback is possible when a learner attempts to demonstrate achievement.

Important is the concept of 'the public domain': 'show the dog the rabbit,' as I have heard it described. We all have criteria by which we judge things, even if we do not consciously know what they are. They are usually vague and imprecise. Students should of course know what are the teacher's criteria by which their work is being judged: the teacher should tell them, and before they do it. If the teacher does not know what they are, he or she needs to clarify them, in everyone's interests. It is unreasonable that students should discover what they are only after they fail to achieve them.

This led some educators to wish to be over-precise about criteria, and it was fashionable to state them as behavioural objectives:

'The carpenter will join two pieces of [specify wood, size, state of preparation, etc.] with dovetail joints. They will use [specify tools] within [time constraints]. Joints will [specify standard and conditions].'

Most behavioural objectives turned out to be less specific. But it was felt they had to be precise enough to eliminate subjective judgement: 'either they did it or they didn't.' The learning and the assessment were to be the same activity. Failure to meet the criteria indicated that the learning was incomplete and needed redoing in some way to be demonstrated again later.

When this was constructed into linear learning programmes, it was felt that if students failed to achieve the criteria it must be the programme that was failing and not the students: learning was to be shaped carefully in predictable and controllable ways.

This focuses on the learning programmes of individuals. Learners can all achieve mastery. The learning proceeds at the pace of individuals. Learning is broken down into small units, and there is immediate feedback of success or failure. Subjectivity is gone. The record of achievement accumulates with achievement of units.

Unfortunately, the process of assessment can then be so cumbersome that it dominates the whole programme. Everything is done for a test to demonstrate criteria. It is one-to-one too: expensive and time-consuming. In fact it relies heavily on the judgement of the assessor who is observing the performance. The elimination of subjectivity depends on precise and clear criteria, well-constructed assessment instruments and recording systems and careful training of the assessor.

It is clear that there must be opportunities for students to show their thinking, even if only to ensure that they can transfer skills they have achieved into different contexts. 'Can do' does require 'doing it intelligently'. The emphasis has now changed to be more concerned with design and thinking, even working in teams, although the 'can do' will still be matched against criteria. It is an important part of the assessment programme to supplement the observation of performance with supporting evidence. This evidence can be obtained by asking questions during the activity or afterwards, either in a written format or orally.

PERFORMANCE CRITERIA

Behaviourist views of achievement require observable behaviour that you can match against standards. Thus, of course, the assessor must be well trained and well briefed. Measurement involves judgement by a subjective judge, perhaps using rating scales. Feedback to the learners indicates where they failed to measure up.

Moderation of such assessment and training of assessors can be hard and costly: reliability is expensive to achieve. The important question is: would another assessor, watching the same performance, make the same judgement?

To differentiate between technical skill and 'doing it intelligently' is also difficult, a matter of judgement. Level A is simpler to observe and measure than Level B: and what of Level C?

In Skinner's behaviourist conditioning teachers impose standards of behaviour on learners, making judgements in order to reinforce desired behaviour. It is no longer a matter of 'doing it'. We have to know how it approximates to expectations of the teacher. But it is the teacher who does the thinking and makes decisions.

If we complicate matters by requiring 'intelligence in the behaviour', rather than conditioned behaviour, we have to find out what the learners know and the decisions they make and why they make them. We have to ask them to tell us, somehow. What criteria then can we impose on this activity? In setting up projects that involve design as well as doing, it is important to be clear what will be expected of students in relation to demonstrating their thinking, and what weight will be attached to that in assessment.

In earlier competence assessment programmes, knowledge was assumed and not tested. It is normal now to test underpinning knowledge and understanding. This, however, is not the same as requiring the demonstration of decision-making and thinking, or the grasp of principles. Most behavioural change does depend on understanding and insight.

It also depends critically on attitude. There is little argument that 'can do' is not the same as 'will do'. Someone may be the finest pianist or surgeon in the world, but what if he or she does not turn up in a theatre to perform, or is unreliable? And what of a nurse, a secretary, an engineer, a teacher? Can we really ignore such things as commitment, confidence, motivation? or the important personality characteristics or the ability to work in teams and organisations with others?

It is all too easy to ignore these aspects in assessment and design. If a learner does it, we should assume these things are happening, since they are necessary for the performance to happen at all.

Maybe they cannot be measured as we attempt to measure cognitive and behavioural change, but they cannot be ignored. If accident statistics remain at a constant level when all sorts of preventative safety measures are introduced (seat-belts, widening of roads and so on), it may be because we are changing perception of danger. There is compensating behaviour: children in adventure play parks, operators of machines, drivers of cars. We need arousal and risk – and excitement, challenge, fun, fulfilment.

Aspects of competence have to be grouped into 'whole behaviour patterns'. It is not possible to achieve individual criteria in a vacuum: they only make any sense together in a context. The criteria must be shared, and everyone must know what they are. And if we are to attempt to observe variables, all the changes in behaviour that make up the competence and the learning, we do need to differentiate somehow what we are trying to observe.

It is common to see competence as operating at a margin between 'can do/cannot do'. For this reason criteria are often set out as lists of tasks. But criteria need not define pass/fail only. Unless they are written as behavioural objectives with specific statements of standards and conditions, they need interpretation by learners and assessors. They act as signposts and directions and can be reinterpreted against tougher standards according to the need, level of responsibility and context of the learning.

PROFILES AND RECORDS OF ACHIEVEMENT

The outcomes of assessment will be recorded, not just as simple registers of criteria which have been knocked down like coconuts in a shy, but as a cumulative portfolio of evidence to support the judgements about maturation and performance that have been made. The whole will be linked by some agreed profiling system.

Much discussion of assessment argues its effectiveness in promoting motivation. Students have to take responsibility for their own learning. They must become self-motivating and self-assessing – but are unlikely to do so if the teacher keeps total control of the assessment process, and indeed of the learning process. After all, the taking of responsibility through self-assessment is the reason for stating performance criteria. Competence programmes assume students will invite assessors to become part of the assessment process when they feel ready, on their terms.

It is the intention to free assessment and certification from the constraints of course programming/time schedules that suit needs of institutions rather than learners. This implies a contract between assessor and learner and others involved, such as employers – a shared responsibility. Hence the importance of agreeing goals, processes and criteria is obvious, as is agreement about what the nature of the evidence will be.

Records of achievement are now standard practice. These profile the achievement, and the better ones also monitor change and predict for the future. Their purpose in the end is to state what this person has done, in what context and with what level of skill and insight, in part to predict what he or she will do in other contexts.

The evidence ought to be available if required: the portfolio the learner has built up of completed tasks and assignments, and all the learning materials and so forth, with assessments made. These provide an over-view of the learning journey completed so far.

Using tests

All teachers require skill and understanding in using techniques for assessing learning achievement and outcomes. Tests usually form important elements of assessment procedures. There are some programmes where tests may represent almost all the evidence of learning achievement. But testing and assessing are not the same: it is possible to assess every aspect of learning in numerous ways, as we have seen, while the purpose of tests is to sample the learning.

Using tests is a complex subject with a large literature of its own, and in this book I can provide only minimal guidance. My purpose here is to indicate a range of procedures that new teachers may find helpful in promoting student learning. Many will find themselves preparing students for tests and examinations set by external bodies, however, or required to produce gradings by the use of internal testing procedures. Should you be in this position, refer to some of the texts identified at the end of this chapter.

Success in external tests depends on 'question-spotting', and on knowing exactly what examiners are looking for. Teachers and learners may try to out-guess the examiners in an elaborate game. Experience counts highly. New teachers must look for advice and help from experienced colleagues in this.

When tests are constructed and administered internally, teachers know what is to be sampled, select accordingly and prepare their students for them. Assessment then drives the learning. It may have beneficial effects or it may not: what matters will be the effect on the learning curves of students. Students need an awareness of their own learning curves, and should be shown how to construct them for themselves. But we are only looking for trends. Where the curve proves very flat or falls rather than rises, they need to take positive action.

RATIONALE

As tests consume time and effort, their relationship to learning has to show cost-benefit. Address questions such as these:

- How much time and effort will it cost? Is it worth that?
- What do I want to know? Why do I want to know that?
- How much information do I need? In what form must it be?
- What alternative ways could I use to get it? Which is best?
- What am I going to do with the information once I've got it?
- Who is it for? Why do they need it? In what form?

Testing is rather like plotting points on a graph, or taking snapshots at moments in time along the learning process. We can distinguish between activities that are separate from the learning, imposed on it to measure some aspect of it, and activities that promote the learning and which also provide feedback.

Tests will be more valuable if they feed back into the learning process. Generally, tests are imposed on the process, and are often used only as end-points. They can be used even more positively to find out where you and your students are starting from: a numeracy test, for example, may be the quickest way of finding out your baseline. You can save a great deal of time in the design of your programme if you have an accurate picture of what your students already know.

The best test is short, focused sharply on specifics, easy to administer and simple to mark. It provides quickly accessible information that can be of use. Elaborate tests take a great deal of time to prepare, administer and mark. By the time any information is available the point of need is past.

The advantage of a properly constructed test is that it can provide a considerable amount of information quickly. Students may, however, see it as an end in itself. They need to be clear how the test relates to agreed learning goals: the process by which they are achieved, and the recording of that achievement. Tests can be very positive, planned as part of the learning process to try to focus the learning by revisiting it. Testing can act to reinforce learning. Many students learn better with such external motivation.

And what if students fail a test? 'You had your chance and you blew it,' is something I have not infrequently heard said to students. Will you merely record a failure and move on, or is it your intention that the learning programme will be renegotiated to ensure that they eventually achieve mastery?

STRATEGY

A decision has to made as to whether students will know about the test, and what kind of information to give them, in order to prepare for it. Springing an occasional test on them may be a useful strategy to keep them up to the mark. It does not always pay off. You may intend to ensure there is consistent effort, rather than simply to test. It may be part of a bigger strategy intended to stimulate them. If it is the only weapon in your armoury it will fail.

Preparing for tests has a short-term effect on learning. Activity will usually increase but fall back sharply after the test. Again testing has to be part of a bigger strategy related to motivation and excitement in learning. Otherwise, learning will be in spurts and rests. In the end you and they must know what part tests play in your overall learning/teaching strategy.

The frequency of testing (or its absence) may determine students' views of the shape and purpose of the programme. If learning is seen to be only for the purpose of testing (as in many British, American and Japanese programmes), the energy disappears. Variation in the use of testing, both in frequency and method, is absolutely essential if tests are to be used effectively. Repetitive patterns ('tell and test') produce wave-like learning curves, while overall the curve remains quite flat. A steadily rising curve or one that leaps with insight is what you need to aim for. Occasional testing may help.

Testing can disrupt the learning process. From a student's point of view, so much effort will be expended in getting geared up for the test that it will be difficult to concentrate after it. Frequently a 'relaxation time' is allowed. This must be costed. Teachers must mark and process tests. Simple tests may be quick; complex tests can take ages. It has to be worth it. And students need to know quickly how they did and what is to happen next.

VALIDATION

All tests need validation: their validity and their content validity have to be established. The students and you need to know that it is fair, tests what it sets out to test, and tests what they set out to learn – not something else. One problem with external tests is that frequently students meet questions, sometimes substantial parts of the test, they have not met before or attempted to learn, although they and the teacher might have done so had they known about it.

Tests are always time-based, so using time effectively is part of the skill. This is true of all testing, of course, and cannot be taken for granted. Students need training in skills required to deal well with tests as with anything else: otherwise they may be tested for the lack of these skills rather than lack of understanding or skill in what the test purports to be about. Performance on a test can be significantly improved simply by practising technique for dealing with the test, as the growth of cramming schools has indicated. A great deal of class-time may also be given over to preparing for external tests. The effect of this on a learning programme has to be evaluated.

People do badly in tests for many reasons: 'nerves', inability to comprehend the questions, failing to read the rubric and so on. Unfamiliarity with the style of the test can also be a handicap: candidates may totally misunderstand what is wanted.

Results of tests can be so important to students and their overall certification that teachers must ensure that candidates do not present a false set of results for any of these reasons.

METHODS OF TESTING

My purpose in identifying a brief list of testing methods is not to suggest that these are to be preferred to others. The essay test, for example, has been used effectively in the appropriate context for very many years. Some examining boards have designed the most elaborate testing schedules for some competence programmes, in particular those in which a partnership is agreed between some assessing/tutoring institution and employers, and the guidance on these tests is published by these boards.

The survey below is of necessity brief, intended to suggest paths to explore. The teacher must learn how to use such techniques by using them, preferably in co-operation with colleagues.

SHORT-ANSWER TESTS

Many techniques of testing have been invented to reduce the time and cost. The purpose of short-answer tests is exactly that. It is quite easy to write and administer them. They are not so easy to validate, however, and they may not prove to be very reliable. One argument for testing relates to syllabus coverage and 'sampling'. A syllabus content is often huge. A final exam, especially an essay-style test, can only sample a tiny part of the learning and may, as we have seen, seriously disadvantage many of the students.

Short-answer tests can cover a great deal more ground, and this is their main use. Such tests are looking for recall and breadth, not depth: Level A with the possibility of Level B, but very unlikely to be Level C. Essays are about depth and will test Level C thinking at least.

Short-answer tests can consolidate learning at Level A. They can identify the misunderstanding or misinterpretation of input and provide feedback, and they can spot a tendency to divergent thinking and behaviour.

To be used well, they need to be sparing and infrequent, and you must be specific about what you wish to discover. Have your questions vetted by a colleague for clarity or ambiguity, and appropriateness to the learning: your validator may show you alternatives you had not thought about.

Such tests are not objective. The students have to be able to express what they think and/or know in writing, and to interpret the questions correctly. Teachers have to interpret answers and respond. This is all highly subjective, but within the context it is a straightforward and uncomplicated business. These tests may not be very reliable as measures of learning without other evidence, however.

OBJECTIVE TESTS

Objectivity in testing depends on the kind of judgements required of the student in responding, and of the teacher in marking the test. Where the correct response requires no judgement on the part of the marker, it is objective. For example, the student may be required to enter correctly words spoken by the teacher as an aural test. Or a response sheet may have gaps in a text, which are numbered so as to relate to lists of possible responses for each gap, and students may be required to select the correct response from each list – a form of multi-choice objective testing. Responses need validation: all should be plausible but only one should be undoubtedly correct. Marking is simple and numeric.

The test can be made valid and reliable because it focuses quite sharply on specific learning: in the first example aural comprehension, while a test involving knowledge of verb forms is described below. Such tests can test a wide range of learning in most subject areas, but mainly at Level A (recall) or Level B (application of rules) where little complexity is involved. It is difficult to design such tests to measure the acquisition of skill.

In languages, for example, the knowledge and application of rules or verb forms is enabling learning: without such knowledge a person cannot use a language correctly (and it must be firmly established), but the ability to use the language effectively in a given context requires the development of a range of other skills and attitudes, which can only be measured validly through observing their use in such a context.

Some objective or quasi-objective testing is straightforward to produce and is effective in giving rapid feedback to teacher and student on specific learning. The gapped handout is an example; this requires students to fill gaps with correct responses. An illustration in language learning:

'From his bedroom window, he (1   ) the man (2   ) the street. The man (3   ) to be old because his back was (4   ) and he (5   ) with the aid of a stick.'

Such material may be used in numerous ways. It is possible to allow students more or less scope for invention. Since the test above is of verb forms, the rubric may require the student to put a verb supplied in simple form into the correct form for a place in the sentence: 'see' as 'saw' for number 1. Or the student may be allowed to choose any appropriate verb. Or, in a more complex test, to control to some extent the content. Where a student has to write something, or perhaps to draw a diagram, to fill the gap, the teacher will have to make judgements about the respones. The test is quasi-objective, the degree of objectivity depending on the freedom of invention allowed.

The marking scheme must identify what exactly the test is testing in order to be valid, since giving marks for inventiveness indicates that that is part of the target learning. Students are surprisingly inventive even with what appear to be straightforward tests, and teachers often have to make judgements about allowing an answer.

The usefulness of the testing of this kind is that it is simple to do. Producing the test does not require special skills, but it does need carefully thinking through in relation to its validity – what exactly is being tested. It is quick to mark – it may be done by the students themselves where there are 'correct' responses – and provides rapid feedback. Used as the main or indeed the only form of assessment, however, such tests may have the unfortunate effect of closing down creativity, unless they are specifically designed to encourage it: learning appears to be about 'right' answers.

Multi-choice objective tests of the kind used by examining boards are best left to experts to compile. Few people have the skills to write them. Items have to be edited for content validity, and edited again, using statistics after trial, to ensure ambiguity is eliminated. Banks of items have to be of sufficient size (which may take years) to ensure that there is coverage of syllabuses using random choice of items.

Compilation and marking of such papers do not involve teachers. To be cost-effective they have to be used with very large numbers of candidates. They are used extensively for testing, but there is not infrequently a mismatch between the nature of the test and the learning it purports to be testing.

Those in common use (and there are many) present a choice of answers, in one form or another. The stimulus or stem may be in words, diagrams or symbols (in maths, for example). A candidate has to choose, usually in such a way that the paper can be marked by a scanner attached to a computer. This allows rapid processing of results. More sophisticated testing programmes allow for some feedback to students and teachers of the results of the test.

Items can be made highly reliable, as ambiguity is erased. There must be an unequivocally 'right' answer, and alternative answers that are plausible but definitely wrong. This removes all possible challenge. Their main use is coverage of syllabus content recall at Level A. In this they can be very effective. It is possible to devise such tests to operate at Level B, but these are more complex to interpret.

ORAL/AURAL TESTS

Ninety per cent of what people do is oral/aural behaviour. We should really put more emphasis on their doing it well, but there has been a reluctance to use oral tests. They are difficult to validate and highly subjective, so unreliable. Aural tests of listening skills are used widely in languages and shorthand (for secretaries), however.

Obviously, the improvement of oral/aural skills is contextual and the test should not be different from the learning activity. If learning goals include 'to take down shorthand from dictation' or 'to comprehend a statement accurately' or 'to make a presentation to an audience', then that is what you must test; no other test will do. And it is very important to make sufficient time available for it to happen.

The first two test listening skills and can be done with largish groups; the last is expensive. Normally orals happen one at a time. It may be possible to find ways out of the dilemma. You can set up some social situations to involve groups, but of course testing what individuals contribute becomes harder.

Oral testing can be done in less formal ways, too: for example, by asking someone to explain what they are doing while you watch a demonstration of a skill, perhaps as part of the test. This is essential when testing 'ability to do it intelligently'. Reliability is hard to prove.

To use an oral test well, you must structure it carefully. This includes time constraints (and thinking time). How much will the students know beforehand? Will they have to think on their feet? How much can they bring to the test to use? Will they need time to set it up? How will the test be organised? How far will the students be able to control the environment? How will the way people are arranged influence what happens? Is it confrontational? If so, what exactly is being tested?

The students need to know what is being tested. For example, in an oral test in language use, the mark-sheet (and there must be one – available to the students too) might set out a format as follows:

Content	Structure	Vocabulary	Accuracy	Overall impression

Examiners put a 'subjective' grade (A, A−, B+ . . . E) for each element, and a total mark is then arrived at by conversion/addition. The structure also allows for weighting. You might wish to set the weight at, say, 3:2:2:2:1. When the grades are converted to a mark for each element, they are then multiplied by the weighting and a final mark arrived at. In this example, if each grade were to be converted to a mark out of 10 and multiplied by the weighting, the total would be a mark out of 100. This sounds complicated but is in fact very simple to do. It allows not only for more disciplined marking than do simple grades, but also for possibility of proper preparation and feedback.

An alternative approach is to identify 'statements' of criteria that the speaker should achieve and to use these in making judgements about the performance. Any number of such elements may be agreed, but complexity must be avoided. The examiner must spend time listening, not filling in boxes: that comes afterwards. In many such approaches also there is a preference for the use of a rating scale (say from 1 to 6) against each of the identified criteria.

SKILLS TESTS

The greater part of skills testing is as part of the learning. To separate testing from learning is not helpful. But there may be occasions when one could set up a new, unfamiliar challenge against the clock, to test not simply acquisition of the skills but transferability of the learning. The main barrier to skill acquisition is repetitive practice. It is difficult to know if a student is 'thinking' at all – doing anything beyond Level A.

The purpose of a 'set-piece' skills test is to test Level B or Level C behaviour. It is usual to allow a reasonably long time scale to test design skills as well as the product. This makes for a more reliable test of overall achievement. Students might be required, for example, to design and build a simulated plumbing installation using learned knowledge and skills. Or to produce a set of documents, as in Case Study 9 in Part 1 (Karen's typewriting class). Or to produce a meal for four guests.

Each test will be set up with specific constraints. Criteria for success should also be carefully explained and agreed. A marking scheme should be produced, which the students should see and understand.

Learning and testing combine here. It is testing many things and promoting such learning as problem-solving, designing and organising things so that they work. Students can see the point of it all. Teachers can test learning within a context. What is included in the mark-sheet depends on context and purpose.

Designing the test, agreeing criteria and constraints, setting standards: all require time and validation.

PROBLEM-SOLVING TESTS

The kind of test just described is really a problem-solving test. This is higher-level skill and behaviour.

The first requirement is to state the problem in a form in which it can be viewed and tackled systematically. It is not unusual for candidates to leap to a solution without first establishing clearly the facts and the constraints. There are good and bad ways of setting about this activity and students need help to learn the good. To be systematic you have to

- explore
- formulate
- design
- make/do
- evaluate –

the same approach I recommended to you for designing teaching and learning programmes within an overall strategy. Students need to learn to explore alternatives, formulate and structure thoughts and ideas, establish the facts, design and plan – and then tackle the problems of doing it. Evaluation should be where you and they revisit the learning to consolidate it.

Such tests can take a multitude of different forms. But to test learning in any field or discipline at Level C, all testing procedures should include a substantial amount of problem-solving. The British Association for Commercial and Industrial Education (BACIE) publishes a very useful set of management and business games that involve a great deal of highly inventive activity like this.

Problem-solving is the most powerful learning activity. Think again about exploring a new department store. What we are doing is posing questions about how to find what we want and where things are – solving problems puzzling us – and the more clearly we know what we want the better. Sir Karl Popper, in *Objective Knowledge: an Evolutionary Approach* shows that any task must start from a problem: we have to ask why it is a problem, and define it clearly. The degree of success we have in tackling (solving) the problem is determined by how clearly we have perceived and set out that problem. To understand also writers on any scientific or social topic such as education and learning, we need to know what the problem was to which they set out to find a solution: what the questions were that they asked, how they arrived at the answers they proposed. Then we need to evaluate those 'answers'.

Popper argues that evolution is best understood in terms of 'trial solutions' to problems met by creatures in their environment. Each is a tentative adaptation to the world the individual lives in. Animals and plants incorporated these tentative solutions into their anatomy and behaviour forming the bases for later solutions, equally tentative. Theories and ideas develop in the same way. Each starts from what a previous theory proposed and challenges it against evidence and new ways of perceiving what is actually going on. For Popper, achievement in all human affairs happens in the same way: in politics, economics or even art, as well as in science and technology. Progress in every field depends crucially on changes taking place under the impetus of critical evaluation of predictions made by theories as against what actually happens; recent history shows how much more successful dynamic, open societies can be than those in which rulers defend unworkable ideologies.

I have encouraged you throughout this book to set up tentative solutions to the learning problems your students face, and to use evaluation critically as feedback to redefine the problems and look for better, more effective solutions. Your perception of what is actually going on in your environment will have changed through this process. So also will the way you approach your students and your preparation.

Well-designed problem-solving activities are to be found in many new requirements by examining boards. Tests, like every other form of assessment, should feed back into the learning process as part of the critical evaluation that is essential to ensure progression to intended learning goals.

For more detailed information about testing procedures there are many useful texts available. The following are obtainable from City and Guilds (Sales Department, 76 Portland Place, London W1N 4AA):

Assessment Handbooks (priced)
1 *Setting Multiple Choice Tests*
2 *Coursework Assessment*
3 *Setting and Moderating Written Question Papers*
4 *Constructing Practical Tests*
5 *Profiling*
6 *APL Handbook – Guidance on the Accreditation of Prior Learning*
A Glossary of Terms

Guide for Candiates (free) – a practical leaflet providing useful information for candidates preparing to take a City and Guilds assessment.

Part 3

The Theory Behind it All

Introduction: Discoveries in Psychology

When I complained to my Head of Division in a Florida college that the sheer size and volume of the humanities syllabus made it unteachable, he replied, 'It's only a survey.' I think he meant it amounted to a 'naming of parts'. They were to be 'covered' briefly, so as to ensure the students had heard about them. What for? I wondered. Why learn these things unless they are to become significant to you in some way?

What I hope to show in this part of the book is that psychological discovery as it can be applied to learning and teaching is exciting and fascinating. It is not 'out there somewhere', but fundamentally important to what teachers do. Even if I had the space of a large book devoted exclusively to it, I could not cover it. I can only provide a glimpse through chinks in the curtains at some major theories of learning. It is my hope you will want to read more, and use what you find out to try to understand what is happening for your students.

A great deal of what happens, even in good teaching, is intuitive. Teachers learn by trial and error and role-modelling, sometimes by *diktat*. They do not always know why something works, but are glad that it does. They are just too busy to be curious, and do not have the time to stand back and think or to read the educational literature. Nor, in any case, will the reading have value unless they think about it in relation to what they decide to do with their students in their context.

This book started the other way about: to try to develop good practice and test theory in teaching before exploring theories in any depth. The test of a theory is whether it works: does it predict usefully what will happen *here*? It is not enough that it should offer an explanation of what *might* be going on. There could be many other equally valid explanations. The history of education is littered with failed theories, even those that were the result of years and years of research.

The model of teaching/learning set out in Parts 1 and 2 is not invention arising simply from my own experience. There is well-documented research in psychology and practical teaching. I have worked closely with many teachers of adults also in many contexts, and I have benefited from their knowledge and experience. It is usual in academic texts to direct the reader through use of footnotes and references to sources for statements and assertions made. I have resisted doing that, as I do not find such texts helpful.

The literature on learning and teaching is vast, however. I have attempted below to direct your attention to those beliefs and thinkers I believe have had an important influence on what has happened: to try to show the sources of the ideas and practice exhibited in the model in this book. Moreover, academic books present a dispassionate, non-advocative description of learning theorists. This survey is intended to go beyond that: there is a thread of argument. Selection and therefore distortion are inevitable. I urge you, where you can, to read original texts for comparison. The 'Suggestions for Further Reading' at the end are intended as a guide, not a comprehensive list.

24 Behaviourism

In the 1900s, psychology was dominated by the school of behaviourism, under the leadership of John B. Watson. The school was inspired by brilliant results in animal psychology achieved by Morgan and Thorndike. Human beings, Watson declared, should be studied like any other animals. 'Behaviour' should be observed like the phenomena in all other natural sciences.

No behaviourist, Watson declared, has observed anything that can be called consciousness, sensation, perception, imagery or will. All such terms are unusable in descriptions of human activity. This assertion was held to be true and self-evident. Experiments were to be confined to objective observations of the results of stimulus and response.

Decision-making was effectively ignored, as was 'thinking it through'. These are mentalistic terms which some examiners still think you cannot test and therefore for the sake of objectivity must ignore. For the same reasons 'goal-seeking', 'the will' and other attitudinal terms cannot be part of the examination/criterion-referencing system, although they were to be accepted by some behaviourists, such as Tolman, as important. Why such puritanism? particularly since they seem to exclude intelligence in the behaviour we are trying to assess (and improve?).

Mental 'representation' or 'conjectural modelling' of the world is an idea the early twentieth-century psychologists tried to eliminate in the effort to give their discipline the appearance of an objective science. 'Any reference to consciousness was carefully excluded for fear it would introduce the scientifically unmanageable idea of a causal principle that was not immediately accessible to public observation' (George Miller in *States of Mind: Conversations with Psychological Investigators*).

The behaviourists developed a programme of research based on the assumption that behaviour of all kinds could be explained in terms of the measurable stimuli impinging on the sense organs and the nerves which controlled the muscles. Stimulus–response bonds most often quoted are reflexes such as the knee-jerk, and the reaction of the iris of the eye to light. There is a stimulus, light, and an immediate unlearned response of the iris muscles. The important thing is that it does not have to be learned.

It is obvious that most behaviour, in all plants and animals, essential for dealing with the world is of this kind. A baby is born with peristalsis in its digestive tract, for example. Without conscious control, it pumps blood around its body and constantly produces the thousands of proteins necessary to its functioning as an organism.

What then is learning? What is it necessary to learn? How is it learned? How does it become embedded so that we do not have to employ consciousness? The behaviourists thought they had discovered the mechanism by which this happened: the **conditioned reflex** – a reflex that was transferred somehow from a direct stimulus to a surrogate stimulus. They believed that, by analysis, it should be possible to show the 'chaining' by which each of these conditioned stimulus–response bonds came to be the behaviour that they were studying, however complex that behaviour might appear to be.

The idea of the conditioned reflex that was built into the doctrine of the behaviourists began with observations of dogs by I. P. Pavlov early this century. In studying the digestive system, he noticed that his dogs would salivate without the presence of food – just the sight of the man who would give them the food would do the trick. Pavlov showed that any stimulus a dog can perceive could be made to evoke salivation after it has been paired with food often enough. Pavlov offered, it seemed, an objective way to explain how ideas become associated: as Pavlov's dogs associated food with seeing the caretaker.

The salivary reflex is not under conscious control. You cannot say: I will now secrete saliva, and thereby cause your mouth to start watering. You could think about dinner, and that might make you salivate: this is a conditioned reflex. Psychologists came to believe that they could build any arbitrary system or hierarchy of behaviour by simply conditioning people in the same way.

Bechterev, a rival of Pavlov's, experimented with voluntary movements, like lifting the paw, rather than involuntary reflexes. Pavlov's ideas, with Bechterev's methodology, were then picked up by John B. Watson and others. In the 1920s, the behaviourists redefined psychology as the science of behaviour, not the science of mental activity. They wanted to exclude the mind from psychology.

As different people introspect differently, they thought a researcher could not rely on what people said about mental activity: 'there's no way I can verify you really had the experience you told me you had.' Behaviourists knew they were conscious, but they thought they could not study conscious experience scientifically. They had to be hard-headed scientists: so nothing was allowed that a physiologist would or could not do.

They thought any complex pattern of behaviour, such as human speech, could with sufficient analysis be reduced to reflexes, and to chains of reflexes. When a stimulus elicits a response, and that response in turn becomes the stimulus to elicit the next response, and so on, the result is a reflex chain. How simple! they thought. People are not complicated after all. Psychologists had discovered the unit of analysis. Given a response they should be able to figure out what the stimulus was that led to it, and so on back up a chain of reflexes. This would allow control of the process.

What was being studied was transfer of response to stimuli of one kind to stimuli of another kind. Learning was defined as **relatively permanent change in behaviour** that could be observed and measured. The programme was to analyse and simplify the complexity of behaviour so as to describe it as chains of stimulus–response bonds. A trained person could then teach by controlling and reinforcing each of the links in such defined chains.

Teaching programmes

The facts are hardly in dispute. Dogs do salivate if they hear the sound of the biscuit barrel. I can be made to feel fear in the cinema by visual or auditory stimulus – made possible by conditioning. It makes it easy for the advertising and propaganda industry to work on people's emotions. **Conditioning happens** – it is very powerful. What is arguable is how it works, what the mechanism is, and how it can be used in teaching/learning. Later psychologists of the behaviourist school sought to extend and modify the early doctrine – to make it viable as a means of instruction.

B. F. Skinner (born in 1904 and formerly Professor of Psychology at Harvard University) set out to identify the 'how'. Skinner argues that a learning process is accelerated by **reinforcement**: a stimulus that increases the probability of a response. He claims that one can describe behaviour in terms of external stimuli and their positive or negative reinforcement.

In **operant conditioning**, the important stimulus is that which immediately follows the response, not that which triggers it. In order to predict how a person will behave, we must look not at his expectation of the consequences that will follow his behaviour, but at what happened as a consequence of similar behaviour in the past. This may seem rather mentalistic after all. What Skinner is trying to avoid is the idea that future expectation – goal-seeking – affects present behaviour. It must relate to what has happened in the past in terms of reinforcement. This shapes our behaviour by using our desires and our fears. The strength of a response can be determined by the intensity of the stimulus. Prolongation or repetition will also increase the intensity of a stimulus.

For instance, if an organism such as a rat is starved, the stimulus of food and the reward of food will be greatly increased. Skinner used this to show how rats can be conditioned to find a path through a maze with food as the stimulus. A rat, which is an exploratory animal, searches a box until by trial and error it discovers how to get food. It can then be conditioned to follow more and more complex paths through a maze to get the food. The experimenter can control the behaviour of the animal and establish patterns in that behaviour. From this, Skinner believed that you could predict behaviour – you could control the process of learning and shape the behaviour as you wished.

The systematic application of reinforcement has been his principal study. Skinner believes that a technology of learning/teaching can be devised. It could be all predictable (in the scientific sense) and so programmed. So teachers should not be learning by experience in the classroom. 'Teachers need the kind of help offered by a scientific analysis of behaviour.' This kind of programme has been attempted, and with some success.

Comment

Does conditioning work? Yes, certainly. Animals and children, and no doubt adults, can be conditioned. It happens in normal nurturing. We observe strong conditioning into sex roles and status expectations. I find it very difficult to prevent making responses that have been conditioned into me, even though I am conscious of it happening. The advertising industry uses emotional engineering to control our responses to their images.

Skinner did it most effectively, at least with rats, by systematic use of his techniques. Parents and teachers use conditioning much more simply, through rewards and punishments, to shape the behaviour they want. People can condition themselves to need salt, nicotine, alcohol – almost anything. With an effort they can also decondition themselves. Much human behaviour in social situations (membership of particular societies, groups, tribes) can be seen to be the result of conditioning.

But powerful as it is, conditioning is not the only type of learning. It cannot be ignored and teachers should take careful note of what has been discovered about reinforcing learned behaviour. As a systematic approach to education or even training, it fails to take into account many other aspects of human behaviour, most notably motivation and attitudinal change. For this reason it tends to fail to achieve the intended programme. Humans develop resistance to conditioning. And it is not clear how conditioning is to promote cognitive and intellectual skills. Surely, teachers need to promote intelligent thinking.

25 Neo-behaviourism: Structural Analysis

Probably the most influential of the neo-behaviourist psychologists since the mid-1960s has been R. Gagné (born in 1916, and Professor of Psychology at the Universities of Princeton and Florida). His concern is the structural analysis of learning processes and the design of teaching models to match the kinds of learning they are intended to facilitate.

He devised a systematised approach to instruction which strongly influences design of many teaching programmes. Learning is seen as 'a change in human disposition or capability, which can be retained, and which is not simply ascribable to the process of growth'. He makes a comparison with organic processes in the body such as digestion to describe a process taking place in the learner's brain. It is a 'total process' – not fragmented but systematically described. It starts for him with **apprehending** what is in the environment – the stimuli – followed by **acquisition**, then **storage** and, finally, **retrieval**. The analogy is a computer program.

Learning is analysed into descriptions of 'changed behaviour in terms of an observable type of human performance', with five major categories of 'human capability that are outcomes of learning':

- verbal information
- intellectual skills
- cognitive strategies
- attitudes
- motor skills.

Clearly, this goes a long way beyond Skinner in identifying a range of types of learning. Each one requires a different learning strategy, and teaching that recognises the type of learning and the strategy in order to match the appropriate process of instruction to it – certainly not simple stimulus–response bonding. It is behaviourist in placing emphasis on a structure imposed from outside. While acknowledging the importance of process in the learning, outcomes are seen as the main criterion of successful instruction. Instruction must be designed with different characteristics 'that depend on which particular class of performance change is the focus of interest'. But the range in the types of learning that are to be 'systematised' is limited.

Gagné sets out eight conditions or types of learning:

1 **signal learning**: stimulus–response at the level of signals
2 **stimulus–response learning**: involves discrimination between stimuli

3 **chaining**: stimulus–response bonds are chained in sequence at a motor level – what others might call 'memory in the muscles'

4 **verbal discrimination association**: verbal chains are formed – involves making of individual links, discrimination and chaining to 'associate' (in Pavlov's sense)

5 **multiple discrimination**: more sophisticated discrimination between apparently similar stimuli – with correct responses

6 **concept learning**: responses to 'classes' of stimuli – recognition of relationships or 'classes'

7 **rule-learning**: chaining concepts: a rule is 'an inferred capability that enables the individual to respond to a class of stimulus situations with a class of performances'

8 **problem-solving**: a natural extension of rule-learning where the most important part of the process takes place within the learner 'who discovers relationships'.

This is a 'hierarchy' of learning. The word is taken from the organisation of priests, and implies a pyramidal structure from many at the base to one at the top. By extension, however, as in this case, it implies that each capability has within it and necessary to it all the previous lower capabilities. For example, I cannot chain stimulus–response bonds unless I am capable of making the individual bonds first.

Gagné proposes use of 'instructional sequences' related to the hierarchy:

- informing the learner as to what form of performance is expected after completion of the learning
- questioning the learner to elicit recall of previously learned concepts
- using cues to elicit the formation of chains of concepts or 'rules'
- questioning the learner so as to obtain demonstration of rules
- requiring the learner to make a verbal statement of the rule.

As a teaching programme this is clearly desperately limited, and entirely teacher-centred. Gagné identifies eight phases in an act of learning which implies voluntary learning activity only:

1 motivation: goal-seeking – induced by creating expectations
2 apprehending: differentiation of stimuli by focusing attention
3 acquisition: storing the learning by encoding it
4 retention: extended memory storage
5 recall: the process of retrieval
6 generalisation: transfer of learning to new contexts
7 performance: demonstration of what has been learned
8 feedback: the process of reinforcement.

Comment on behaviourism

Gagné's programming of learning derives from how he believes the teaching–learning interface operates. Certainly, statement of learning goals is of major importance – but who identifies the goals? The teacher? Gagné sees the teacher as the designer and manager of the process of instruction, the provider of immediate feedback to the learner to reinforce learning (Skinner-style), and also the assessor of learning outcomes. Assessment is the teacher's prerogative.

This is an attempt to 'systematise' instruction. A great deal of effort in training in particular has gone into such systems. It has dominated much of the provision. There is little room for dynamic or organic change within such a programme. It has within it an implied conditioning of the learning through the process of shaping and reinforcement.

Nor does it acknowledge that humans are exploratory animals. Decision-making is for the instructor. How can this produce independent learners, let alone independent thinkers? The emphasis in the end is on demonstrable, observable performance. Those aspects of learning which Gagné identifies as important, such as the developing of cognitive strategies and attitudes, since they are not demonstrable in performance are ignored in instructional/ assessment/feedback programming.

The eight phases of instruction appear to relate systematically to outside rather than inside need – to the American style of instruction: 'tell and test' orthodox right answers. Where then are 'discoveries of relationships' or 'leaps ahead beyond the evidence'? It would be impossible to imagine 'leaps' that miss out whole parts of the chaining.

Yet we know that the human mind does make such leaps. Often enough we leap to conclusions, usually with very inadequate evidence, and then fill in the gaps in the chain afterwards. Desperately untidy for such a system as Gagné proposes. Where is 'trust in the students'?

Science, it was thought, worked by the accumulation of experimental 'facts', analysis, theorising, the demonstration of proofs, and replication: a misconception of how science works that was prevalent until the last war. The whole behaviourist programme was based on this misconception. Behaviourists thought they could build up a supremely thorough-going system which would inevitably be effective, since it was designed on the basis of 'scientific' research. It could be systematised: each building block was to be made up of conditioned behavioural patterns, using reinforcement techniques (totally teacher-centred stuff). Gagné appears, like Darwin and Freud, to wish to impose a rigid finality that cannot allow of challenge from the learner.

Dynamic, unpredictable change must imply unpredictable outcomes. You cannot make the outcomes totally shape the learning process, unless your purpose is conditioning to preconceived patterns of behaviour – indoctrination. How much of *what* people actually learn, let alone *how* they learn it, is really in the control of teachers? Do teachers need to perceive a much more modest role for themselves?

Unfortunately for the behaviourists, science just does not work as they thought. It tends to generate hypotheses, sometimes 'hunches', and look for evidence to support or invalidate the hypotheses. It starts from questions and/or guesses rather than from evidence: top down, not bottom up.

Sir Karl Popper in 1958, in *The Logic of Scientific Discovery*, proposed a new philosophy of science. Scientific method since Bacon had been thought of as demonstration of proofs, and research was concerned with proving the theory correct; scandals occurred when all contradictory evidence was suppressed. To be scientific for Popper a theory must be falsifiable, not verifiable. The proper business of science is the rejection of hypothesis. It starts with a conjectural hunch that often goes way beyond the available information; then the programme is set up to check the hypothesis against the world – does it explain the facts? will it predict what will happen if . . . ? A good theory will predict events under given circumstances. The test is whether or not the prediction is false.

Einstein's theory of gravity made very different predictions from Newton's. For example, he said light rays from distant stars would be bent if they passed close to the sun. This prediction was tested during an eclipse in 1919. Measurement was very difficult but it seemed to confirm Einstein against Newton. He was also correct in predicting that clocks would run slow in spacecraft. But Newton's equations are easier to use and more practical than Einstein's, so Newton is preferred in our everyday world.

Scientific theories, since Einstein and Heisenberg's Uncertainty Principle in relation to the structure of the atom, are no longer expected to demonstrate objective truth: it is enough that they work. So long as they will predict what will happen they are useful, and that is what is required. The great optimism about being able to explain everything has largely died.

Gagné's insistence on matching teaching to intended learning and analysis of 'how that is intended to happen' is extremely important. We must surely do the analysis. We must understand how to design a strategy of learning.

We must agree learning goals with students. They must be signposts rather than goalposts, since we cannot predict what will happen or how the goals will need to be redefined as the process evolves. And in any case a point of arrival is also the next point of departure. Nothing is once for all.

We also need to use feedback in a formative way. This is not to reinforce the learning in the behaviourist meaning and technique. That implies that we seek to shape the learning to teachers' predetermined models. Feedback is better seen as more in the nature of a mirror, to allow the students to match what they are doing against models and criteria that we have agreed with them and which they perceive. This will enable them to measure their progress and so to improve whatever they are setting out to learn – to set about learning consciously and intelligently, and so take responsibility for their own learning.

26 Insight Learning: Gestalt

Intellectual progress – psychology is no exception – takes place by challenge and defence. The school that arose in vehement opposition to the behaviourists was the Gestalt school.

Where Skinner spent many years studying rats, experimenters who wanted to challenge Watson and his school studied chimpanzees – our nearest cousins. I once had a very 'intelligent' cat who discovered how to get me out of bed in the middle of the night by rapping the knocker on the front door of my house: he climbed up the slats and lifted it with a paw. I certainly did not condition him to do it. How did he learn it?

Kohler (1887–1967) was interested in the ability of chimpanzees to solve problems (*The Mentality of Apes*, 1925). Since they could not tell experimenters their introspections, he observed their behaviour and created his own hypothesis to explain it. You may well have seen these experiments, since they were filmed. One was to give a chimpanzee the problem of getting bananas that were suspended out of the ape's reach. To solve this the animal placed boxes one on top of another.

How would you explain what the ape did? Surely not by stimulus–response chaining. Had the ape had experience before that had been developed through reinforcement to produce a capacity to make such inventive use of the environment? Or was it creative thinking of some kind? Was there a reorganisation in the brain or 'mind' of structures in the world? Did the ape perceive a different relationship of objects to make an 'artificial tree' that it could climb?

Another experiment used the ape's frustration at not being able to reach a bunch of fruit outside the cage. The ape apparently 'experimented'. Some jointed sticks had been provided, and after several attempts it succeeded in putting them together to reach the fruit. Studies of behaviour of similar kinds have been filmed in the wild, with various animals. What hypothesis could one put together to explain this? How would you explain problem-solving of this kind?

It was like my cat's 'experimenting' with the knocker on my front door. Kohler saw this behaviour as 'not connected with previous trial and error', not linked step-by-step into a chain, nor as reinforced patterning. In order for it to be stimulus–response bonding such links are necessary. Could it have been recall of past learning? and if so, of what kind of learning?

Kohler called it **insight learning**. It was, he thought, a restructuring in the mind to see how the whole thing might work: Eureka! I've got it. We have the experience ourselves quite frequently. It happens, in a **Gestalt**: when the structural essence of the total situation posed by the problem is perceived by the learner. You will have experiences like this with pets of your own, and similar personal experiences to reflect on.

We quite often use the phrase: 'Oh! I see it now!' This implies some kind of visualising of the problem in a new way. We see how the bits make sense together. For Gestaltists, 'the whole is greater than the sum of the parts'. It is 'seeing the whole' that makes sense of the parts.

What distinguishes insight learning for these theorists is that:

- the solution is a sudden leap, as if pieces were fitting together
- once it has been accomplished, it is easier to solve similar problems
- it leads to permanence in learning – it appears to become part of our way of dealing with the world – and we can transfer that learning to unfamiliar situations, in different contexts.

In other words, it appears to be about how we *subsequently* do things. It seems to improve our intellectual problem-solving skills and processes. The transferability is essential: cognitive skill becomes applicable to other contexts.

This suggests that if we want to improve people's skills we need to look at how people deal with things 'in the whole', and not try to improve skill by analysing it into constituent bits. It doesn't work that way. Gestaltists argued that a phenomenon like learning has to be studied as an organised, complex structure which changes as a whole by sudden leaps from one state of being to another. The pattern of activity that made this leap happen they called **insight**.

Certainly most things, from the simplest to the most complex such as human behaviour, are much more easily grasped and understood when we have a view of them as a whole. We cannot even begin to see what each bit does on its own; we can understand it only in relationship to the whole. There are multitudes of things of which the whole is not analysable into its constituent parts. For instance, a picture is perceived only as a whole. So is a piece of music, or tree. Analysis of constituents and processes helps you to appreciate it more, but to take it apart is to destroy it.

Comment on Gestalt

The Gestaltists' explanation of how learning happens is important. They saw it as a dynamic process: not linking nor even associating with previous experience, but a creative restructuring that arises from thinking through problems. Challenge is part of learning. For them, the acquisition and retention of insight form the core of the learning process. Since this comes about through problem-solving, it will be most effective when learners are challenged by being given problems to find solutions for, questions rather than answers.

It demands a very different kind of learning programme from that proposed by Gagné's structural analysis. It must be dynamic and open in terms of any predicted learning. It is difficult to predict how a mind will restructure its experience. It involves productive thinking. A dynamic, creative process is involved. All decision-making will therefore be seen as a **creative response** to situations.

It is creative because it involves making a new structure of the problem in order to invent or discover a solution. The process is cumulative. This is contrasted with rote-learning, in which creativity is suppressed. It can be seen to happen when we are faced with a familiar object in an unfamiliar guise. We might have to rotate it in our mind's eye or picture it some new way to recognise it. It is a favourite game of local newspapers to present such picture puzzles to their readers: where is this?

Capacity for creative thinking will be present in most learners. This capacity is in the student, and is to be brought out; it is not in the teacher to be transferred to the learner by some techniques of knowledge transfer. How should the teacher attempt to bring it out, rather than to teach it or to put it in? Asking a question of this kind changes the perspective of teaching entirely.

Productive thinking involves learners grasping the essential relationships within a problem, grouping them into 'wholes' and restructuring the problem to find solutions. But we quite often might need to break down a problem into related stages in order to tackle it successfully. We may not be able to grasp the whole of something if it is too big.

Teaching/learning strategies

Much of what makes a 'person' is a result of conditioning, whether it is consciously done by parents, teachers, employers, peer groups, churches, advertising companies and so forth, or just a series of pressures to conform, such as sex-role conditioning. It is helpful to understand the mechanism involved. Unlearning such reinforced behaviour is extremely difficult, particularly if it is accompanied by a mind-set of beliefs and attitudes.

Clearly, there is a place for rote-learning. It may be the quickest way to lay a 'sound' foundation of accepted knowledge. But again, there are real problems in overwhelming students with too much information at one time. And unless they use the new information it will remain 'in a memory box'. Indoctrination approaches to teaching clearly suppress creativity – are in fact intended to do so. Memory rote-learning has an important place in the laying of foundations, let's say in number work, but used as a major means of instruction it stifles the very learning we are trying to assist.

But it is fairly easy to test. Creativity is not testable. It relies too much on personal judgement, and is only indirectly observable as outcomes. It is obvious too that unless you have a sound basis of information to build your speculations on you will offer solutions that make no sense, no matter how creative you are.

As in science, the main criterion of feasibility in a theory is: does it explain the facts? It must make predictions that stand up to facts. It does not require insight learning to memorise facts. But that seems a poor reason to require *only* memorising of facts – or opinions masquerading as facts.

Problem-solving is a powerful tool of learning. It is creative, related to success as an organism in the world, to social behaviour as a social animal, to intellectual growth and development of skills and capacities – and through all this to self-esteem and independence. It has the additional advantage that we can use it to foster sharing and team-efforts, which are essential in our technological environment.

So in designing learning programmes, we must vary approaches to learning and fit them together to create successful learning strategies.

Right answers

The major problem with the Gestalt approach, as it turns out, is that there is frequently too little information for the learners to have a view of the 'whole'. They have to make a leap with insufficient evidence (insufficiency of evidence hardly ever stops one, of course). Or the whole may be just too big a leap to make – we have to take smaller whole lumps, and hope to build them up into a greater whole later. I wonder if such a strategy would be acceptable as Gestalt?

One consequence is that we often end up with the wrong 'whole' – a delusion or a misconception of what it is we are about – which may lead us off in a totally unprofitable direction. Insight is fine when we leap to the 'right' answer. What do we do in such a description of the learning process if, as is often the case, the answer is wrong in whole or in part? Ensuring that students have the correct response is the intention of reinforcement. The transmission of 'non-false' information/knowledge is important if we are to avoid serious problems in later learning. It must be correct, if only because it is so hard to unlearn once it is established.

One of the great difficulties with discovery learning and problem-solving is this: at what point should the teacher intervene if it becomes obvious that the students are on the wrong track? How important is it that they do find the correct solution at the end of their effort? Obviously, wheels without an axle or bearings or gearing may well be ineffective for the purpose intended. The students need to have that pointed out.

The other great problem is that it can be very slow as well as very fast. Teachers (and students) easily become impatient. I remember well a student saying to me twenty-five years ago, 'Sir, why don't you just tell us the answer? It'll be so much quicker.'

The method is intended to accelerate the learning by a sudden leap in which the whole of the thing falls into place. This is how we often learn: we make a sudden leap beyond the evidence, and fill in the gap in retrospect between where we were and where we have arrived, with our knowledge of the 'whole' to guide us.

In support of the approach it is easy to show that a leap to a conclusion, and cutting out a great deal of rather tedious unit-building, is efficient as a methodology *as long as a student does fill in the gaps afterwards*. Frequently this last condition is unfulfilled, and gaps remain which later prove to be very inhibiting of future progress.

It may be very slow because students may not be very good at formulating or visualising the problem – discovering the questions or a method of looking for answers. They may go down blind alleys or run up against gaps in their knowledge or understanding that inhibit progress. If they are working in a group they may have conflicting gestalts or paths of enquiry to follow.

Teachers will want to provide 'teacher's Gestalt' to hasten the process. A major problem may then be that the gap between where the learner is now and where the teacher is may be so wide as to make 'teacher's Gestalt' incomprehensible to the student. Teachers usually start from what *they* know, *their* picture of the world, and provide it as an insight for students. Or they may offer an author's 'picture of it all', a textbook solution.

This is the standard practice in complex subjects such as history, English literature, sociology and engineering science. The amount of detail is so huge that it is far too time-consuming a process to build up the students' 'picture of it all' by taking a tedious slow march through the details. In any case, from the practical point of learning it, it is much easier to understand the detail and to know what you are looking for in the detail if you have a picture in the head of the whole thing. 'You can't see the wood for the trees.' It is a fact that too much information is confusing.

But we have to ensure that we do understand where the student is starting from: how he or she may 'make the leap' to the Gestalt, and what has to happen then in terms of 'filling in the gap'. And this is not easy to do if we have no view of what the gap consists of, or even that gaps exist.

This is part of what is wrong with providing teacher's or the textbook's 'right' answers. They may make perfect sense to the teacher and the author because they are restructuring information that is already possessed to make a new 'whole'. On the face of it, it looks like an efficient approach because it accelerates the students to a conclusion they might otherwise take a long time to reach, or which they might never reach at all because of lack of skill or information.

But the whole without the evidential information makes little sense – especially if students do not know *what* the questions are to which these are the 'right' answers. Textbooks rarely state the questions: too often, answers are to be learned as facts when they are truly one person's reconstruction of the world to make sense of facts. Teachers may be pleased with the efficiency of what they appear to have done but in Gestalt terms it is an illusion of knowledge, since the students have not actually made any leap at all.

They can only do that if they restructure their own 'picture of it all'. They must process information themselves; they must restructure their conceptual framework for it to become usable knowledge. To memorise and then to repeat accurately what they have memorised is not insight, although it is the way many examining systems work.

Enabling students to achieve insight learning provides a formidable challenge to teachers – which explains why it so infrequently occurs.

27 Cognitive Development: Concrete and Formal Thinking

Jean Piaget (1896–1980, for fifty years Professor at the University of Geneva and Director of the Rousseau Institute) studied hundreds of children, trying to understand how they learned. Like gestaltists, he believed that all children are born with certain **innate mental structures** that determine the shape of their cognitive development. These structures provide their motivation to interact with the environment, and guide the growth of their knowledge about the world. But Piaget thought the **shape of the mind** was also affected by the environment in which the child grew up. Children construct grammar in their minds as they learn to talk, because their genes allow them to. He took a middle road in the prevailing 'nature–nurture' controversy.

Piaget concentrated his attention on the mind. He paid little attention to behaviour itself. It was the mental functioning controlling behaviour that interested him. 'The child is not shaped by the parents,' he said, 'the child is the teacher.' Your social environment merely provides the inputs; your mind interprets and reshapes these inputs to create the knowledge you presently have. He was much more impressed by similarities in all children than by individual differences. Intellectual development in every child, according to him, will proceed through four clearly defined stages. These occur in giant steps; they are not the slow and steady accumulation of knowledge and information. The four developmental stages of cognitive development are as follows:

1 the sensory–motor period: birth to 24 months
2 the pre-operational stage: two to seven years of age
3 the stage of concrete operations: eight to twelve years of age
4 the stage of formal operations: twelve years onwards.

Piaget maintained that the *average* age at which children attain each maturational level was about the same in all cultures. All infants explore and respond to their environment directly and rather automatically. Children explore the physical and maternal world up to around the age of eighteen months, when they truly begin to 'think': they thus build an internal representation of the external world, and learn to 'manipulate' objects in their minds.

Between the ages of two and seven children acquire sophisticated language which gives them the ability to deal with many aspects of the world in symbols, by talking and thinking about objects rather than having to manipulate them directly. They can remember past events and anticipate their happening again. But they exhibit only egocentric reasoning: they cannot differentiate between self and the environment.

By the time children reach six or seven they begin to acquire 'concepts' and see the objects 'out there', but only gradually perceive them in relationships. A new object (two halves of a ball, say) they believe to be new objects and so expect them to weigh more than the original whole ball. They *perceive* weight and number in a non-adult way. Counting is not the same as the concept of number. In infant and primary schools, for this reason, a great deal of effort goes into teaching number by concrete examples, by handling objects.

At about the age of twelve, Piaget believed for *all* children, a cognitive leap occurs. They begin to use abstractions to manipulate thinking about the world. People can then solve problems in their minds by isolating the important variables so as to manipulate them mentally or perceptually. Now at last individuals can draw meaningful conclusions from purely abstract or hypothetical data. They can now deal effectively with questions about how, what and why. Piaget identified this change as being able to reason 'formally', using abstractions, instead of seeing the world and themselves in 'concrete' or 'real out there' terms.

Is it true?

The main problem is that Piaget did not conduct experimental research under the controlled conditions that present psychological research uses. Such research does not confirm his assertions. Many of his basic assumptions are suspect: in particular, that there are 'general structures of the mind'. There are also so many exceptions to his general rules.

But his are challenging ideas. I have found that many adults cannot deal with abstract conceptualisations; they see things in concrete terms, or even 'me and the world' terms. They can deal well with counting objects, but not with number concepts. Perhaps as many as eight out of twelve adults have failed to make this cognitive leap. Assumptions we make about ability to cope with learning goals and programmes that we teachers set up for them have to take account of such readiness; to recognise cognitive growth.

The recent change to the National Curriculum in Science in the United Kingdom has led to a crash training programme for science teachers: biologists have to relearn physics to integrate it into science teaching again. To do so, they have to explore new student-centred methods and projects. Thinking scientifically is impossible unless you can deal in abstractions, and can perceive variables and differentiate between them. To do a science experiment you must isolate one variable you wish to study and try to keep everything else unaltered, so as to measure change in that variable alone. This implies quite complex thought processes. The problem comes sharply back: so many students have not made the leap from concrete to formal thinking by the time they come to do GCSE (age sixteen), and they cannot deal with abstract ideas effectively.

The old input/output approach to memory training allowed teachers to get students through exams in science without real understanding of most of it. The new GCSE will not allow that. Pupils have to conceptualise and design a method for investigating phenomena. You cannot do that without formal as against concrete thinking. Teachers therefore must tackle this cognitive change first.

The cognitive development problem exists, but not as Piaget envisaged; nor is the problem confined to science. *All* creative thinking involves the ability to conceptualise and use abstractions. It relates in fundamental ways to vocabulary – the ability to use words and symbols.

28 Perception

Common sense and my experience tell me that if I run headlong into a wall, I will do myself harm. But a nursing training officer once told me of patients she had known who had walked straight through walls without apparent harm to themselves; perhaps they did not perceive a wall to be an obstacle to them because of their 'insanity' at the time.

How far is what actually happens related to what we expect to happen? Does the learning come from experience – the way we investigate the world? or from inborn ways of visualising? from cultural beliefs? Why do some people have such a different view of the world from ours? How is it that people walk on hot coals without apparent harm, or put skewers through their faces without bleeding?

Creatures receive information about the world from sense organs, of which for humans the eyes are the most powerful. It was probably because they used sight in preference to the other senses that our ancestors took to walking upright: to get a better look at things. Dogs, by contrast, evolved the ability to differentiate smells, to which they are a thousand times more sensitive than we are. Sight is not so important to them. We may wonder what their picture of the world would be like. It would be fascinating if dogs could describe their 'view' of things.

Would we recognise any of it? Could we even have a common language when concepts for them would relate to smells we cannot smell, and concepts for us to colours they cannot see? It is encouraging to think that all humans seem to be able to use the same conceptual ideas – which suggests they have a similar experience of the world from which to derive them.

On the other hand, that common experience relates to physical capacity for sensing the world which excludes a great part of the available information. We are becoming familiar with very different pictures of the world because of television, probably the most powerful educational tool we have. There are images of galaxies and stars from radio telescopes, X-rays of the human skeleton, brain scanning using sound waves, and heat-imaging using infra-red light that appears to be used by snakes and other creatures. These are all converted into visual images we can deal with, using visible light. We cannot have direct sensory access to those images of the world. Similarly, we 'hear' sound-echoing used by bats and dolphins to picture their world or for navigation, but only by changing the frequencies to what our ears can actually hear. Are we in fact genetically programmed to have a particular perception and therefore knowledge of the world we live in?

We cling to our familiar picture of the world, brought to us only by visible light (the light we can see), as a true picture: the *only* picture. From a purely practical angle, what else can we do? But what has it to say about what the physical world is really like? Enormous parts of the information about even the most everyday aspects of our environment are not accessible to us through our senses. Or, if they are, we ignore them.

Clearly, our brains select from the experiences we have. Someone who loses the ability to see may become much more aware of the other senses: may hear things and smell things of which the sighted person is unaware. You can demonstrate this very easily to yourself. Make a tape-recording of an ordinary hour in a room while you are busy doing things there. Listen to it afterwards; you will hear so many things you did not notice at the time: clocks ticking, birds singing in the garden, the noise of footsteps or chairs moving, the sound of your own voice. Similar things can be learned by closing your eyes and exploring by touch only.

You normally filter nearly all of this out, presumably because there has to be a limit to the amount of information about your environment that your brain and nervous system can process. So much of what is there you do not 'see' or 'hear' or 'feel' or 'smell'. What you select is what you need at the time.

What do we do with the information, such as it is, when we get it? How do we see the world, for instance? Do we have direct access even by vision to an external reality? Vision was once thought of as the experience of a spectator, seated behind a screen, watching a perfectly formed image of the world. What is wrong with this idea? We are forced to ask: how does the spectator see what is on the screen? The same way I see – a 'spectator' looking at another screen in his eye? And then another 'spectator', another screen *ad infinitum*, an infinite regression? It cannot operate like that.

Jonathan Miller in *States of Mind* gives the example of someone driving along a wet road. He *sees* a three-dimensional scene of slippery tarmac. What he actually *sees*, the image in the eye, is neither slippery nor three-dimensional. This can only mean that the person is subjectively and actively creating it by conjuring up a 'model in the head' of what is there. I gave, in Part 1, another example of driving: of lights coming towards you at night. The amount of sensory information is very small indeed. Yet you usually have no problem with it. You build an image of a vehicle to which the lights belong and decide what you have to do, according to what you think that vehicle is and what it is going to do.

Without an image of it all in your head you could not deal with it. It is the same with a slippery road. You see it as 'wet' or 'slippery' because of your previous experience of such things. You may be wrong. It could be a mirage caused by heat on the road: I expect you have seen that too. But given alternative explanations, you normally go for the most common first. These are 'alternative perceptual fictions'. They are fictions because you have invented them as explanations of what you actually see. What your eye receives is light: directly received from the headlights, received by reflection from the wet road. The eye makes an image on the retina.

What happens then? is the important question. An analogy may help. Think of how a telephone works on a principle of coding and decoding signals. Sound waves, coded as electrical impulses, are sent down a wire and decoded back into sound at the other end. Similarly, the optic nerves must take information coded as chemical messages from retinal cells. Nerves that run from the retina are part of the brain, not separate from it. They are the means by which the central nervous system receives this coded information. What kind of code? By a complicated chemistry, the light seems to trigger pulses of electrical energy that are transmitted along the nerves and have to be decoded in the brain. The brain does not decode them back into light! What does it do with them?

All sorts of interesting things, obviously. For one thing the retinal image must be upside down, since the lens works much like a camera lens. Look through a camera lens and you will see that. Why don't you see the world that way up? Then again, the image must be constantly changing. You cannot hold your eyes still – they flicker. What happens when you move your gaze around the world? Try starting at one end of a wall and letting your gaze travel along to the other end: does the wall appear to move? The image on the retina of your eyes is streaming past in reverse and upside down. How is it that you see a stationary wall?

How, in addition, do you see it as a solid wall, if all that the retina has to go on is light reflected from the surfaces? What a complicated business it must be! We see a three-dimensional world. Having two eyes makes it possible for us to see objects in perspective, but how does it work? If you put a patch over one eye, you still see the world as three-dimensional even if you find it hard to judge distances.

Your brain must in some way set up a constructed image of the world you are perceiving. It has to *know* somehow that the world is solid and motionless: it is your eyes that are moving across it. You will have experienced the confusion of not knowing whether it is you moving or the world when you were sitting in a train at a station and another train next to you appeared to move. After all, before Copernicus everyone thought the earth was motionless and the sun went around it. That was their hypothesis; his was different.

Your mind/brain interprets sense data to make them match the image it has constructed. If they fail to match, you become confused: you look for other information to help you. You look out of the other window of the train; you try various other models to see if they match. This seems to be what your brain does, without your thinking about it: it tests out alternative hypotheses, it generates explanations or assumptions about what is there.

What you actually do is to explore the world, set up hypotheses or models of what appears to be there and then test to see how well it all matches. For much of the time, too, the hypotheses are constructed from very inadequate information. Even when there is very little sense data – as with the lights coming towards us in the car at night – we still make hypotheses.

Look at the drawings made by young children. There is a pattern to the way all children make drawings of the world around them. Fascinating studies have been made of this. Why are the people in the drawings so similar? and the houses? Where do children get their images from? Are they representing some inbuilt, innate, models?

This is how Gestalt theorists explained it. Either all children see people and houses very differently from the way adults see them, or they deal with what they see differently. Are the 'models in the head' they use different from those of adults? If they are the same for all children, where do they come from? Or maybe it is physiological, something to do with their ability to co-ordinate hand muscles.

As we grow we accumulate experience: we appear to create more sophisticated models of reality to enable us to deal with the world and make sense of it. We certainly must have a larger and larger range of models to choose from, unless our experience is very restricted even in adult life. T. E. Lawrence in *The Seven Pillars of Wisdom* told how the tribesmen of the desert, who were brought up without representational images of people (it is taboo in Islam to make images of people) could not make any sense of a drawing he did of their Sheikh. The best guess one made was that it was a foot. They apparently could not 'see' it. Lawrence said that their ability to visualise people had atrophied.

Professor Richard Gregory of Bristol University worked with visual puzzles. He writes in *States of Mind*, 'It turns out that the generation of fictions is very important for seeing the richness of reality from the very limited amount of data, or information, which the senses can handle or have available to them. So generation of fiction is intimately bound up with generation of fact.' He identifies four kinds of illusion. Here are just two: ambiguity and fiction.

Try your own 'perceptual brain language' on the illustrations in Figure 8. The three boxes look like three-dimensional objects, but they are just lines on a flat piece of paper: how does that happen? Gregory wrote, 'Sometimes you find one face looks like the front and then suddenly it'll flip and become the back. You can make it happen when you blink, or when you move your eye about; it will also flip entirely spontaneously.' Try!

It is the ambiguity that we have problems with. We set up and test one of the possible alternative hypotheses of how this cube 'is', in a fictitious three-dimensional world we also create for it. We test out another, equally probable, hypothesis. We cannot come to a definite conclusion with the available evidence, so we try again . . . and again.

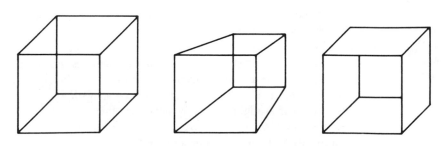

Fig. 8   Ambiguities

We do all this quite unconsciously too. It just keeps flipping from one to another. It is very difficult for us to control it. Try! This suggests that the part of the brain that is testing the hypotheses is not the same part we use to take conscious control, or even to think about what is happening and why. Is there a duality in the mind?

The 'Rubin vase' in Figure 9 shows two different kinds of object, the vase and a pair of faces, in profile. These are actually two different objects, and to get this to work, says Gregory, the objects must have roughly equal probabilities. The brain switches and tries out the two hypotheses.

Figure 10 was devised by an Italian psychologist, Gaetano Kanizsa. The central triangle in each of the figures is an illusion. Although we see the edges as sharp and clear, they are not there. There's no actual brightness difference across the edges: the triangle must be constructed by the observer, says

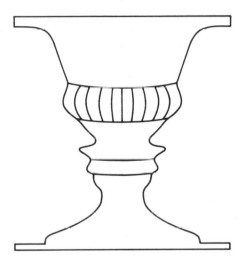

Fig. 9   The Rubin vase (from *Synopleveda Figures*, S. Rubin, 1915)

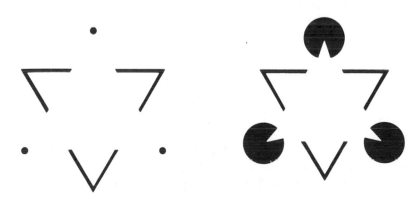

Fig. 10   The Kanizsa figures (from *Synopleveda Figures*, S. Rubin, 1915)

Gregory. The lines seem to curve if you simply reduce the angles of white in the dark sectors: the visual system seems to join up an imaginary triangle with curved sides.

You actually *see* a white triangle, although all that there is on the paper is gaps in a black triangle and some little bits out of black circles. I have tried this with Japanese university students who have never seen it before: they also see the triangles, so it is not cultural conditioning. It seems to be a genetically determined trait in humans to make these hypotheses of 'the world out there'.

'If it's a figure that's got surprising gaps which are unlikely to occur by chance, it's more likely there's something getting in the way, producing gaps, than that something is missing. This is the way the brain deals with experience. It is normally very useful to go on *seeing* parts of objects, or at least to believe that they're there, when they're hidden by something nearer,' says Gregory in *States of Mind*. Otherwise, we have to believe in bits of objects existing, like the Cheshire Cat's grin – impossible!

Hypothesising

Professor Gregory has described many more visual experiments of this kind. The main conclusion he comes to is that **perceptions are predictive hypotheses**. The test of a scientific theory is whether it can successfully predict what will happen. We appear to behave in this fashion in perceiving our world: we make hypotheses and then test them out. As Gregory points out, in the Kanizsa figures it is *absence* of signals that makes us 'see' the overlying triangles. We hypothesise the existence of the triangles to explain the gaps. And this is not something over which we can take conscious control.

Even if we know something is wrong we cannot will ourselves to *not* see it. You cannot stop yourself from seeing the white triangles that are not there. It is as if knowledge of the world or objects is built into the brain somehow, together with the rules for making guesses and matching which we cannot have access to in our consciousness. We cannot observe inside our brains to watch ourselves think.

Gregory comments in *States of Mind* that the process of evolution has created brain structures, just as it has shaped our noses so that we do not drown when it rains. We have noses like roofs to keep out falling rain; why not brain structures that 'incorporate a more and more accurate model of the universe in which it lives'? The brain seems to have 'rule-observing processes which in brain language are more and more accurate pictures of the world'.

It exhibits pattern-making processes also. Are they the same? I suggested in Chapter 18 that the two hemispheres of the brain appear to have different functions or preferences related to pattern-making (images) and rule-making. Does this help to explain some of the enigmas of perception?

Teaching/learning

It is essential that teachers know how people perceive the world if they are to help students to learn. A carpenter works with the grain of the wood in order to shape it successfully. We must work with the normal processes of learning if we are not to create problems for students rather than to help them learn.

Since our normal behaviour in learning is to explore, setting up and then testing hypotheses, we should recognise this in the strategies we devise in teaching/learning. Think, again, about the baby as it explores its world using all its senses; think too about the adults in Tony's class (Case Study 4).

People learn by testing hypotheses, but they have to want to. What drives them to put a great deal of effort into it is equally complex. No doubt a part is played by dissatisfaction: we modify hypotheses or models when they do not fit. If people are very happy in the conditions as they are (and with what the world is for them), they are not likely to change. It may or may not be a good thing for them to continue with their present models of the world and the way that affects their behaviour in it. It may be that the models they have are appropriate for their need. Needs change, however, and then there is a need for more appropriate models.

Teachers must remember that change is painful. There are costs in terms of self-image, adjustment, insecurity and so on. Students need our support as they deal with change. But since change is permanent, at least so long as we continue to evolve new technology, teachers will always be needed.

29 The Cognitive Revolution

We make progress in thinking about a new idea according to the kinds of analogies we have available to us: what we can compare it with that is already familiar. We use analogies all the time. It is an ancient practice. Plato's approach to problems in philosophy was to argue by analogies. His most famous is of the citizens who are in a cave and only see shadows on the wall. What will they make of the person who goes out into the light and comes back to tell them of the wonders he has seen in the real world out there? Of course, they will reject him as deluded.

For Plato our world was merely shadows: 'ideas' existed in a 'real' (i.e. a permanent and unchanging) world accessible only to a disciplined intellect. Our world lacked permanence: everything was in constant flux. The concept of a permanent, 'real' other world of the mind is the basis of many great religions. It has provided a fertile ground for the mind–body controversy.

The revolution that occurred in psychology was the result of the invention of machines that appeared to behave intelligently. That made it possible to use taboo words like 'purpose' and 'goal-seeking', excluded from use in discussion of psychological behaviour since they were seen as mentalistic concepts – not demonstrable, objective, scientifically acceptable evidence.

Ever since Newton's time, it was thought that if you couldn't point to an object or some phenomenon, see an example of it in the physical world, you had better ignore it. You could not study it scientifically. Behaviourists said: introspection is all very well, but show me 'a goal' out there.

Once you have radar that locks on to a target, or an automatic pilot that is designed to keep you on a predetermined course, you can show that purpose and goal-seeking are eminently respectable 'out there' ideas that explain what happens. The new machines made it perfectly sensible to say: Look! it went for that target. The word 'target' is about the future. So is the future somehow controlling the present? In what sense do we talk of cause and effect if a cause is in the future?

Machine-talk has crept into thinking about our mental behaviour. The language of 'coding and decoding of information' comes from information theory – intended to improve radio signalling, and applied to processing by computers. Some experimenters in teaching techniques, such as Edward de Bono, see the brain as largely a pattern-making instrument that works by encoding information into patterns which it can then store and retrieve in order to match with sense data as it arrives and is processed in the brain.

226

Here the analogy is computers that use processors to encode information and facilitate memory storage of the coded data: with retrieval systems so as to match new data to coded data in order to systematise it. Is the brain a computer? Is what is going on similar to the 'artificial intelligence' of a computer system? Or is the use of analogy distorting our thinking about complex behaviour, by applying a simplifying model that we feel able to work with? Can it be that simple?

What is the process of encoding like? De Bono thinks of the brain as being responsive to patterns that become etched into the fabric of the brain in some way. His simile is of water that makes deeper and deeper channels in a substance. Where the channels go depends as much on the qualities of the substance (its resistance) as on the incidence of the water. Material that is soft will be channelled into more easily. The brain by analogy may be more receptive to establishing some patterns than to others.

In *Lateral Thinking*, he argues that the brain encodes into recognisable patterns. When new sense data is received there is a matching process with encoded patterns. Clearly, the least resistance will occur where the deepest channels have formed from previous experience. So we tend to have preferred ways of seeing the world. They are not innate but the result of experience, whereas the Gestalt theorists would have argued for innate brain structures that programme us to perceive the world in a particular way.

De Bono sees the activity of the brain as setting up hypotheses related to such pattern-matching behaviour. His view of creative thinking is totally different from that of the gestalt school. It is not about the 'whole' at all, but about patterns that may build into wholes. The major problem he sees is that we will hypothesise the 'wrong' pattern, and that this will inhibit our making sense of things when new information arrives.

One effective way of avoiding this happening, since we are now aware of it, is to try to avoid setting up a hypothesis that an experience is of a specific pattern: what he calls **vertical thinking**. Once you have set yourself on a particular path by such a hypothesis you will block out all other possible patterns and so are very likely to miss another more useful pattern that makes better sense of the whole. You should aim to keep your options open, to allow your mind to generate numbers of different patterns out of the experience. It can then match against a range of possible coded patterns as additional sense data provide additional information. This he calls **lateral thinking**: it proceeds on a broad as against a narrow front.

Would he quarrel then with Professor Jerome Bruner? who comments in *States of Mind* that the most practical thing you can do is to have an hypothesis that you can reject on the basis of experience. This clearly echoes Popper's view of science.

Bruner (born in 1915, and Professor of Psychology at Harvard and Cambridge) argues that we 'perceive' the world by active selection from sensory information. It depends on setting up hypotheses and testing them out, as described by Richard Gregory. Previous experience is the key to what actually is perceived. And it is also strongly determined by the society in which the individual lives – by its culture.

So **knowledge is seen as a continuing process in the brain**, not a product. It cannot be packaged in 'lumps' to be put into some new brain in some way. It has to involve active processing on the part of the learner. The brain of any individual will be selective, according to such intangibles as needs, values and attitudes. Many of these are made part of a person by cultural factors in the society he or she grows up in.

Thus learning will depend on how far these attitudinal aspects of behaviour will affect what the individual does with the new information or new sensory data. There will be rejection of those parts that are found threatening or culturally difficult to deal with.

New studies on attention and alerting showed how the brain deals with the 'information–knowledge' process. 'Arousal of the nervous system with active scanning was seen to occur when the model of the world stored in the brain was violated in some way, i.e., when it was inconsistent with the incoming information,' wrote Gregory. How does the process work?

- There must be seeking of some kind.
- There is a selective mechanism.
- There is a means of reorganising the concepts already established to accommodate the new information to produce modified concepts – and from these 'internal models' of the external world.
- The process involves hypothesising to explain incoming information, and some testing of the new models/concepts to see how far they are meaningful when used to explain the world of experience.

Not patterns, but 'internal models of reality'. Bruner argues that physicists came to realise that 'the data of physics were related to the models in the physicist's head – the models he had constructed in order to build his theory of the physical world'. 'Post-war psychologists were into mentalistic matters such as the selective filtering of experience, the construction of selective representations of the world in memory, strategies for co-ordinating information. Its sum total amounted to "the Cognitive Revolution" ' (R. Bruner in *States of Mind*). Bruner dates this from 1932, the year in which Heisenberg was awarded the Nobel prize for physics for his statement of the Uncertainty Principle: a revolution in the way scientists viewed the ability to observe the world, one outcome of which was to question whether the observer was in fact creating the phenomena he was attempting to study by the method he used for observing them.

As the science of computing began to grow, it was possible to see 'stimuli' as forms of 'input'. Their significance depended on how you coded the input, where you put it for storage, how you retrieved it and how you matched it with other coded inputs. You could store not only inputs in the memory of the computer, but instructions as well. Instructions were like thought processes.

Bruner has a very different view of **competence** from that being advocated at present in the United Kingdom. Competence, he believes, is what students should be learning, rather than particular performances: central to the attainment of that end is the acquisition of correct modes of thinking. In this, there is a central role for perception.

We live in an amazingly complex world. The brain can only deal with a limited amount of information at any one time – there is 'limited channel capacity'. An internal model of the world will make it possible to 'chunk' information into manageable packets, and to use this model to guide the search for, and processing of, information constantly arriving. If this is what is in fact happening in physics, clearly 'objective, out there' becomes more a matter of 'interaction between the observer and the environment'.

If perception involves actively exploring the world with our senses, there must be some mechanism in the brain which enables us to tell the difference between sensations which result from what *we* do – our own movement – and sensations that result from the world's movement. If we explore the world with our eyes, the world does not seem to move. We are constantly moving and so are our eyes, but we never get the impression of the world moving. 'Neurological mechanisms which anticipate the state of affairs which will result from a forthcoming action are called "feed-forward" mechanisms to distinguish them from "feed-back" mechanisms which provide information about the result of such movements. In fact, the comparison between feed-forward and feed-back represents one of the most important processes in the nervous system. The difference between what was intended and what actually occurred is what we process to correct the movement' (R. Bruner in *States of Mind*).

Learning behaviour relates to the learner's ability to create strategies: defining goals and ways of achieving them. This will involve feed-forward and feed-back. We might see Kohler's chimpanzees in this light. It also is necessary for learners to have a conceptual model to work towards. They must analyse available information and think about what is to happen. They must be prepared to take risks, to test out the hypotheses and so on – to come back from failure and try again – to explore and experiment.

This is essentially a creative process. Since what we are striving for are models which are transferable to enable us to deal with changing conditions and new situations, learners must be taught to see single instances in terms of principles and generalisations. They must develop the cognitive skills that enable them to grasp principles and to apply them to concrete instances in changing contexts: adaptability.

Learning is mainly cognitive: acquiring information, transforming it by the assimilation of it with previous knowledge, and checking how the knowledge structure now constituted works in relation to explaining new situations.

It is not very helpful to separate learning 'about' something from the process of learning to do it. It is better to learn physics by doing what physicists do. And it is the same with teaching: you learn to generalise about teaching by having experience of teaching. Realism and discovery come from actively doing what you are setting out to understand. So long as you do then reflect cognitively on the experience, matching what you expected to happen with what actually happened.

Telling the student about it in an expository way may be useful in terms of 'alerting and attention' (what I hope is happening now for you reading this book), but it will only become a part of your mental 'model of it all' through experience. Only then can it be transferred and become usable.

Bruner proposed a 'spiral curriculum'. By this he meant that learning had to be constantly revisited. If knowledge is a process, so is acquisition of skills, attitude formation, and so on. They are all part of growth. The most commonly occurring mathematical figure in nature, particularly in living organisms, is the spiral. This is because organisms grow by multiplying cells and that creates, mathematically, a spiral.

No learning is once for all. We have to revisit it constantly to reshape our skills and knowledge. Rudiments early, and Bruner insists that learners must proceed by mastering each learning task or skill. The concept of mastery is a dynamic one: it is related to growth and maturity. Although learning does not occur as a continuum, but by spurts and periods of consolidation, mastery at each point is essential. Gaps in learning can and must be overcome by revisiting. Development and redevelopment matter.

The model I have developed for this book attempts to interpret discoveries such as these about the human capacity to learn into practice in teaching.

Appendices

Appendix 1

TASK 24: A major study

Your own field of expertise will be experiencing development and change along with everything else. It is essential you keep up with what is happening. Documents produced by examining boards or other bodies providing guidance to teachers, tutors or senior staff who undertake training roles as new initiatives in education and training are introduced. How familiar are you with these? Where can you find them? Can you use them to make practical, workable schemes of teaching and learning programmes?

What other information is there? How can you discover that and use it to help you make sense of what you are setting out to do?

First, make a list or a collection of relevant documents – at least know where they are kept and how to get hold of them.

Second, try to identify what it is you need to find out and where to look for the information you need.

This will change with time. So you need to review your needs.

Third, at an appropriate time, which you must decide, undertake some research in depth into initiatives in your field as they affect what you as teacher or trainer need to do.

Appendix 2: Curriculum Design and Competence

Welcome to the end of this part of your journey. What you have been exploring is your role as teacher. I hope you found plenty to stimulate and interest you on the way. What you have learned will depend on what you have done, and how busy and active you have been in using the programme of Activities and Tasks in the book.

You have probably discovered a great deal about yourself. Whenever I ask student teachers to evaluate their learning on a programme, such as the one I set up here, they always tell me that they have learned most about themselves. They discover strengths and talent and many surprising things. They learn how to cope with demands made by circumstances and other people. They learn how to take control of what they and others are doing.

I hope you also have gained insight and skills. You should have a new way of looking at things, be more observant, able to distance yourself and take a critical view. And you should have learned the skills of evaluation.

Where to now?

Every arrival is also a point of departure. We evaluate in order to decide what to do 'now'. We can always be better. Learning is for tomorrow, next year. After all, we cannot change the past.

TASK 25: Curriculum design

With a group of colleagues design a curriculum to use in your own context. It should use the learning you have achieved from this case study you have now completed, and exhibit the good practice and principles of design that we have explored together.

Revisiting and consolidating learning is essential. This activity is intended to make that happen. But there is really no point in learning something as complex as teaching well to engage students actively in their learning, unless you make it habitual.

The most urgent activity for teachers now is to design curriculum for their students. The curriculum must motivate them. It must be designed to help them learn efficiently. The design should integrate all the elements of learning and syllabus content so as to provide a coherent and effective learning experience.

You will have developed the knowledge and skill to design it. But you cannot integrate all elements of syllabus content unless you have a shared curriculum design with your colleagues. There are many skills and roles in teaching and many still to learn.

Competence frame

A strategy is an over-view, a model in the head if you like, which enables us to know what we are trying to do or how we perceive it happening. Although there are many strategies that may be used in the design of curriculum, some are more effective than others. In considering curriculum design for students at any level, it is helpful to have a view of the 'whole' as well as the parts. What is to change here? Surely, behaviour as a whole.

I have used the word 'competence' repeatedly throughout this book. You may still be a little vague as to what the word means. This may be because competence is a developing concept; the meaning and use of the term change with time and with who is using it and for what purpose. Most words tend to work like that. My own use of the word derives from a view I take of what is involved in demonstrating competence in a role. I designed a diagram (Figure 11, overleaf) to present visually an over-view of it.

Competence can be viewed in a narrow sense – 'can do' statements related to specific, defined tasks – or in a broad sweep: 'able to take responsibility for . . . '. I choose to use the latter mainly for the reason that training in specific tasks is highly contextual and does not allow for transferability to new contexts. Nor does it address the problem of 'Can do . . . intelligently'. Whereas if we consider roles that people occupy, we can design training that is generic and will be transferable from one context and level of responsibility to another.

Analysis is fairly easy to do. We can break down behaviour into constituent parts. Identifying criteria does just that. We can, if we wish, train parts and test them. What is more difficult to do is to put the parts back together, to synthesise them into the behaviour as a whole that we really are trying to achieve.

The language used in discussion of competence shifts. There is much more emphasis now on 'effectiveness in a role'. This is to recognise that tasks do not make sense in a vacuum – they relate to context and role. It is the role that integrates the parts.

But there is much more to effectiveness in a role than technical skill in achieving specified tasks. To identify what is required a person needs a conceptual framework – that is, to be able to grasp what the role is about, to understand what purpose it serves and what are the essential qualities and attitudes that a person needs in order to fulfil the role successfully. Insight into the way this role fits with roles of other people is essential; so is an understanding of the theory as well as the practice, the underpinning knowledge that enables him or her to use skills and expertise intelligently: to think through problems, set targets, design action plans, get properly organised.

235

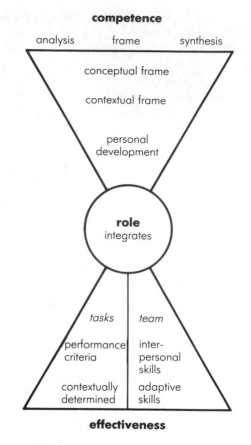

competence

analysis   frame   synthesis

conceptual frame

contextual frame

personal
development

role
integrates

tasks   team

performance
criteria

inter-
personal
skills

contextually
determined

adaptive
skills

effectiveness

Fig. 11   A competence frame

1 Let's look at an example. If I say the words 'personal assistant', you will immediately have a view of what the person is likely to be doing; there is a concept that you understand. Anyone who is to undertake such a role has to work with this concept. But there are so many more concepts, understanding, insights that he or she will be expected to grasp to become effective in the role. Training must develop this conceptual grasp/framework.

2 There is no such thing as 'personal assistant', an abstract concept; there are only particular people who are engaged in specific contexts. Their role depends critically on the role of others, especially the person they assist.

Without full understanding of the context, and the demands that are made in the context and by others, we cannot design any training programme related to tasks, as we do not know what the trainee will be expected to do or at what level of competence. Will the trainee be required to keep accounts? use a word processor or a fax machine? What skills will need to be developed? It depends on what the context requires. So much training has had to guess and provide for general possibilities that it often happens that the skills someone really needs are not included while others are practised that are never used – or the context demands things are done quite another way.

So the conceptual frame is modified by the contextual frame. In designing training, we must attempt to develop tasks that are generic and transferable (and develop insight and skills that are equally transferable), but that require learners to interpret them in their own context to make sense of them.

3 This cannot be all, however. We appoint people, not personal assistants. The person in the role makes it what it is. If that person is to be effective, he or she has to develop those personal qualities that the role demands. These require growth that results from experience by using experience intelligently. A training course must concentrate on self-assessment, taking responsibility for one's own learning. It cannot be set up so that external assessors test task competence.

4 Once we have a mechanism for developing the framework for a design that will deliver effectiveness in role, we can then analyse what tasks and technical skills the role requires. We can set about developing them, ensuring if we can that learning is transferable to other contexts.

We can also apply quite demanding performance criteria. But we should ensure that the criteria identify good practice in fulfilling aspects of the role. The tasks have to become habitual: the skills are a means to an end – to do the job.

5 At low levels of responsibility, that may be enough. There is clearly an absolute necessity that people do have sufficient insight and skill to do the job properly.

But it is rare for people to be isolated, working on their own. The great majority work as part of a team. A personal assistant can only be as good as the boss. Together, they may form a good team (or not). In terms of effectiveness, it is essential that they do.

At all levels beyond that of no responsibility at all, there is a pressing demand for the development of interpersonal skills. How they work depends again on the context. Training programmes must, however, concentrate on those learning activities that will develop these skills.

6 But no amount of good practice and skill is much use if, when circumstances change or new challenges arise, they become outdated and an obstacle rather than a help. Dinosaurs were among the most successful creatures ever to evolve. Why did they become extinct? It seems that they could not adapt to the catastrophic changes that happened in their environment.

This has happened so frequently in the past decades in our highly technological and rapidly changing world. Dinosaurs die: adaptable mammals thrive. Training in tasks may make for highly proficient skilled workers so long as things stay the same. Adaptability requires problem-solving skills, and the ability to design and take control of what you do. Training programmes have to make sure learners are able to adapt.

I hope it is clear that the design of the programme in this book for teachers exhibits the logic of the above argument. Competent teachers have to be effective in the roles they undertake.

When you design curriculum for your students, take an over-view of what as a whole they need to know. How far will your programme help them to achieve effectiveness in the roles they will occupy?

Suggestions for Further Reading

Annett, J. *Feedback and Human Behaviour*, Penguin (Harmondsworth), 1969

Ardrey, R. *The Social Contract*, Fontana (London), 1971

Ausubel, D. *Educational Psychology: A Cognitive View*, Holt, Rinehart and Winston (New York), 1968

Belbin, R. M. *Management Teams: Why they Succeed or Fail*, Heinemann (London), 1981

Berelson, B., and Steiner, G. *Human Behaviour: Inventory of Scientific Findings*, Harcourt Brace Jovanovich (New York), 1964

Berne, E. *Games People Play: Psychology of Human Relationships*, Grove Press (New York), 1964; Penguin (Harmondsworth), 1968

Bligh, D. *What's the Use of Lectures?*, D. A. Bligh (London), 1971; Penguin (Harmondsworth), 1972

Block, J. H. *Mastery Learning: Theory and Practice*, Holt, Rinehart and Winston (New York), 1971

Brady, M. *What's Worth Teaching?*, SUNY Press (New York), 1989

Bruner, J. S. *The Process of Education*, John Wiley (New York), 1977
Actual Minds, Possible Worlds, John Wiley (New York), 1986

Buzan, T. *Use Your Head*, BBC Books (London), 2nd edn, 1989

Chapman, A. H. *Put Offs and Come Ons*, Putnam Berkley (New York), 1968

Coating, B. F. *Science and Human Behaviour*, Macmillan (London), 1953

Davies, I. K. *The Management of Learning*, McGraw-Hill (New York), 1971

de Bono, E. *Lateral Thinking: a Textbook of Creativity*, Penguin (Harmondsworth), 1977

Ebel, R. L. *Essentials of Educational Measurement*, Prentice-Hall (New Jersey), 1972

Edney, P. *A Systems Analysis of Training*, Pitman (London), 1972

Gagné, R. M. *The Conditions of Learning*, Holt, Rinehart and Winston (New York), 1973

Gelb, M. *Present Yourself*, Guild Publishing (London), 1988

Goldner, B. *The Strategy of Creative Thinking*, Prentice-Hall (New Jersey), 1963

Gregory, R. L. *Eye and Brain*, Weidenfeld and Nicolson (London), 1977
The Intelligent Eye, Weidenfeld and Nicolson (London), 1970

Hall, E. T. *Silent Language*, Fawcett, Premier Books (New York), 1959

Handy, C. *The Gods of Management*, Pan Books (London), 1979

Herzberg, F. *Work and the Nature of Man*, World (New York), 1966

Hilgard, E. and Bower, G. *Theories of Learning*, Appleton-Century-Crofts (New York), 1966

Hills, P. *Teaching and Learning as a Communication Process*, Croom Helm (London), 1979

Hoffman, B. *The Tyranny of Testing*, Crowell-Collier Press (New York), 1962

Hollander, E. P. *Leadership Dynamics*, The Free Press (New York), 1978

Hoyle, F. *The Intelligent Universe*, Joseph (London), 1983

Hudson, B. (ed.) *Assessment Techniques*, Methuen (London), 1973

Kohler, W. *The Mentality of Apes*, Harcourt Brace Jovanovich (New York), 1925

Magee, B. *Popper*, Fontana (London), 2nd edn, 1985

Maslow, A. *Motivation and Personality*, Harper and Row (New York), 1954

McConnell, J. V. *Understanding Human Behaviour*, Holt, Rinehart and Winston (New York), 1983

Miller, G. A. *Psychology: The Science of Mental Life*, Harper and Row (New York), 1962; Penguin (Harmondsworth), 1966

Miller, J. *States of Mind, Conversations with Psychological Investigators*, BBC Books (London), 1983

Morris, D. *Manwatching*, Panther Books (London), 1978

Moseley, D. *Helping With Learning Difficulties*, Open University Press (Milton Keynes), 1976

Nash, R. *Classrooms Observed*, Routledge & Kegan Paul (London), 1972

Nierenberg, G. I. *The Complete Negotiator*, Souvenir Press (London), 1987

Oborne, D. J. *Ergonomics of Work*, John Wiley (New York), 1982

Peng, T. H. *Fun With Chinese Characters:* Straits Times Collection, Federal Publications (Singapore), 1980

Piaget, J. *Language and Thought in the Child*, Routledge & Kegan Paul (London), 1926

Behaviour and Evolution, Routledge & Kegan Paul (London), 1979

Popper, K. *The Logic of Scientific Discovery*, Hutchinson (London), 1972

Objective Knowledge: an Evolutionary Approach, Oxford University Press (Oxford), 1981

Rackham, N., Honey, P. and Colbert, M. J. *Developing Interactive Skills*, Wellens Publishing (Northampton), 1971

Reynolds, V. *The Biology of Human Action*, Freeman (Oxford), 1980

Rowntree, D. *Assessing Students: How Shall we Know Them?*, Harper and Row (London), 1977

Satterly, D. *Assessment in Schools*, Blackwell (Oxford), 1981

Shannon, C. and Weaver, W. *The Mathematical Theory of Communication*, University of Illinois Press (Illinois), 1949

Shostrom, E. *Man – the Manipulator*, Bantam (London), 1967

Skinner, B. F. *The Technology of Teaching*, Appleton-Century-Crofts (New York), 1968

Sperry, L. *Learning Performance and Individual Differences: Essays and Readings*, Scot Foresman (Glenview Ill.), 1972

Watson, J. B. *Behaviourism*, J. B. Lippincott (Philadelphia), 1924

Wertheimer, M. *Productive Thinking*, Harper (New York), 1945

Whitehead, A. N. *The Aims of Education and Other Essays*, Williams and Norgate (London), 1950

Willmott, A. S. and Fowles, D. E. *The Objective Interpretation of Test Performance*, NFER Publishing (Windsor), 1974
Woodcock, M. *Team Development Manual*, Gower Press (Farnborough), 1979

Index

abstract thinking 33–4, 217–18
achievement *see* records of
   achievement
activities 9
ambiguity
   of information 159
   visual 222–4
antique pottery (case study) 28–9
appraisal 181–2
assessment 89–93, 180–81, 183–98
   choice of methods for 184
   criteria for 91–2, 93, 186–9
   evidence for 90–91
   formative and summative 183
   hierarchy of 184
   learning a part of 51
   of discussions 128
   of lectures 115–16
   of mastery 185
   of resource-based learning 138
   of skills 124
   reliability and validity of 185–6
   timing of 92
   weighting of 184–5
   work-based 143
   see also tests
attention 81–2
attitudes 188
attitudinal barriers 157–8
audibility 72, 82, 162–3
audio-visual aids 161–3
   see also visual aids
aural tests 195–6
AVA *see* audio-visual aids

barriers
   of language 178–9

to communication 115, 157–60
to learning 6, 7, 79–80, 120–21
Bechterev 204
behavioural change 24, 25, 105
behaviourism 108, 188, 203–6, 209
   see also neo-behaviourism
boardwork 83, 84, 162–3, 166
body language 32, 76
brain
   pattern- and rule-making
      activities 15, 148, 150–51,
      224, 226–7
   role in perception 221, 222–4
Bruner, J. S. 174, 227, 228–9, 230

case studies 9, 98
chaining (reflexes) 204, 208
chalkboard *see* boardwork
class visits 19–22
coffee break 77
cognitive change 105
cognitive development 216–18
cognitive learning 108, 226–30
communication 74–84, 125
   barriers to 115, 157–60
   skills 74; lesson plan 55–6
   with and within groups 170–79
competence 113, 188–9, 228
   in teachers 62, 113
competence frame 235–8
competition 108, 129–30
   see also games
concentration curves 72–3
conditioning 204–6, 213
consolidation of learning 21–2, 36
context of communication 171